D1278632

Compliments of Sprint. Dedicated to
helping your business do more business.

HOW TO REALLY
DELIVER
SUPERIOR
CUSTOMER
SERVICE

How to Really *Deliver Superior Customer Service*

Copyright © 1994 Goldhirsh Group, Inc.

All rights reserved.

Printed in the United States of America.

No part of this book may be used or reproduced in any manner whatsoever without written permission except in the case of brief quotations embodied in critical articles and reviews. For information, write *Inc.* Publishing, Attn: Permissions Manager, 38 Commercial Wharf, Boston, MA 02110–3883.

Text design by Susan L. Dahl
Cover design by S. Laird Jenkins Corporation, Lynne G. Waring

Portions of this book were originally published in *Inc.* magazine. For information about purchasing back issues, please call 617–248–8426.

This publication is designed to provide accurate and authoritative information in regard to the subject matter covered. It is sold with the understanding that the publisher is not engaged in rendering legal, accounting, or other professional service. If legal advice or other expert assistance is required, the services of a competent professional should be sought.

ISBN: 1–880394–14–6

First Edition

1 2 3 4 5 6 7 8 9 10

Acknowledgments

I would like to acknowledge the help and support of several individuals in pulling together into a cohesive whole the score of contributions that make up *How to* Really *Deliver Superior Customer Service*.

If it is true that every writer needs an editor, so too does every editor need an editor. So I thank my editor, Brad Ketchum, Jr. for his unerring direction and insight, not just on this book but on a variety of projects over the 20 years that I have been fortunate enough to have worked with him professionally.

Experts who have contributed to this book are acknowledged chapter by chapter as well as in the expert appendix. The heart of this volume is its case studies. These case studies, adapted and updated for the book, originally appeared in *Inc.* magazine. For their meticulous research and fine craft, I thank Edward O. Welles for his story on PDQ Printing; John Case for his stories on Intuit Inc., Phelps County Bank, and Leegin Creative Leather Products, Inc.; Paul E. Brown for his story on Direct Tire Sales; and Joel Kotkin for his story on Dell Computer Corp.

Jennifer Zampell deserves my thanks for the day-to-day support that enabled me to fulfill my promises to assorted experts and colleagues. Susan Dahl is to be congratulated for her design talents. Susan has done a fine job of transforming letters, numbers, and bytes into a hands-on workbook that is inviting, approachable, clean, and easy to navigate.

My gratitude also goes to Michael O'Loughlin and Jacqueline Lapidus, fact-checker and copy editor, respectively. And, finally, for Hilary Glazer, I breathe a sigh of relief as I utter my thanks. Without Hilary's eye for detail, scheduling, and deadlines, this book would not exist. She made my job easier by anticipating problems and finding solutions before they hit my desk. For me, Hilary personifies customer service excellence.

John R. Halbrooks
November 1994

Contents

Introduction

As I write this introduction to *How to* Really *Deliver Superior Customer Service*, I am struck by an article in the *New York Times* about a gathering of customers this coming weekend. The customers, some 25,000 strong, will be streaming into the town of Spring Hill, Tenn. from around the country to celebrate the fact that they all bought the same product. Some of these travelers will have driven hundreds of miles. One 22-car caravan set out from Nevada for the 1,800-mile journey to Tennessee.

Whether by caravan or singly, everyone making this trip to Spring Hill comes by car, for that is what they all have in common. These pilgrims all own Saturns. They are making their pilgrimage, rolling mile by rolling mile, to Mecca. For it was here at Saturn's Spring Hill plant that each of these cars rolled off the assembly line.

Think about that for a moment.

Thousands of Saturn owners, some driving thousands of miles, gather in a sleepy Tennessee town. These fanatics — for that is what they call themselves — are celebrating a collective "homecoming" with a hoedown in a hayfield. To country and western and rhythm and blues these Saturn owners will chow down on hot dogs and tour the Saturn factory. And they'll pay good money for the privilege. To help defray the cost of the celebration, the General Motors Corp. will charge Saturn owners $34 per adult and $17 per child (entry to the amusement park at Opryland is included, accommodations are not).

Meanwhile, groupies who can't afford the time or expense of the trip to Spring Hill will do their bonding at mini-homecoming celebrations hosted by Saturn dealerships across the country. These parties are expected to draw another 100,000 Saturns, many packed with entire families.

Has this sunk in yet?

We're talking car owners here, but not owners of Silver Shadows and Stutz Bearcats. Not even Corvettes and Mustangs. This is the Saturn, a well-designed, moderately priced automobile but certainly not the kind of car that turns heads when it drives by. How to explain it? What has GM done to create this frenzied pride of ownership? How did GM create a car cult? The answer is as prosaic as it is surprising: GM did it with good old customer service.

Imagine experimenting with a novel concept like customer service in the automobile industry! Talk about daring! Can't you just hear top management's reaction to the wild suggestion that GM try introducing customer service in its car dealerships? That's a bit like suggesting Mary Poppins as the undercover agent to infiltrate a drug ring.

In every survey ever conducted to rank professions on trustworthiness, Americans place car dealers at the bottom, down there with politicians. Yet, when Saturn owners are asked to explain the intensity of their feelings for their cars, they frequently mention their dealers. Saturn dealers actually host barbecues for their customers. Saturn dealers routinely offer free seminars to educate first-time buyers.

Saturn dealers also do something that is taboo in the industry — they do not bargain. The price you pay for a Saturn is the sticker price. This revolutionary concept — a no-haggle price policy — has been greeted with cheers by many customers, particularly women, who appreciate a less confrontational, less stressful car buying experience.

Just how passionate are Saturn owners? According to surveys of customers by the company, 80% of the 60,000 owners of Saturns insist that their next car will be a Saturn, too.

Saturn's success should demonstrate to any business in America the power of customer service as a business strategy. After all, if you can make people feel good about their car dealers, is there anything customer service cannot achieve?

Saturn's experience also indicates how widely customer service is welcomed in business in the United States and around the world. As companies embrace customer service, it has become the business buzzword of the 1990s. But don't be fooled. This is no fad. Indeed, it is quite the opposite. Once the automobile arrived, the days of the horse and buggy were numbered. Service is an easily acquired taste that quickly becomes a habit consumers are unwilling to give up.

The Saturn is not the only story attracting media attention. Consider the 24-hour customer support telephone line IBM just introduced for its users in 1994. Dell Computer Corp., one of the case studies that anchors *How to* Really *Deliver Superior Customer Service,* introduced the concept of 24-hour customer service 10 years ago, when it was founded. Today, Dell is a $2.9-billion international corporation because it understood that computers are not merely a commodity. Dell understood that computers had to be custom-built and that customers had to be offered extraordinary customer service. IBM now receives about 9,000 calls each day from customers. Dell, by contrast, fields something on the order of 35,000 customer calls a day.

One of the expert contributors to this book estimates that only 16% of all businesses actually deliver on the promise of customer service. All claim the mantle, but only the Sixteen Percenters deserve to wear it. The good news is that businesses that develop customer service strategies will gain an edge in today's increasingly competitive marketplace. The bad news is that there is no rest for the weary.

As our expert writes, "New competitors are busy building better and better mousetraps. Answering the phone in three rings, please and thank you, phone calls returned immediately, on-time delivery, order accuracy, speed of service, business knowledge, company flexibility, expertise, and all the other components of service delivered beyond the product generate customer focus, customer service, and customer satisfaction long term. And they are all fast becoming routine."

In this hands-on workbook, you will read about six businesses that have employed customer service strategies to achieve startling heights of performance. The case studies anchor the six chapters that make up the book. Accompanying each case study are consultant analyses — the "Expert's Insight." In soliciting these contributions, we asked the experts to play off the case studies to test, challenge, question, and provoke.

A "Good Form" concludes each chapter. "Good Forms" are precisely that — actual forms that businesses have created, modified, or adapted to accomplish a particular customer service task. Hopefully, you will modify or adapt these forms for use in your company to augment or improve your customer service strategies.

Sharpen your pencils!

J.R.H.

Other business books from Inc. *Magazine*

How to *Really* Create a Successful Business Plan
• By David E. Gumpert

How to *Really* Start Your Own Business
• By David E. Gumpert

How to *Really* Create a Successful Marketing Plan
• By David E. Gumpert

Anatomy of a Start-Up
Why Some New Businesses Succeed and Others Fail:
27 Real-life Case Studies
• Edited by Elizabeth K. Longsworth

**301 Great Management Ideas from
America's Most Innovative Small Companies**
• Introduction by Tom Peters
• Edited by Sara P. Noble

**Managing People: 101 Proven Ideas for Making
You and Your People More Productive**
From America's Smartest Small Companies
• Edited by Sara P. Noble

**How to *Really* Recruit, Motivate, and Lead
Your Team: Managing People**
• Edited by Ruth G. Newman with
  Bradford W. Ketchum, Jr.

To receive a complete listing of *Inc.* Business Books and Videos, please
call 1–800–468–0800, ext. 5007. Or write to *Inc.* Business Resources,
P.O. Box 1365, Dept. 5007, Wilkes-Barre, PA 18703-1365.

Turning Customers Into Apostles

Ostensibly, the product at Intuit Inc., the Menlo Park, Calif. micro-computer software manufacturer, is personal-finance management software. Its true product, however, is unalloyed customer service. By distilling customer service to its purest form, Intuit has turned its customers into salespeople. If there are flaws to this gem, they are invisible to the naked eye.

When Intuit's founder, Scott Cook, decided to enter the field of personal finance management software in the mid-1980s, the market was crowded with quality products. No surprise, then, that Cook had trouble launching his new company (see Founder's Insight, p. 17). But Cook's audacious goal was to venture beyond simply offering customers a quality product. He intended to give his customers top-flight service as well. No new mousetrap. Just unmatched customer service.

No company can grow to $230 million in sales on the strength of service alone. But extraordinary service can differentiate a product. Extraordinary service can give a company an aura or cachet that creates formidable word-of-mouth advertising. Extraordinary service can, in short, create such good will for a company that customers line up to buy its products.

By carrying the concept of customer service to almost absurd lengths, Intuit has honed Quicken, its personal finance management software, to such a point that its owners have become "apostles" of the company. Intuit's apostles sing the praises of Quicken near and far. The result of that enthusiasm — and one of the intangible benefits of quality customer service — is that six years after the company was founded, Intuit still employed only two salespeople.

Like an archaeologist, Scott Cook went to work with the simplest of tools to strip away layers of dirt and sand to reveal truths about his customers. The tools used at Intuit are not expensive. It's what Cook and his employees accomplish with those tools that sets them apart from everyone else. Cook and his employees meticulously pick through trash heaps of data to retrieve nuggets of information they can use to improve the company's products and service. By sifting mountains of sand to its competitors' molehills, Intuit understands its customers better than any other company in the field.

Scott Cook would never have succeeded with Intuit if he had not been able to communicate his customer service philosophy to his management team and employees. The extent to which a leader can imbue the culture of his company with such a philosophy, notes JoAnna Brandi (see p. 25), determines its potency. When employees internalize a concept, it becomes a powerful tool.

What distinguishes Intuit from most other companies, according to Deborah B. Taylor (see p. 18), is the company's attention to detail. Taylor argues that 84% of all U.S. businesses fail to "more than satisfy" their customers because they overlook four critical "missing links" in quality customer service.

Wes Zimmerman (see p. 29) believes Intuit's success can be replicated in any company, large or small. The principles are universal.

The name Intuit could not have been more appropriate for the company Scott Cook launched a decade ago. Cook sensed an opportunity in the field of personal finance management software. He understood intuitively that it is impossible to offend customers by paying them too much attention.

Imagine a Company Called Intuit

Imagine a company that can bring products to market that are higher in quality and lower in price than those of the competition. Imagine that this company's products are direct hits with its customers. And imagine that this company is able to support its products flawlessly after the sale. Imagine a company called Intuit.

Suppose your company could really satisfy its customers. Suppose you could provide a product or service that was better than they expected, for less money than anybody else charged. Suppose that every time you brought out something new it was just what buyers wanted. Suppose your after-sale service was so good that customers with problems went away feeling better than before.

What would happen? Easy — you'd own your marketplace. People would buy from you over and over again, would relish the experience, would never even dream about doing business with anybody else. They would proselytize on your behalf, telling their friends and associates to buy from you. You'd hardly need salespeople.

Impossible, you say. Farfetched. Then again, you haven't met Scott Cook, and you probably don't know much about his company, Intuit Inc. All those statements apply to Intuit. Better yet, Cook has figured out how to build that kind of customer orientation into the organizational bricks and mortar of his company.

"Operating without a safety net," the 41-year-old president calls it.

Or "the Toyota approach." Or simply "getting it right." Whatever — it's partly a matter of management techniques, partly a matter of fundamental philosophy. And it's what sets Cook's company way, way apart from the competition.

Intuit makes microcomputer software. Its flagship product is Quicken, a program that allows consumers and small businesses to write checks and keep track of their finances on a personal computer. Owning the marketplace? Quicken is the most successful personal-finance program ever written, holding a market share estimated at 60% to 70%. "It has become the brand-name product in what would otherwise be a commodity business," says Jeffrey Tarter, editor of the industry publication *Softletter.* "It's the Kleenex or Xerox of its market."

Intuit, not surprisingly, has been exploding. With its acquisition last year of Chipsoft Inc., maker of TurboTax and MacInTax, Intuit has engineered the merger of companies that produce the best-selling personal-finance management software and best-selling tax preparation software. By the end of this fiscal year on July 31, Intuit expects to post sales of $160 million. Chipsoft will do another $70 million on its own. Under the Intuit banner, the merged companies will do better than $230 million in total revenues in 1994.

Granted, the software industry has always been populated by hot-shot fast-growth companies. But Intuit doesn't fit the conventional mold. Unlike, say, Lotus, it started without venture capital or other early advantages (see Founder's Insight, "Wager: One Company" on page 17). Unlike VisiCorp or Wordstar, it has dominated its marketplace through several generations of software, beating back waves of would-be competitors. Consumers yank Quicken off the shelves virtually unbidden. Intuit sold close to a million units in 1990. Four years later, more than six million units of Quicken have been sold, more than the combined total of all other personal-finance software.

So what moves the goods? Asked that question, founder and chairman Scott Cook peers mock-earnestly through his thick glasses, allowing only the hint of a grin to cross his face. "Really," he says innocently, "we have hundreds of thousands of salespeople. They're our customers."

Suddenly missionary-sober, he adds that he wants his customers to be "apostles" for Quicken. Intuit's mission is to "make customers feel so good about the product they'll go and tell five friends to buy it."

And as to what would make a customer feel that good, which is to say better than most customers feel about any product or service — well, the only way to understand it may be to watch Cook and his company at work.

Real Women Write Checks

The year is 1984; the place Palo Alto, Calif., not far from Intuit's current hometown of Menlo Park. Cook and three colleagues are in a room with a bunch of computers and several well-dressed women. The women — members of the Palo Alto Junior League — are not what you'd call computer nuts; some have never even touched one of the machines before. But today, after croissants and orange juice, they are sitting at the keyboards, trying to use the computers to write checks. Cook and his colleagues watch but don't help.

Cook — a Harvard M.B.A., a Procter & Gamble-trained marketer — is a bit on edge. In a way, his fledgling company depends on what he learns here. His epiphany, a year or so earlier, was simplicity itself. More and more consumers and small businesses were buying PCs. All those computer buyers wrote checks and kept financial records. Outfitted with the right software, a computer should be able to automate such tasks. The only rub: a few dozen check-writing programs were already on the market, and Cook had no money to elbow them aside. If he wanted to start a software company — and he did — he would have to offer customers something his competitors didn't.

Wondering what that something might be, Cook and a newly hired assistant began placing telephone calls to middle- and upper-middle-income households. They didn't stop until the calls numbered in the hundreds — and until they began hearing the same responses over and over.

The vast majority of respondents said they did financial work every month, they didn't like spending so much time on it, and they would consider using a computer to do the work. But they couldn't be bothered with learning a complex program, and they certainly didn't want to spend more time on the chore than they were spending now. Curious, Cook assembled a panel of computer buffs to test the most popular programs then available, writing checks and keeping records first by computer and then by hand. Sure enough, in every case, the computer was slower.

Conclusion: There was a market out there, already big and undoubtedly growing bigger, a market capable of appealing to Cook's P&G-honed aspirations. But if he wanted to reach that potential mass market, his program had better be fast, cheap, hassle-free, and above all easy to use, so easy that anyone could sit down at the computer and start writing checks.

Now he's watching very intently as the Junior Leaguers stare at the unfamiliar keys. He and his chief programmer, a recent Stanford graduate named Tom Proulx (rhymes with true), have developed a prototype, and today's trial is one of many to see how well they've done. If the women flunk, so does the program.

For a while the test goes swimmingly. The women hunt and peck, but they don't have much trouble selecting "write checks" from a menu on the screen. The outline of a check appears, and the cursor jumps neatly from date to payee to amount. Anyone who has ever written a paper check, they discover, can write one with this new software. And the computer's check register looks just like an ordinary checkbook.

Then, alas, they go to print the checks they've written. Cook and the others have loaded up the printers with specially prepared checks, and the testers find "print checks" on the menu. But the first check prints too high, or maybe too low. To a woman they fumble with the printers; to a woman they make the problem worse. What's the matter with this computer? The checks just won't line up right.

Cook cringes. So does Proulx; so does Tom LeFevre, another colleague present at the creation.

"We knew one thing," recalls Proulx. "If people had that much trouble the first time they used the program, they'd never use it again."

"Scott looked at Tom and me," adds LeFevre. "He said, 'You guys figure out a way to solve that problem.' His tone said, And don't come back until you do."

> HOT TIP

Want to let your customers know how committed you are to serving them? For the past four years, J.W. Kisling, CEO of Multiplex Inc., a St. Louis maker of beverage-dispensing equipment for the food-service industry, has listed the home phone numbers of the company's 16 directors and officers in its catalog. Next to the list is a suggestion to call in case of emergency — if satisfaction can't be had from an area manager. "The secret," Kisling confides, "is we only get a couple of calls a year. But seeing it in writing impresses the hell out of our customers."

Survey, Poll, Focus. . . Survey, Poll, Focus

Jump cut: 1990. Proulx and LeFevre have long since resolved the alignment problem, developing a fancy bit of programming (patented and still unique in the industry) that makes the computer line the checks up automatically. And Quicken has long since been released, upgraded, and released again. It has climbed to the top of the best-seller charts; it has won industry awards. Intuit is making a lot of money selling not only the programs but upgrades, special checks, and other supplies.

Yet now Alex Young, a product-development manager for the next release of Quicken, is sitting in the home of a man he doesn't know, watching him open a shrink-wrapped box.

Maybe it was the P&G training, maybe the lesson of the Junior Leaguers, maybe just the impact of the original market research. Whatever the reason, figuring out how to satisfy customers has become Cook's, and Intuit's, obsession. The company runs an annual customer survey, asking which of Quicken's features buyers use and don't use, like and don't like. It polls dealers anonymously, asking what personal-finance programs they recommend and why. It compiles data from customers who call in with problems or write in with suggestions. It runs focus groups, usually consisting of people who aren't Quicken customers but (according to Intuit) ought to be. Information from all those sources flows directly to product-development teams (working on the next version of Quicken), to the documentation department (which regularly updates the manual), and to marketing.

The company also tests its programs relentlessly. And not just the so-called alpha and beta testing commonly practiced by most software companies — tests that are designed primarily to locate bugs in the programming — but tests at a much earlier stage of product development. Get in some experienced Quicken users — see if this new version is going to confuse them in any way. Get in some Junior League-style novices. What's their reaction to a certain screen? "You watch their eyebrows, where they hesitate, where they have a quizzical look," says Cook. "Every glitch, every momentary hesitation is our fault."

That'll do it, you might think. Not that all the research costs so much — only the big sample surveys represent much of a cash outlay, in the neighborhood of $150,000 a year. But surely Intuit has been finding out all it possibly can about its customers' experiences with the product?

Not so. "There's still a group of people we were missing," says product manager Mari Latterell. "People just setting the program up. In fact, we didn't really know how easy it was to get started with Quicken. When you survey customers, they've been using it for six months or a year and won't remember. When you bring in testers, you have them in an artificial situation. They aren't entering their own data in their own homes."

That's why Latterell, imbued with Cook's market-research mission, proposed the Follow-Me-Home program, in which Quicken buyers from local stores are asked to let an Intuit representative observe them when they first use Quicken. And why Alex Young, who volunteered to participate, is now watching his new acquaintance unwrap the shrink-wrapped Quicken box.

Today Young will spend five hours with his subject, longer than any of the dozen or so other employees who have so far followed customers home. Sitting behind the customer, he watches and listens. Customer confronts the program's main menu. (Confusion, notes Young: He thinks the word register, meaning the check register, has something to do with the product-registration card.) Customer begins to enter data from his checkbook. (Problem: He tries to enter a balance manually. You can't do that; once the opening balance is entered, the program calculates the balances automatically.) Customer tries to print checks (He prints more samples than he needs to.) Finally, the day is done, and the customer is happy. As part of the deal, Young is now allowed to offer a little help and advice.

Young and Intuit, for their part, have their payoff: a thick sheaf of notes on the myriad ways that the next incarnation of Quicken, already the most popular program on the market, might be made just a tiny bit easier for first-time users.

"If people don't use the product," observes Tom LeFevre, "they won't tell their friends to use it, either."

Suna Kneisley, senior customer-support specialist, can't quite believe her fax machine. A customer she has just spoken with wants to know how to put his various records onto Quicken and has just faxed her nine pages' worth of data. It's a Friday; no way can she go through it all today. Oh, well. She calls the customer and leaves a message: She'll take it home with her over the weekend and get back to him Monday. Monday, she has the answers he wants.

Technical-support reps such as Kneisley are Intuit's front-line employees, like waiters in a restaurant or reservation clerks at an airline. There are 40 of them, almost a quarter of the company's 175-person work force. You've just bought a new printer, and you can't get it to work with Quicken? Call tech support. You've damaged a disk and lost some data? Call tech support. The response you get, of course, will define your attitude toward Quicken and Intuit, probably forever.

So ask yourself: How much is it worth to the company when a customer gets a response like Kneisley's — not only that she'll answer a request going well beyond the ordinary, but that she'll take it home and work on it over the weekend?

Kneisley, 24, had been at Intuit only five months when this particular request came in. No matter — she had already absorbed the messages that Cook has built somehow into the very structure of his company: Intuit stands or falls with what happens in tech support. Do whatever you need to do to satisfy the customer. The messages are hammered home in several different ways:

• Thank-you letters from customers are read aloud, circulated throughout the company, and then framed and posted on the wall. Kneisley's colleague Debbie Peak gets a letter because she faxed a customer some printer information, then thought to call the next day to make sure it had arrived safely. Kneisley herself gets one from a woman who damaged four years' worth of data; working at home with a special data-recovery program, Kneisley salvaged the material.

• Virtually everyone in the company, from Cook on down, spends a few hours each month working the customer service lines, underscoring by example the importance of what the department does. "I was hired in September," recalls Victor Gee, who started as a rep and is now a supervisor in tech support. "That same month Scott came by and start-ed taking calls, too. I thought, What other company would have the president do the same thing I'm doing?" Every few months, moreover, each employee is taken to lunch by a top manager. Lunch with a Dork, employees have christened the program — but its message is not lost. "My last one was with Scott," says customer-support specialist Dwight Joseph. "He brings his notebook with him, and he writes down what you say, any ideas you might have. It's pretty gratifying."

• A torrent of statistics — daily write-ups, weekly summaries, hand-lettered charts covering a whole quarter — tracks the tech-support department's performance for all to see. How many callers have to wait longer than 60 seconds? How many give up? At the company's Monday morning meetings, says Cook, "the first four numbers we go through have to do with customer service. Even before we get to revenues. It cre-ates real peer pressure to improve service — people see how we're doing each week."

At a lot of companies, pressure to improve customer service creates a white-collar sweatshop: Harried managers browbeat supervisors; super-visors keep an iron grip on employees. Intuit, by contrast, is structured to encourage cooperation and to make improvements through innova-tion rather than through tighter controls. Greg Ceniceroz, recently pro-moted from tech-support rep to product specialist, is assigned the job of figuring out how to cut down on the average time spent with each cus-tomer. His first step toward a solution: a big loose-leaf reference binder containing answers to customers' most frequent questions, for every rep's desk. He encourages reps to submit questions for inclusion in the binder and makes sure those who do get a public thank-you.

Kneisley, meanwhile, notices that management is looking for a vol-unteer to chair a group dubbed the Innovative Ideas Committee, which has been charged with collating and following up on every product-improvement idea emanating from the tech-support department and from Quicken users. She writes a four-page proposal about what she thinks the group ought to do, and gets the job. "We worked with her to set the committee's objectives," says Tom LeFevre, "since she had been here only a few months. But she was very interested. And the more interested people are, the better job they'll do."

Involvement of that sort, of course, translates into a sense of ownership more valuable and more productive than any amount of iron-grip supervision. "Most of us work at least 50 hours a week," says Kneisley. "We don't get any extra compensation. But we do have a profit-sharing plan, and if Intuit does well, we will, too."

Intuit's latest promotional campaign: Send for a copy of Quicken. Pay only an $8 shipping-and-handling charge. If you don't think you're doing useful work within a few minutes, don't pay for the product. No, not "send it back for a refund." Keep it. Just don't pay for it.

Why would a company do this?

"It's like the Japanese," Cook says. "It's like the Japanese assembly lines, where they have only two hours' worth of inventory. There's no margin for error — they have to have super-reliability from their suppliers." Cook goes to his bookshelf, pulling out a copy of *The Machine That Changed the World,* a book on the auto industry that discusses Toyota's "lean production" system. "What we're doing is the Toyota approach. We take away the safety net. If you do that, you have to get it right."

Tech support, for example. Here are 40 people answering all kinds of crazy questions — for free. Here is a $500,000 state-of-the-art telephone system, installed in late 1989 just so callers won't have to wait so long. This isn't normal: Nearly all of Intuit's competitors put a limit on tech support, some charging for it and some curtailing it so many months after purchase. And nearly every company with an after-sale call-in line doesn't mind keeping customers waiting for a few minutes.

But then, those companies have a safety net. "Most software companies would go broke if they didn't charge for tech support," argues Cook. "We said, we're not going to charge. If our customers have problems, we pay. That makes us get the product right the first time."

Take the product itself. For $50 or less — sometimes as low as $20 on store-sponsored special sales — you can buy a copy of Quicken. In its latest form, you get a program capable not only of writing checks but of

> **HOT TIP**
>
> *Frank Meeks, president and owner of Domino's Pizza Team Washington Inc., a 53-store chain in the Washington, D.C. metropolitan area, has always understood the consequences of alienating customers. For employees, however, such concepts often prove abstract. So Meeks tries to talk real numbers with his employees. For example, he estimates that many customers patronize his shops twice weekly, which means they spend close to $1,000 a year. Each unhappy customer, then, represents $1,000 in lost revenue annually. Actually, losses are greater still, since each unhappy customer tells about a dozen other people about his or her experience.*

tracking investments, generating profit-and-loss statements, and doing a dozen other chores a small-business owner or financially sophisticated consumer might want to do on a computer. You also get a 460-page manual, the right to regular upgrades at modest cost, and access to unlimited help. Once again: abnormal. Quicken's chief competitor lists for three and a half times as much as Quicken, and Quicken's price could probably double before Intuit noticed much of a sales decline.

But that would be a safety net. "We sell an inexpensive product, and we offer free customer support," says Alex Young. "We have to make sure it's right when it goes out the door." Suddenly, refinements like the Follow-Me-Home program make perfect sense.

And finally, look at Intuit's marketing. The no-pay ad, for example. "We heard from our focus groups that people really didn't believe the product could be so easy to use," recalls Mari Latterell. "After all, software never is. So we did this big advertising campaign — 'You'll be using Quicken in six minutes or it's free.' The goal was to put our money where our mouth is." Even the company's tiny sales force — two people — begins to seem comprehensible. Outside salespeople could push more product into stores, maybe. But depending on pull-through marketing means the company can't survive without satisfying its customers. "When someone comes in and thanks a clerk for selling him Quicken," says marketing vice-president John Monson, "there's nothing a salesperson could do that would come close to being as powerful a recommendation."

By some reckonings, Intuit's approach to customer satisfaction is costly. Technical support and other departments that have customer contact (the one taking orders for checks, for example) cost the company more than 10% of revenues, or upwards of $3 million a year. The testing, surveys, fancy telephone systems, focus groups, and other stay-close-to-the-customer expenses add another $1 million to $2 million. A corporate raider concerned only with the next quarter's earnings would buy up Intuit, cut back on all such expenditures, and boost profits anywhere from 50% to 100%.

"That," says Scott Cook, "is the advantage of owning the company. When you own the company, you take the long view."

Preaching the Gospel of Customer Service

Jump cut: 1994. Bill Strauss is talking from his car phone en route to a meeting somewhere in California. Strauss is vice president of operations and customer service for Intuit. He's been with the company for about seven months, having been recruited about the time Intuit acquired Chipsoft. Since Strauss joined Intuit, Scott Cook, now 41 years old, has stepped aside as president and CEO. Bill Campbell, a former executive of Apple Computer Inc., assumed that position in April. Cook remains as chairman.

"Scott hired a new president to free himself up to get close to the customer," says Strauss. "He wants to get back down to tech support. A new president cuts him loose to pursue those things he loves, which is customer service."

Customers remain Intuit's best salespeople today. "Word-of-mouth recommendation is the number one reason customers buy our products today," says Strauss, "just as it was the number one reason they bought our products in 1991."

Strauss contends that customer service is never a function of systems. It is ultimately a matter of attitude. And that attitude starts at the top, with Scott Cook. At every meeting he holds, Cook preaches customer service. It is an attitude that is reinforced every day at Intuit.

"There are two philosophies at Intuit," says Strauss. "The first is, Do right by the customer. The second is, Do right by the employee. We treat our employees well here. There is not a lot of bureaucracy. Employees have a lot of freedom. Our dress code is relaxed, because we want our employees to be comfortable. We want them focused on our customers."

If Intuit has made accommodations to growth, with the addition of processes and systems, those systems have never been permitted to interfere with customer interaction. For example, the company looks for ways to reduce the time employees spend on each phone call. Reducing phone time, of course, is in the best interests of Intuit and its customers. "We do make an effort to cut the time we spend on customer calls," says Strauss. "But that effort is invisible to the customer. Let's just say that no employee at Intuit has ever been reprimanded for spending too much time with a customer."

Strauss believes that Intuit could continue to grow and sustain its culture of superior customer service even if Scott Cook were not at the head of the company. "If he were to retire," says Strauss, "Intuit would continue to prosper, because Scott has either hired customer service or developed it in his management team. Being around Scott, customer service becomes second nature at every level of the company."

Take the company's QuickBooks software. When Intuit designed this accounting package for small business, a strange thing happened. "You won't find a single debit or credit in the program," says Strauss. "It drives accountants crazy. But we didn't design this program for accountants. We designed it for the beautician whose core competency is hairdressing, not accounting. She doesn't care about debits or credits, because she doesn't think that way." Now *that's* customer service. ∎

WAGER: ONE COMPANY

A make-it or break-it ad campaign brings Intuit
back from the brink and launches a phenomenon

MAY 1, 1985. Nine years later, Scott Cook still remembers the date. "It was the worst day of my life," he says.

Who would disagree? His company, Intuit, was less than two years old. And he had to tell his seven employees he could no longer pay their salaries.

Cook knew he had a promising product, an easy-to-use check-writing program for personal computers. What he didn't have was money.

The dozens of venture capitalists he had approached scarcely gave him a second glance. The $350,000 he himself had sunk into Intuit, a sum pieced together from life savings and home-equity credit, from credit cards and loans from his father, was nearly gone. Without money, he had no distribution channels and no customers. What computer store would carry an unknown software product — unsupported by advertising?

Intuit's sales so far had been a kind of good-news-bad-news joke. The good news: Cook had persuaded a few banks to sell the program in their lobbies. Each one ordered several hundred copies

for inventory when it signed up, generating a little cash. The bad news: Banks were lousy at selling software, so reorders were slim. Knowing he had to get the program into computer stores, he scrambled to sell to just a few more banks.

By the summer of 1986 Cook's efforts had just barely paid off. The little company had $125,000, enough to start an ad campaign. By rights he and his colleagues should have done some tests. But there was no time, not if they wanted to catch the Christmas selling season. So early in the fall they took the $125,000 — all of it — and spent it on one make-or-break ad campaign. Cook wrote the ad himself. If it didn't work . . . nah, better not to think too hard about that.

Well, Lady Luck was smiling that fall. Or maybe Cook's extraordinary efforts to create a product that would truly satisfy its buyers were on the money. Whatever the reason, the ad launched Intuit's program on what turned out to be a brilliant career.

"The company," says Cook of the now $230-million business, "grew a bunch." ∎

The Missing Links
of Customer Satisfaction

by Deborah B. Taylor

What is most striking about the explosive growth of Intuit Inc., the Menlo Park, Calif. microcomputer software manufacturer, is how perfectly ordinary its business strategy is. Intuit has succeeded famously by paying attention to its customers. Yet every company today boasts of doing just that. Customer focus, customer service, and customer satisfaction are on everyone's lips.

But lip service, not customer service, is what most companies deliver today. The importance of customer service is widely recognized in business. Fully 91% of all businesses have some sort of customer-service theme, customer-satisfaction program, or customer-focused training in place. What separates the wheat of Intuit from the chaff of other companies is execution.

Reading a case study about a company like Intuit is inspiring. Following its lead can be daunting. If the challenge were simple, more companies would provide the high-quality customer service that Intuit routinely affords its customers. Only 16% of U.S. companies feel they have been successful in applying and producing the desired results with customers. For the most part, customers do not find doing business a "pleasant buying experience." The service, the courtesy, the convenience, the speed, and the outcome of the experience routinely fail to meet customer expectations. And this is true in 1994, ten years after customer service was recognized as a powerful new strategic tool in business.

Businesses today spend significant amounts of energy and resources

Deborah B. Taylor is managing partner of the Taylor Consulting Group Inc., Cedar Rapids, Iowa.

on customer service programs, themes, and training. But for the most part, their efforts are cosmetic. What they achieve is a perception of customer satisfaction. They *look* like customer service-oriented organizations. Few businesses really are.

The competitive edge in customer service today is "more than satisfied." But only 16% of businesses achieve that level of service. The 84% of businesses that fail to achieve competitive-edge customer service are neglecting the four critical "missing links" of customer satisfaction: Execution, Raising the Bar, Immediacy, and Commitment. The four missing links are not new. They are simply not being applied.

The Execution Factor

Businesses do not do what they know how to do. This truth is what separates a company like Intuit from most other companies. Companies fail to use, apply, and execute the programs, themes, standards, and training that they claim they have implemented. Many 'doers' feel the new customer satisfaction efforts are just one more program, one more 'hype' or training activity that will run its course and disappear. A company's doers may understand friendly service, problem-solving, accuracy in work, timeliness of response, but they do not execute those skills.

Even when doers are willing to execute, a lack of supervision and accountability sends the message that these skills are not a priority at the company. As a result, resources are wasted and customers dissatisfied. When a failure to service occurs, management generally solves the problem without involving the doer, which only perpetuates a system that is fundamentally flawed. Unless doers are empowered and disciplined to make every customer more than satisfied, customer service is just a slogan.

Doers must be made accountable and responsible for more-than-satisfied customers on every customer contact to enhance the return on a company's investment in customer service. Intuit Inc. ensures that customers are more than satisfied every single time they interact with the company. That intensity has made it a member of the exclusive Sixteen Percenters. But there are other examples.

The Ritz Carlton hotel group, for instance, is well known for its excellence in service. At the Ritz, doers understand the importance of the execution factor. Every employee in housekeeping is graded on a measurable reward system based on criteria of most importance to guests of the Ritz Carlton. (Like Intuit, the Ritz is meticulous about asking its guests what services they consider important.)

Or consider Nestlé, the giant food products company. In a market where a gain of one or two share points is considered phenomenal performance, Nestlé gained 24 share points over a six-year period in which it was outspent in advertising, seven to one, by competitors. Nestlé's secret weapon? Direct interaction with customers.

Or take Ryder Truck. Recently, the large, well-entrenched vehicle leasing firm was slipping deeper and deeper into the red as a result of double-digit losses. Did they change management? Of course they did. Did they advertise? Of course they did. Ryder did all the things turnaround companies do to turn around. But if you ask what Ryder did specifically to turn double-digit losses into double-digit profits in a single year, the company will tell you, "We refocused our entire organization around meeting the needs and wants of our customers."

This is what Scott Cook is talking about when he compares Intuit's management style to the Japanese. The Toyota approach, says Cook, removes the safety net. When there is no margin for error, you have to get it right the first time. And that is how a company more than satisfies its customers.

The Retton Factor

Unfortunately, no sooner do you get the hang of customer service than the rules change. Today's more than satisfactory level of service will probably not cut the mustard tomorrow. Companies must extend a level of customer service based on the current competitive environment and new customer demands. IBM understands this only too well today, for as IBM continued to operate at existing customer service standards, companies like Dell Computer, Gateway 2000, and AST entered the marketplace willing and eager to extend a new level of customer service. Insensitive to its customers' desires for cheaper machines, less technology, greater availability, and 24-hour service, IBM faltered.

As 1984 Olympic Gold Medal gymnast Mary Lou Retton so aptly puts it, "A gold medal performance in one Olympics is merely a routine in the next." Retton says we must constantly "raise the bar." We must constantly improve and be sensitive to a changing market. Antiquated customer satisfaction criteria are a common flaw in businesses that fail to live up to promises of customer service.

By contrast, Intuit raises the bar with its Follow-Me-Home program. This program actually sends service personnel to customer homes to stand in the user's shoes, to witness and understand the current needs of the company's target audience. It is not the program, but the process of learning, that makes Intuit successful. At Intuit, the learning process is continuous and ongoing. The learning process reaps a harvest of learned needs. The actions that Intuit executes to solve problems and meet needs are what has enabled this company to acquire more than five million users in less than ten years in business.

The Immediacy Factor

Intuit and all businesses that deliver outstanding levels of customer service and customer focus recognize "do it now" components. Growth in revenue, market share, and customer base can all be attributed to a "do it now" attitude. Intuit recognized the impact of the Immediacy Factor early on through focus groups, proactive customer follow-up support (the Bounce Back Program), and an extreme client focus. Intuit created an environment in which the basis of every employee's responsibility, every action, and every decision was to satisfy the customer's needs better, immediately. If the decision, action, or responsibility does not in some way enable Intuit to better serve the customer, it is considered unnecessary.

The Intuit corporate culture demands action. Intuit understands that the "customer response" or technical support department is managed as the team which learns the customer's changing needs. Without a culture of action, Intuit could not continually improve to meet new customer demands. Companies that react immediately to an opportunity can achieve excellence in customer focus, customer service, and customer satisfaction. Businesses that endlessly analyze opportunities or those that must seek several levels of approval will frustrate customers who are more demanding than ever before. Today, companies that fail to react quickly to opportunities are destined to watch competitors seize their customers.

The Commitment Factor

At Intuit, the minimum standard of performance is "more-than-satisfied" customers. The Ritz Carlton calls its policy the "act-at-first-notice concept." The Ritz Carlton empowers all of its employees to take whatever action they deem necessary in a crisis to obtain "instant customer pacification." With such empowerment, Ritz Carlton employees understand that "more than satisfied" is not a level of performance toward which to strive but performance expected on a day-to-day basis.

The Commitment Factor in the solutions matrix of the Taylor More (than) Satisfied Customer Matrix (TMTSCM) poses the question: "How will we do in our business if it is our competitors who are able to do these things?" The answer is that we would falter. As a result, companies such as Intuit and the Ritz Carlton have no choice but to deliver outstanding service to achieve more-than-satisfied customers 100% of the time.

Misconceptions

Certain business myths retard a firm in its efforts to identify and satisfy its customers' needs profitably. One such myth is the belief that client satisfaction is always tied to product features and price factors. The fact is that it is impossible to sustain a competitive advantage in product or price. It can't be done. As successful as it is, even Intuit is too product feature-reliant for customer satisfaction. It is what you do for your customer beyond the product that sustains a competitive advantage long term. What you do to satisfy the unique needs of your customers over time — the empathy component — secures a competitive advantage.

If the idea that a customer will do business with a salesperson because the two like each other was ever valid, it is a myth today. If a client is not sold and served ethically and professionally, if the provided products and services are not related to customer needs, there is no way customers will become loyal, satisfied customers.

That is underscored by the fact that in most of the companies that believe they "more than satisfy" their customers — the Sixteen Percenters — sales and service people did not sell on the basis of emotion, but on the basis of logic. They did not ask for a customer's business unless they could help improve the prospect's business.

Intuit and other Sixteen Percenters enjoy a bonus as customer service-oriented firms. In many cases, the Sixteen Percenters have recruited their customers as an ancillary sales force. These firms provide so great a value in

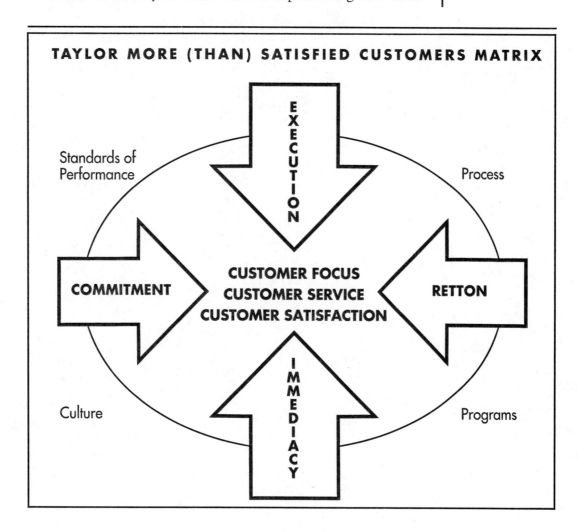

sales and service to their customers that their customers recommend their products to new customers. It is difficult to place a value on this sort of word-of-mouth advertising.

But rather than rest on their laurels, Sixteen Percenters should bear in mind that new competitors are busy building better and better mouse-traps. Answering the telephone in three rings, please and thank you, phone calls returned immediately, on-time delivery, order accuracy, speed of service, business knowledge, company flexibility, expertise, and all the other components of service delivered beyond the product generate cus-tomer focus, customer service, and customer satisfaction long term.

And they are all fast becoming routine. ■

The Intuitive Culture

by JoAnna Brandi

Why, when customer service is so strategically necessary in business, are there so few true practitioners of the craft? What differentiates those companies that have learned the customer service lingo from companies that deliver on the promise? The answer comes down to a corporate culture that focuses so intently on the customer that customer service is a consideration of every business decision.

The success Scott Cook has enjoyed in getting his employees at Intuit to share in his obsession with customer service is grounded in the culture he has developed at the company.

Corporate culture is the foundation of customer service. Corporate culture is a set of beliefs and attitudes that employees of a company embrace. And embrace is the right word, because the degree to which employees internalize a philosophy determines the potency of a company's culture.

It follows that culture begins with the founder of a company and is an extension of the founder's personal values and perceptions. Bill Strauss, now vice president of customer service at Intuit, talks about how Cook has imbued his employees with his commitment to the customer. Strauss says Cook has either instilled his culture of customer service in employees or hired that quality.

"Culture is the soul of an enterprise," says Stephen Harper, Professor of Management at the University of North Carolina at Wilmington and author of the McGraw-Hill *Guide to Managing Growth in Your Emerging Business*. When a company holds contradictory values and beliefs, employees work at cross-purposes. But a convergence of values and

JoAnna Brandi is president of Integrated Marketing Systems Inc., Sea Cliff, N.Y.

beliefs, attitudes and behavior, as has occurred at Intuit, can create a focus of laser-like intensity.

Culture, like the words agriculture, cultivate, and even cult, share the same Latin root, *colere*, meaning to grow or nourish. For ten years now, Scott Cook has nourished an environment at Intuit where service to customers flourishes, where employees feel good about coming to work in the morning and proud to be a part of what they consider a noble enterprise. In the final analysis, both customers and the bottom line have blossomed.

Professor Harper believes the best corporate cultures are found in companies with crystal-clear vision. In these companies, everyone knows where the company is going and what is expected of them. Employees know what work is rewarded and what actions are not acceptable.

According to John Monson, vice president and general manager of the Business Products Group at Intuit, the motivation of employees can be reduced to a phrase. "We aspire to making the lives of our customers better," he says. Not satisfying customers, not pleasing customers, not getting them to buy the product again, but improving their lives. "That's what personally motivates Scott," says Monson, "and that's what personally motivates me."

This commitment to customers relates directly to the bottom line. "If you make customers' lives fundamentally better," Monson says, "in a way they're willing to pay for, then you've earned the right to make money."

Intuit has certainly done that. It has also experienced rapid growth. For several years, the company tripled in size. Recently the company has been growing at 40%. Late in 1993, Intuit merged with Chipsoft. But significant growth and mergers can often threaten corporate culture by bringing on board large numbers of new employees who do not share the values and beliefs that led to the company's success. Mergers bring together entire companies, often with a clash of cultures.

To avoid such a schism, management decided to borrow a page from its own philosophy. What Intuit had done so well by its customers, namely, listening to them, it decided to try with employees. The compa-

EXERCISE
Do you have what it takes to serve your customers?

Put an X on the line closest to how you score for each item. Connect the lines and draw a circle around the three highest and the three lowest scoring items. List the highest scored items under "three greatest strengths," and your lowest list under "three improvement opportunities." Make a commitment to boost your strengths and use your improvement opportunities to eliminate weaknesses.

	20 ⊥ 40 ⊥ 60 ⊥ 80 ⊥ 100
Communicates clearly	_____
Understanding and caring	_____
Sensitive to feelings	_____
Takes responsibility	_____
Organizes priorities	_____
Mindset is flexible	_____
Enthusiastically shares ideas	_____
Relationship builder	_____
Competent	_____
Actively listens	_____
Reliable	_____
Energy level is high	_____
Empathic	_____
Xtra step	_____
Problem solvers	_____
Expects to succeed	_____
Respects others	_____
Turns a crisis into an opportunity	_____

Three Greatest Strengths:

1._____

2._____

3._____

Three Improvement Opportunities:

1._____

2._____

3._____

ny developed a process known by the acronym VMOVA, which stands for Vision, Mission, Operating Values, and Achievement.

The company began with an all-day brainstorming session with a small core of employees. A team consisting of the executive committee and an equal number of people from every department in the company spent several months sifting through the information the employees had shared. Then all employees were included in a vision process in which they were encouraged to look out into the future. As they peered into that future, Intuit asked its employees to be revolutionary, rather than evolutionary, in their thinking.

Monson admits that the process took "five times longer" than had been expected. And he cautions patience for managers who wish to develop a new vision for their companies. "Be inclusive," he says, adding, "I think the investment is worthwhile."

In time, Intuit will know how worthwhile the process was. The company has committed to certain changes. And it has committed to going through the process again. That, of course, is the key to making a vision work in any organization. The vision must be relevant. Employees must clearly understand the part they play in the success of the company.

Will Intuit's vision, its new culture, be self-sustaining? Will the company continue to grow, prosper, and delight its customers? Will customers continue to enjoy the experience of using Intuit products so much that they become salespeople for the company? Only time will tell, but when a company is willing constantly to re-examine itself, its goals, and its processes, the likelihood is that its culture will remain vibrant and its employees enthusiastic. ■

Creating the
"Perception of a Difference"

by Wesley W. Zimmerman

We are all customers of someone. We give continuing business to certain suppliers because we perceive a desirable difference in them. When that "perception of a difference" is sharply focused, we ignore price differences and willingly pay our favorite suppliers up to 15% more because they satisfy us. While product is important, it is the service these suppliers provide that is the key to our satisfaction, particularly when we buy several different products from the same supplier. We develop expectations about service. When these expectations are met by the supplier's employees, our feelings toward the supplier remain positive even when a product proves unsatisfactory, because we know we can return it or have it replaced.

Intuit is a master of using "perception of a difference" to promote its products. The company has been extraordinarily successful in controlling and then fulfilling the expectations of its customers. Conducting research to determine what potential customers would expect from a product like Quicken, Intuit then developed a product to meet those expectations.

Intuit tells potential customers they will be doing useful work within a few minutes of loading Quicken into their computers. The customer's expectations fall within a relatively narrow range: I can very quickly use this software to pay my bills and save time in the process. The "difference" that Intuit customers perceive is sharply focused at the end of that first day using its products. This "perception of a difference"

Wesley W. Zimmerman is chairman of WZA Inc., Scottsdale, Ariz.

remains sharply focused, because the customer's expectations are fulfilled by Intuit's customer service group on every call for help.

Intuit's follow-up customer service is effective because it reinforces the customer's ability to do "useful work" quickly, thereby fulfilling the customer's expectations on a continuing basis. This is the only reason any customer service is effective. Most companies and customer service organizations find it impossible to develop a list of tasks or criteria that define good customer service. When asked for a definition of good service, a customer's first words, spoken or unspoken, will be: "I expect…"

Customer Service vs. Customer Satisfaction

Success in any business depends on satisfying customers with a product and/or service.

A satisfied customer is one whose expectations have been met. To meet a customer's expectations we must know what those expectations are, when, why, and how they are changed. With this knowledge we can design successful products and deliver service that creates lifetime customers.

Traditional customer service fixes problems, straightens out procedural glitches, corrects errors of commission and omission, and provides information. It is essentially product and "I" (vendor) centered. It satisfies customer requests but doesn't necessarily create customer satisfaction. Customer service is reactive. Creating customer satisfaction is proactive.

Customer satisfaction is "you" (customer) centered and focuses on meeting the customer's expectations. It recognizes that the product or service purchased is usually a tool for use in creating satisfaction. Customer service that satisfies requires sensitivity on the part of every person involved in the creation and delivery of the product and/or service.

Every satisfied customer strengthens the perception of a difference that sets us apart from our competition. People make that difference. When each member of a company's team realizes that they make a difference, it becomes possible to satisfy customer expectations. Creating and maintaining this focus is management's greatest challenge.

People listen to customers.

People design and build products.

People perform service.

People create expectations.

People satisfy expectations.

People create the perception of a difference when they want to!

As owner, principal, CEO, president, or manager, your task is to encourage your people to create the perception of a difference. Scott Cook has done this at Intuit. In your company, *you* are the difference!

EXERCISE

The Challenge: Customer Expectations

1. **How many of your people have a distinct customer clientele who specifically name them when calling for service or a reservation, or when they come into your store?** _____

2. **Are these customers satisfied when someone else handles their requests?**

   Yes _____ No _____ Why?

   _____

   _____

   _____

3. **Does a detailed record of the requested person's service, to this specific customer, exist for use by a replacement person?**

   Yes _____ No _____

4. **Is this record current?**

   Yes _____ No _____ Why not?

   _____

   _____

   _____

5. When will it be current?

_____

_____

6. What do you think a new customer expects about your product in terms of:

functionality? _____

quality? _____

support? _____

overall? _____

7. Is this what you think they should expect?

Yes _____ No _____ Why?

_____

_____

_____

8. Objectively, what would your expectation be?

_____

_____

_____

9. What do you think a new customer expects about your service?

responsiveness? _____

friendliness? _____

competence of people? _____

thoughtfulness? _____

overall? _____

10. Is this what you think they should expect?

Yes _____ No _____ Why?

_____

_____

_____

11. Objectively, what would your expectation be?

_____

_____

_____

In the Intuit Case Study:

How did Scott Cook, the company president, check the validity of his own expectations for his product and support service?

_____

_____

_____

There are many ways to determine what the majority of customers expect and will expect from a product or service. The product or nature of the service will determine the approach, to some extent. However, the success of the product or service will be directly related to how well it enables buyers/customers to meet their expectations.

A tractor that truly satisfies a Kansas wheat farmer will be totally dissatisfying to an apple grower. The size, power, and maneuverability requirements are completely different. However, the service support that satisfies both will be similar because there are periods within the growing cycle of wheat and apples when time is critical and tractor downtime can have disastrous effects on the farmer's profitability.

If customer expectations were stable, it would be relatively easy to develop and maintain consistent, high customer satisfaction. Unfortunately, customer expectations are not stable.

EXERCISE

Customer Expectations: Avoiding the Oversell

Get a copy of the latest advertisement for your product or service, look at it and answer these questions.

1. **What will your customer expect from your product and/or service after reading it quickly?**

   _____

   _____

   _____

2. **What will he/she expect after reading it carefully?**

   _____

   _____

   _____

3. **Are the two expectations the same?** Yes _____ No _____

4. **Do you want them to be the same?** Yes _____ No _____ **Why?**

   _____

   _____

   _____

5. Do your customer service personnel understand the customer's expectations?

Yes_____ No _____

6. Will your product, service, and team meet these expectations?

Yes _____ No _____ Why?

_____

_____

_____

7. Will your product, service, and team satisfy your present/old customers when these expectations are added to expectations they had before reading your ad?

Yes _____ No _____ Why?

_____

_____

These questions must be answered before approving any advertising copy because the advertisement affects and changes the expectations of your customer and prospective customer. Intuit's promotion for Quicken, for example, told customers to "pay only an $8 shipping-and-handling charge. If you don't think you're doing useful work within a few minutes, don't pay for the product. No, not 'send it back for a refund.' Keep it. Just don't pay for it."

What do you expect after reading it quickly?
Read it carefully — what do you expect now?

Initially, I expect to be able to try a product for $8. After reading the ad carefully, I expect the product to be extremely simple, easy to use, and very useful. I'd better not order it until I'm sure I want something that does what it is designed to do, because I'll be conscience-bound to pay the full price plus the $8. This producer is that certain of its capability. These are my expectations after reading this ad. The product and service must meet these expectations if I am to be a satisfied customer.

Mail Order or Personal Selling — The Same Challenge

Every advertisement, sales brochure, and statement made by a salesperson creates expectations. If a prospect converts all the input from these sources into expectations, becoming a satisfied customer may be difficult. Advertising copywriters have become so adept in the use of modifiers and disclaimers that many people do not set expectations on such printed input. However, once they come to trust a salesperson, they tend to convert everything the salesperson has said since their first contact into expectations. (Occasionally some expectations get set in actions, not words.)

What does this tell you?

1. Are your salespeople educated sufficiently about your product and/or service to be able to create expectations that can be met?

Yes _____ No _____ Why?

_____

_____

_____

2. How many salespeople do you have?   _____

This number should include everyone who contacts a customer by phone, fax, presentations, demonstrations, and proposal creation. If you sell using catalogs, include the people who write the catalog copy, product descriptions, etc. (Feel free to draw a line through your first number and write in the new figure.)

For several decades, Sears, Roebuck & Co. (now Sears) was

tremendously successful. Its sales growth and profitability were fueled by satisfied customers who made 60% to 80% of their Sears purchases from the catalog without talking to a human. These customers were satisfied and claimed that Sears gave the best service in the world. That service consisted primarily of prompt shipment of products that met the customer's expectations. Prompt shipment is and was relatively easy (computers didn't exist then). Satisfying customer expectations was no easier then than it is today.

The Sears secret was in the way it set and controlled customer expectations. Whenever possible, products were offered under quality designations of good, better, and best. The catalog product descriptions included accurate pictures and text that detailed the use, wearability, and value of the product in relation to the good, better, or best quality designation in a manner the reader/buyer could relate to. For instance, the thread count per inch and quality of cotton used in the threads was stated for sheets. Good Quality was 100% cotton with 120 threads per inch. Better Quality was a 100% blend of regular and long fiber cotton with 160 threads per inch. The Best Quality was 100% long staple cotton with 240 threads per inch. They also used name differentiation, e.g. Sears Tools vs. Craftsman Tools, Kenmore vs. Lady Kenmore appliances.

These descriptions justified the prices listed and enabled the customer to order based on quality versus price. The customer's expectations were set within Sears's ability to meet them. If the customer opened the box, liked the style, but decided that better quality was more desirable than the good quality he/she had ordered, the item could be returned and the better quality ordered with a check for the difference enclosed.

Any item could be returned with or without explanation for full, prompt refund including shipping charges both ways. Warranty service was prompt and, where appropriate, consisted of exchange with a new product or a loaner for use while the repair was made. If this didn't satisfy, the purchase price and shipping charges were refunded promptly. The customer was satisfied because his/her expectations were controlled and met consistently. Sears was synonymous with quality for the price. It was not perceived as the low-priced source. It was profitable.

Customer service is not limited to fixing problems. The perception of a desirable difference that forms on the first contact with a prospect gains us the right to create and meet his/her expectations of our products and service. When we are successful in this, the prospect becomes a customer. Our customer service begins with designing and building products to meet customer expectations and continues with support service and product revisions that continue to meet expectations. All of this builds customer satisfaction.

It is not always possible to control the customer's expectations as well as Sears did. Competitors, our own statements, and our success in serving customers create changes in their expectations. Therefore, only a consistent effort by 100% of our team can create satisfied lifetime customers.

It is also essential to ask customers continually what their expectations are (since they are likely to change), and get regular feedback from them. ■

Notes

1

The Rigorous Customer-Complaint Form

Customers with complaints become apostles for the competition. When Jim Thompson realized this truth in 1990, he challenged his employees to get a grip on customer complaints. His company, Electronic Controls Co. (ECCO), based in Boise, Idaho, designs, manufactures, and markets amber strobe lights for utility vehicles and backup alarms for trucks that beep when the driver shifts into reverse. And like most businesses, ECCO was hearing its share of customer complaints.

ECCO's customer-service reps, who fielded the complaints, were authorized to issue credit memos, ship replacement products or parts overnight, or do whatever else was necessary to placate customers. That was fine as far as it went, but it didn't go far enough for Thompson, then president. There was no record of the complaints or the reps' response to them. Thompson's concern was that the underlying problems that provoked the complaints in the first place still lurked, almost certain to prompt future gripes.

"We sensed we were getting the same complaints over and over, but we weren't sure," says Ed Zimmer, then in charge of sales and marketing, which includes customer service. "Our challenge was to track them and make them go away. We needed the statistics because, you know, if something gets measured, it gets done."

So the customer-service team devised a form to capture the core data — the customer's name and account number, the complaint itself, and ECCO's corrective action. As patterns emerged, the form was improved. For instance, check-off boxes were added for the most common complaints.

Customers with complaints become apostles for the competition.

Zimmer, who considers the form an "active document," encourages such innovation. "It's better to have the form designed by the people who use it," he says. "We revise it at least once a year. And we decided to put a lot more effort into how we handled the complaints. Instead of a 'corrective action' that responded to complaints individually and specifically, we adopted a 'first response corrective action,' to correct the root causes of problems."

Now in its fifth generation, the form provides a way to tabulate complaints and deal systematically with them. ECCO tracks the information in two ways. A sales-team secretary enters each complaint into the computer's database, and Lori Hicks, the customer-service team leader, files the original hard copy of each open-and-shut case in a binder with the "closed" cases. The complaints that merit further consideration go into the "open" binder. Hicks uses the database to generate a monthly customer-satisfaction report that lists complaints by category and by frequency of occurrence.

"Once we know what the most common complaints are, we can identify what's causing them," says Zimmer, now president and chief operating officer. "We take our top three problems and assign corrective-action teams to solve them. Then our biggest problem goes away and number four becomes number three. In a recent 12-month period, we'd had 33 complaints about shipments that were either over or under the right quantity, but in the past six months, since we redesigned our packing slips and added a second check of each box before it gets sealed, we've had only six such complaints."

1 GOOD FORMS

ECCO president Ed Zimmer explains the form:

At first we routed the filled-out forms to everybody in sales and all department heads, but that took too long. Then we realized that everyone who really needed to see the complaints was on one of these three teams — leadership, production, or sales.

About 95% of the complaints are phoned in. Most of them, like this example, come into the customer-service area, but we provide pads of these forms to anyone who might talk to a customer. Even our engineering people have them, because someone might call with a technical question about installation and make a complaint. I have a pad at my desk, too, because sometimes customers demand to speak to the president.

Complaints that don't fit into one of the common categories are marked "other." But if an unusual complaint increases in frequency, it can end up with its own box. "Competitive comparison" is a relatively new category that used to be covered by the "other" choice.

ECCO CUSTOMER COMPLAINT FORM

Leadership Team Review: _____ Mtg. Date: 7/19 Production Team Review _____ Mtg. Date: 7/14
Sales Team Review: _____ Mtg. Date: 7/14 Copies Requested by: _____

Taken By: JA) Complaint Date: 7/14/93 Invoice #: 97604 S.O. # 020316
Ship Date: 7/2 Customer P.O. #: 930706 Phone: 243-4224 (314)
Customer: Translectric Location: Jackson, MO
Contact Name: Tom Mirley ECCO Account Mgr.: Dan McCann

COMPLAINT: ☹ (Please Check)

☐ Alarm ☐ Light ☐ Contract ☒ Service

PRODUCT LINE:

PRODUCT: **SERVICE**
☐ Electrical Interference
☐ Concern over early failure
☐ Warning labels missing
☐ No/wrong box labels
☐ Not boxed correctly
☐ Parts missing from kit
☐ Not labeled correctly
☐ Other:

☐ Transit time too long
☐ Incorrect part shipped
☐ Out of inventory
☐ Short/over shipments
☐ Unit priced incorrectly
☒ Freight charge incorrect
☐ Sent order to wrong cust.
☐ Order not rec'd/entered

☐ Handling charge
☐ Incomplete shipment
☐ Competitive comparison
☐ Competitive pricing
☐ Past due shipment

DELIVERY
☐ Error by carrier
☐ Other:

We ask for a root-cause analysis when we see a complaint that's pretty frequent or one that we feel is becoming a severe problem. That's how we discovered that our badly designed packing slip promoted mistakes and that we'd ended up shipping the wrong amounts repeatedly. Those complaints go into the "open" binder, which the director of sales and marketing, Dan McCann, and I review at least monthly. Anything still open after a month gets pretty high attention. We expect these teams to react quickly.

The team is usually two or three people, from the area where the root cause appears to be, who are in a position to implement corrective action. If it looks like a materials problem, for example, then we assign people from the materials team or the purchasing department, and so on. Those people report back to a member of the leadership team, who can either approve their corrective action or have them keep working on it.

We try to take corrective action on the first phone call. It's important to apologize and to make sure you understand the problem. Sometimes, unhappy customers are merely looking for a place to vent frustration. They feel better when they get the chance to do it. You can't assume you know how they feel or that you know the severity of this complaint to them. So we want to satisfy each customer right away. This complaint was filed by one of our customers who is entitled to freight-free shipments on orders over a certain dollar amount. Our sales and marketing people are authorized and trained to deal with complaints, and there's no dollar limit on what they can do. They can't make a mistake so big that it's worse than having an unhappy customer out there, telling other people about us.

"Track for trend" is for complaints that don't come up very often and aren't really serious, like a dented box. If we suddenly see several customers with this same complaint, however, then we might assign a corrective-action team to hunt for the root cause. Generally, these are internal problems, mistakes we made. They just go into the "closed complaint" binder.

If, for example, we sent three boxes and the shipper delivered only two, we'd consider it an external error that required no more investigation.

Before each Monday leadership-group meeting, the sales and marketing department and probably the production department have already reviewed the newly filed complaints. Sometimes those departments recommend solutions. But the leadership team assigns a corrective-action team to each serious or frequent problem. For each complaint, we have three possible courses of action.

We leave this blank until the root cause has been identified and corrective action is in place. It completes the loop. Only a member of the leadership team can authorize closing a complaint.

We keep each hard copy in the binder for six months after the complaint is closed. We figure that's long enough. But the information is never purged from the computer. We have all the complaints in our database, going back to when we started this.

The little happy faces are just a personal touch. ∎

FIRST RESPONSE CORRECTIVE ACTION: will fax a copy of the freight bill for immediate credit to his account. apologized customer

MANAGEMENT REVIEW RESPONSE:
Suspected Root Cause: Customer set up incorrectly in computer

☐ Track for trend (CLOSED)
☑ Requires root cause analysis and further corrective action (OPEN)
☐ No further corrective action required (CLOSED)

CORRECTIVE ACTION TEAM: Lori Hicks, George Forbes

ROOT CAUSE CORRECTIVE ACTION: Customer file corrected and continuing training held in customer service.

Complaint Closed: Date: 8-23-93 Authorization: Dan McCa Purge Date: 2/94

Notes

_____

_____

_____

_____

_____

_____

_____

_____

_____

_____

_____

_____

_____

_____

_____

_____

_____

_____

_____

_____

_____

_____

CHAPTER

2

Who Are Your Real Customers?

If Leegin Creative Leather Products' history contains a lesson for business people, it is this: You can't provide quality customer service unless you know who your customers are. Leegin (pronounced *legion*) Leather was a $10-million belt maker for years. Then CEO Jerry Kohl made a discovery. He discovered that his customers were not the specialty stores that ordered and sold Leegin's belts. Those specialty stores were his salespeople's customers. Jerry Kohl's customers (Leegin's true customers) were Leegin's salespeople themselves.

When Kohl understood this truth, he had to revamp his company inside and out. To take care of his customers, Kohl empowered them with technology — sending them out on the road with laptop computers. Those laptops sent a surge of power through his salespeople. Suddenly, they could provide their customers with a wealth of information that turned Leegin belts into profit centers in their specialty stores. But once Leegin's sales force had this new power, they needed a new level of support from the home office and plant to take advantage of it. It was this level of support that required Kohl to completely revamp the systems and functions and teams at corporate headquarters.

How did he reorganize Leegin Leather to support his customers (his sales force), so that they could deliver superb customer service to their customers? And what impact has such a reorganization had on Leegin Leather? The answers are the core of this case

What impresses consultants Martha Rogers and Don Peppers (see p. 64) about the way Kohl transformed his company is the shift in his strategic thinking. Rogers and Peppers contend that Kohl's success hinged on his realization that as a belt manufacturer, Leegin was managing a product, a product much like many others on the market. When he understood that he must manage his relationship with customers (what Rogers and Peppers call 1:1 Marketing) rather than manage his product, a tectonic shift occurred in his approach to business. The results have been volcanic.

After you read about Leegin's transformation and study the Rogers-Peppers lesson in 1:1 Marketing, consider the advice consultant Bruce Hodes (see p. 75) offers about the value of teams in organizations in the 1990s. Hodes insists that the quality of the service you provide your customers largely depends on how well your customer service people work together as a team.

A Business Transformed

First you figure out what you can do to break away from the pack in your industry. Then you teach your salespeople how to make your product indispensable to customers. And then, as Jerry Kohl of Leegin discovered, you learn that those steps are just the beginning.

For much of the 1980s, Leegin Creative Leather Products in Industry, Calif., just drifted along. Leegin's sales, expressed in millions, read like the judges' scorecards at a figure-skating contest. Nine point five. Nine point seven. Nine point three. Year after year the $10-million barrier seemed impervious, and Leegin condemned to steady-state purgatory. Just an everyday company in the apparel trade, so it appeared, due to be snapped up by a competitor or driven under by imports.

Then, suddenly, the heavens beckoned. In 1987 the company hit $10.8 million; in 1988, $15 million; in 1989, $20 million. Every year thereafter brought similar bursts. By the end of the 1993 fiscal year, Leegin had recorded revenues of $60 million, six times its mid-1980s level. This year, the company expects to do about $70 million. Profits, too, have grown apace. Leegin's pretax income in the last three years has hovered around 10% of sales. Its debt-to-equity ratio dropped from 3:1 in 1989 to 1.1:1 in 1993.

Leegin makes leather belts, which is to say it does business in a fiercely competitive marketplace, an industry propelled partly by fashion but mostly by buyers' unchanging need to hold up their trousers. The company has neither uncovered nor created a burning new trend or technology to which to hitch its rocket. It hasn't signed up any deep-pocketed investors; it hasn't landed any make-or-break accounts, no Wal-Mart or Sears or J.C. Penney. (Leegin's 15 biggest customers account for less than one-third of its business.) Nor has the global economy boosted its growth. Leegin's customers, several thousand specialty stores and a handful of mail-order houses, are nearly all domestic. It makes most of its belts in its California factory.

Oh, and one other thing: Leegin never advertises. There isn't even a sign on the company's building. "The belt industry hardly knows who we are," says Kohl, exaggerating only a little.

So, what's the secret? You could say — accurately — that Leegin's salespeople can do things with computers that most salespeople only dream of. You could note how the office and the factory have been reorganized to support sales rather than undermine them. But those are parts. And ultimately, to understand what has happened, you have to see Leegin whole, the way its zealous leader, Kohl, sees it, as a company that has undergone and is still undergoing a self-directed metamorphosis. Leegin has quietly but surely been transforming itself from just another belt company to a supplier that its customers will find indispensable, maybe even irreplaceable. Leegin is eating its competitors' dinner because Kohl isn't afraid to throw out or reinvent any part of the company that interferes with that objective.

Kohl always wanted to sell to specialty stores. He had run one himself, started before he even finished high school, with his girlfriend, Terri, now his wife of 24 years. It was a psychedelic shop, with T-shirts and paraphernalia for the youth trade, opened up each day as soon as its owners got out of class. At age 19 Kohl bought into Leegin, a tiny leather company he did business with, and set out to supply the specialty clothing and leather-goods market. Two years later he and Terri bought out the founders.

Leegin grew — a little. It was a tough business. Customers had to be called on by salespeople; catalogs and telemarketing alone wouldn't do the trick. But the stores were small, and Leegin's line was limited. Salespeople found themselves traveling long distances to write up small orders. Every time a salesperson quit, Kohl lost dozens of accounts. Back at the plant, Leegin's designers kept turning out new styles, since any clothing retailer likes something fresh for the season. But the proliferation of products threatened to choke the factory with work in process. A batch of belts could take more than a month to wend its way through cutting, sewing, and every other department.

Bogged Down in Paper Blizzard

Then there was the office, which by the early 1980s had turned into a jumble of fiefdoms and foul-ups worthy of a Charlie Chaplin movie. Orders awaiting fulfillment were jammed into a clipboard on the wall. Invoices were cranked out in sextuplicate. A simple request from a customer — "add a belt to my last order," say — went from customer service (which filled out a form) to order processing (which looked up the style and price information) to data processing (which entered it in the computer) back to order processing (for verification) and back to customer service (which was the only department allowed to talk with customers). The round-trip took weeks.

Like employees and managers all over America, Leegin's workers passed the buck and covered their rears. Salespeople on the road griped about lost orders and lousy manufacturing quality. People in the office accused the salespeople and one another of sloppiness, and the factory workers of incompetence. On the line, production employees pursued their own idea of them and us. They'd come in, put on their Walkmans, and wait to be given work.

If ever a company seemed stuck, it was Leegin. The nine-point-something numbers reflected it: For six straight years its sales scarcely budged. Kohl, however, was about to get himself unstuck. In the summer of 1986 he went off to Harvard Business School for the first of three annual sessions in the Owner/President Management Program. Kohl had never been to college, and this was a once-in-a-lifetime experience. There were compelling case studies, smart professors, late-night study sessions. There were a hundred other businesspeople with whom to swap ideas. Soon, bells began to ring.

Leegin was a belt manufacturer just like every other belt manufacturer, Kohl realized. As long as that was true, the company would never grow. But it didn't have to be just like the others. Frank Perdue, the poultry magnate, had come to Harvard a few times to learn how he could differentiate his chickens from all the other chickens on the market. If Perdue could differentiate chickens, of all things, couldn't he, Jerry Kohl, differentiate belts? And if that was his goal, were his main problems, as he had once thought, how to make the plant and office a little more efficient, and how to add a few more salespeople?

Of course not. Not by any stretch of his fertile imagination. Rather, Kohl began to see, what he had to do was something entirely different. He had to create a new kind of belt company — a company that offered customers a level of service and a variety of products they couldn't get anywhere else. He had to make it so that customers had no conceivable reason to go to a competitor.

That would mean reshaping the daily interactions and relationships between his salespeople and the stores they serviced, for it was in those interactions and relationships that Leegin's rubber met its road. Salespeople, Kohl could see, would have to have more to give their customers. They'd have to learn how and where the stores made money, then help them make more.

But new tires alone wouldn't make a clunker into a chariot. And if salespeople were to have more to offer, the office and the plant would have to back them up. At the time, all three facets of Leegin's operations were a mess. "Somehow," Kohl muses, "we had to make each one different."

Today, each one is about as different as it can be. And though the whole may outshine the sum of the parts, the parts themselves can be pretty dazzling. Come on the road, for example, with Perry Patton, 33, a Leegin salesman for the past eight years, now nosing his new white Mercury Villager around the freeways of Los Angeles. Among his stops, this February day, is a trendy men's clothing store known as Sporting Club, on Santa Monica Boulevard in West Hollywood

Patton's first job at the store is to take inventory. Like a bread supplier in a supermarket, he and a young trainee go through Sporting Club's belt racks, counting and straightening.

His second job is a little more unusual. Unpacking his laptop computer, Patton punches up the Sporting Club account and records the count for each style number as it appears on the screen. Soon the little computer's portable printer is spewing out reports: Sporting Club's orders in the past 12 months (about $20,000 wholesale). Current sales volume, compared with last season's and last year's (up). Number of belts sold — by individual style, by category, by color, by nearly anything that Patton and Sporting Club co-owner Don Zuidema might want to see.

Patton's third job? Selling, which is now mostly a matter of consulting the numbers and making informed judgments. Leegin's One World and Honest lines are doing best in Zuidema's stores. Black is hotter than brown right now. Patton shows Zuidema some new styles that fit with the top sellers, and a few others that his computer indicates are doing well in similar stores. Studying the reports, Patton points out that Zuidema's sales as a percentage of inventory are too high: Sporting Club may be losing customers who can't find a belt in a given size.

Computers Don't Lie

To Zuidema, the information provided by Patton's computer has changed the nature of the vendor-customer relationship on two critical counts. One, the objectivity of the numbers engenders trust. "If we're not selling dress belts," Zuidema points out, "there's no reason for him to push dress belts on us." Two, the information allows Zuidema to tailor his inventory and thus maximize sales in what was traditionally a forgotten corner of the business. "Thanks to them, we make a lot of money in the small space we use for belts. It's probably one of the most profitable centers in the store." On this day, Zuidema scans Patton's numbers and listens to his pitch on new styles. Then he places an order for $7,000 worth of belts.

Kohl, who still describes himself as a belt salesman, always figured that computers could revolutionize selling. But off-the-shelf software for

> **HOT TIP**

When J.W. Kisling, CEO of $26 million Multiplex Co., Ballwin, Mo., gives tours of the beverage dispenser manufacturing facility, he invariably stops at a workstation to chat with one of the company's 120 factory employees. "It impresses a customer to see that our employees can explain what's going on around them. Everybody's a salesman here."

personal computers never seemed to deliver what he needed. Frustrated, he taught himself to program. When the first portables appeared, he bought one and began experimenting. He asked salespeople what they would like a computer to do, then wrote the software to do it. Soon he was asking for volunteers to take a portable computer out on the road.

Guinea pig number one was Vicki Schubert, saleswoman for the San Francisco Bay area. Guinea pig number two: Perry Patton. There were times when each was ready to chuck the first machines through a store window. On one grim day Schubert visited a small chain's seven stores, spent hours taking and recording inventory, then punched the keys to combine all the stores' records into one for her presentation. All the data vanished — for good.

Despite such mishaps, the volunteers soon saw firsthand how much paperwork the computers could save them and how the information they held could help in selling. One salesman wanted no part of it and left. The others — egged on and trained by the early users — gradually climbed on board. Kohl kept revising the software and replacing the hardware, no expense spared. He told salespeople to call him or another programmer anytime, day or night, if they encountered a problem.

Orders by Modem

Today Leegin's 75 outside salespeople enter orders directly into those notebook computers, no paper required. They transmit the orders to the office by modem every night, along with messages to anyone in the company they need to contact. Information flows both ways. The central computer updates the salespeople on phone-in orders and payment records and credit problems in their territories. It provides daily information on belt availability, no small matter in a company that now produces more than 1,000 styles in a range of sizes. ("That lets me say, 'Those belts you sold? I can get them back in here right away,' " explains Patton.) It automatically updates the portables' software, correcting bugs and adding features. Recently, Kohl added a database to track the competition and asked salespeople to note on their screens who else was selling belts in each store. Now, he boasts, "I can tell you not only what we sold yesterday in Chicago but every other company that's selling belts in Chicago."

To sales managers such as Doug Patton — Perry's older brother — the computers provide daily data on how the troops are doing: Number of accounts visited, by store type. Number of categories sold. (Too few categories probably means stores are missing some sales.) Recurring problems will be grist for one of the 10 or so training-and-discussion sessions salespeople attend each year.

To Kohl, the computers provide instant market information: "We know what to manufacture, because we know what's selling." They also create an account database that remains with Leegin when salespeople leave. Most important, the computers further his strategic objective, which is to make Leegin indispensable to its customers. "Our goal was to know more about the stores' business than they know themselves." Where belts are concerned, acknowledges Zuidema, Leegin does.

How many companies have boosted sales only to watch their production and support systems crumble? At Leegin, the office and the factory were already stretched to capacity. If the new computers made salespeople more productive — or if, as Kohl expected, the machines made it easier to add and train new ones — the company would probably face meltdown. Every problem would be shunted off from one department to another. Everyone would have an excuse.

So in September 1988, at the beginning of the holiday production season, an apparel company's busiest, most frantic time, Jerry Kohl issued marching orders. Leegin would have no more order processing, no more customer-service or credit and collection departments. All those functions would be folded into one job, account specialist. A pair of account specialists would cover a territory. They would be responsible for everything that customers or salespeople might need from the office. All by themselves.

Panic set in. Some people's worst fears abruptly came true. The jobs they were accustomed to vanished. They had no chance of qualifying for the new ones. Three of the dozen or so office workers left right away. Three more were let go later on. Those chosen for the new jobs plunged into classes, for many the first since high school. How to process an order. How to approve credit or collect a bill. For four months the group met two or three times a week, often from 6 a.m. to 8 a.m.

The panic subsided into chronic, efficiency-killing anxiety. Queasy about asking for money, the fledgling account specialists postponed collection calls. Unnerved by demanding customers, they pulled "picking tickets" — shipping instructions — from the computer and walked them into the warehouse, highlighting special requests and penciling in changes as they went. Shipping clerks found themselves dealing with 12 different people, each with an urgent need, several times a day. Some orders went out twice. Some never went out at all.

If Kohl had doubts, he doesn't remember them. "You lose some people as they get frustrated," he says breezily. "But we were getting people to feel more a part of the company." Just such single-mindedness, of course, was probably what made the whole thing work. Even after the initial training period, classes continued, once a week, for two hours at a crack, in communications and computer skills and a dozen other topics. (They continue to this day.) Kohl and information-systems director Kimmi Pitchford constantly refined the office's software, streamlining procedures, allowing the specialists to record idiosyncratic but critical information about every account ("pays bills late but always pays").

Leegin Express

Maybe most important, Kohl spent money to help account specialists meet customer needs more easily. He built up hefty inventories of Leegin's fastest-moving styles, then introduced Leegin Express, a program that guarantees shipment of those styles in 10 working days. Three years ago, Kohl and a team from the office developed procedures for a "quick ship" program, allowing orders in before 1 p.m. to go out the same day. Today Leegin Express accounts for some 60% of the company's business. About 80 quick-ship orders are filled every day.

Leegin's office is noisy and crowded, with 16 account specialists crammed into a space scarcely larger than a good-sized living room. But watch an employee such as Theresa Van Frankfoort at work, and you get a sense of what has changed. Van Frankfoort and her partner — who are known as the Blue Team — handle the Pacific states plus Arizona, roughly 1,000 accounts in all. They take orders, schedule shipments, approve credit, handle collections, authorize returns, answer salespeople's questions, solve problems such as lost invoices, and perform a dozen other tasks, most with a phone call or a few keystrokes. Charts on the wall track each team's key measures — credits issued, accounts receivable, cash collected, and so on. Overwhelming? At times it is, acknowledges Van Frankfoort, who in the evening finds herself jotting notes about things to accomplish the next day. The payoff is that the responsibilities — and the customers — are hers. "I love what I'm doing," she says. "I know the customers and they know me."

The attractions of the one-stop shopping provided by Van Frankfoort and her colleagues aren't lost on the customers. "I don't need Perry to come in," says Lottie Shamie, manager of a western-goods store that is among Patton's top accounts. "I can call and place an order, and they ship it right out. Even if it's just one belt. Another company we deal with, their orders get messed up all the time and I'm constantly returning stuff."

In the factory the transformation probably started the day Mickey Zaldivar, Chava Sanchez, and the other bosses went out to clean up the cafeteria. Or maybe it was earlier than that; Zaldivar says things began to change "the day Jerry came back from Harvard."

Whatever the key event, the facts aren't in dispute. Kohl began talking to manufacturing director Zaldivar and production manager Sanchez about what he was learning. He gave them books on subjects such as quality and empowerment. Before long the two men found themselves going on retreats, talking to consultants, and taking seminars, often with the plant's dozen or so supervisors. A workbook in a course on continuous improvement suggested the group give employees a live demonstration of the importance of housekeeping. At an appointed time, the managers and supervisors marched into the lunchroom There they swept and polished the floor, scrubbed the walls, and set flower vases on the tables

Change Was in the Air

"Everybody stopped working," recalls Zaldivar with a chuckle. "There was this silence. 'Have you guys gone crazy or what?' " But the exercise conveyed an inescapable fact: Change was in the air. Now Zaldivar could begin experimenting.

Since belts require a lot of hand labor, Leegin's factory is in many ways old-fashioned. Workers toil over cutters, punch presses, and sewing machines. In the past, employees stayed in one functional department. They cut or sewed or punched or dyed all manner of belts as they came through, and collected a wage determined by a complicated system of piece rates. Wanting to change all that — and brimming with up-to-the-minute ideas of empowerment and teamwork — Zaldivar and Sanchez handpicked 20 experienced workers and put them in charge of a complete belt line. From then on, Sanchez and Zaldivar announced, those workers would own that category of belts and would monitor their own production. All would be paid an hourly wage, based on what they were earning before.

The experiment produced a little good news: Quality levels in that category of belts rose sharply. But the bad news was dismal. Output dropped like a stone. Unused to working as a team — and with no financial incentive to hustle — the group turned out half what the managers had expected. Once again, it was September, the company's busiest time. With production falling, deliveries had to be postponed.

Zaldivar and Sanchez, disciples of a stubborn mentor, didn't quit. They divided the group of 20 into four or five subgroups. They instituted a group-incentive wage. Soon output was up to the hoped-for level; eventually it climbed even higher. In another six months the two men started a second team, this one with only 10 or 12 people. That seemed to go more smoothly. Slowly, carefully, a line at a time, they pressed on. For each line, production systems were mapped out. Machinery was tagged and moved. People were selected and cross-trained. By 1990 most of the plant had been transformed into minifactories, work cells responsible for categories of belts from start to finish.

> **HOT TIP**
>
> *G.O.D. (Guaranteed Overnight Delivery), a truck company based in Kearny, N.J., wanted to prove to its customers that its guarantee means something. So, in every monthly report it issues to customers, it details the previous month's deliveries, including any missed or late. If any mistakes were made, G.O.D. automatically includes a refund check with the itemized report — without being asked. The check is made out to the shipping or traffic manager, rather than accounting, because purchasing makes the buying decisions. Not only does this policy give G.O.D. salespeople clout, but it reminds customers' purchasing agents that G.O.D. is an overnight delivery service.*

Change Is Always Difficult

Care alone couldn't eliminate the costs, either human or financial. A couple of the plant's 12 supervisors wanted no part of the changes and had to be replaced. Employees, suddenly asked to chart production levels and several other variables, were baffled and resentful. Zaldivar hired a consultant to teach basic math skills and graphing. Since most of the hourly workers are native Spanish speakers, classes were conducted in Spanish. Later he brought the local school district in to teach English. All this training and instruction took place on company time.

Today the factory is as cluttered as ever; workers are jammed together as closely as the account specialists in the office. But Zaldivar, walking through the plant, points out the signs and symbols of a transformed organization. See the computer terminals scattered around the plant? Everyone can use them. On-line information helps the teams figure out daily priorities. Workers punch in batch numbers as the belts move along, so managers know where everything is.

Oh, and check out these boards. That's where the teams chart cost, delivery, quality, absenteeism, and safety. Every day each team meets for a few minutes to go over any problems. Every week the lead people review the numbers with managers. Says Zaldivar: "We'll have a meeting where everyone announces the figures, and Chava sits there with a laptop putting them in the computer. At the end of the meeting he pops out a report, and the lead people then go back and discuss the numbers with their teams.

"Three or four years ago," he concludes, "it took us about six weeks to put an order through. Now it's a week and a half, and we want to get down to two or three days." Quality is up, too. Customers can see the difference and the reason for it. "Under their modular manufacturing setup they have the same people working on each type of construction," says Mary Beth Adams, a product manager for Lands' End. "That really assures us that the quality is there."

Part of Leegin's story — and Kohl's accomplishment — is told in the numbers, the dry figures of throughput and receivables and sales per account, gathered and charted by the day and the week in the Industry headquarters. What's curious on this score is that a compulsive counter like Kohl can't quite say how much the transformation of his company cost. The cost of computerizing his business he figures at more than $1 million dollars, all told. The reorganization and training of account specialists and factory workers, he isn't sure about. Press him and he shrugs. The company has always made money, he says, sometimes more, sometimes less, and it owes the bank less than it used to. What's to worry about? Which may, of course, be exactly the attitude you need when you're investing in something hard to put a price tag on.

Leegin now makes more than 1,000 styles of belts, up from a couple hundred in the bad old days. It sells to more than 7,000 accounts, up from maybe 2,000. It doesn't advertise, because it doesn't need to: a salesperson visits the stores at least once a season. A new telemarketing operation keeps the company in touch with stores that are too small, or too remote, for a visit. Quality levels, delivery times, and prices are among the best in the industry, say buyers such as international merchandising manager Rodney Lane of L.L. Bean.

Computer-Toting Soldiers

That kind of capability itself makes Leegin difficult, maybe impossible, to compete with. "We have 75 soldiers out there," says Kohl, "and each soldier calls on three customers a day. Unless you have the ability to call on 225 customers a day" — not to mention the ability to provide them with up-to-the-minute sales information, or the ability to produce and ship thousands of orders a week, including 250 for a single belt — "how are you going to compete with me?" Indeed, the company has slowly been acquiring lines from competitors who decided not to try.

But Leegin's real advantage is that it has become a moving target, poised for continual improvement on any number of fronts. The company recently introduced a line of handbags, for example. And why not? It has a distribution channel to women's specialty stores. It has the expertise to help the stores merchandise the bags. It can gather instant information, via the laptops, on how well they sell. Planned refinements of office and production systems should allow the company to expand in other ways, too — by adding more belt lines, say, or by continuing to add salespeople.

Jerry Kohl, in addition to his many other traits, is a business junkie, a voracious reader of business magazines and eager attender of conferences, a man who swaps stories of manufacturing and selling and customer service the way others talk about baseball or movies. Somehow, all the information he gathers seems like more grist for the company-changing mill, the single-minded and in some ways single-handed metamorphosis he has set in motion at Leegin Creative Leather Products. ■

KOHL'S CREED: KNOW YOUR CUSTOMER ONE-TO-ONE

Years ago, a vendor canceled an order because our prices had gone up. I called him up to tell him he couldn't just cancel an order. I was holding a signed purchase order from him. He said, "Jerry, I don't know you from Adam. I don't know your name. You're nothing more than a number to me. If I knew you, sure, you're right, I couldn't cancel my order. But I don't know you." And then I heard him tearing the PO in half over the phone.

When I heard that PO being torn in half, it changed the way I do business. From that day on, I knew that I had to know who my customers are and they had to know me.

Knowing your customers really means knowing two things: First, you have to identify your customers. Second, you have to understand what you want your relationship with your customers to be.

My customers are not my company's customers. I truly believe that my customers are my 75 salespeople out there selling my belts. I have 7,000 accounts buying my belts, but they are the customers of my salespeople. In my business, people don't just call up to buy belts. Without my 75 salespeople out there in stores, I wouldn't be in business.

I want to build a doctor-patient relationship with Leegin's customers. I want salespeople who have a good bedside manner. Do you remember Dr. Marcus Welby on television from your childhood? If you were Welby's patient and you had brain surgery, Welby wouldn't have performed the surgery because he wasn't a brain surgeon. But he would have been at your bedside.

That's not the case today. Today, when you go to see your doctor, he or she refers you to another doctor, who refers you to a specialist. When you wake up from surgery today, chances are you won't even recognize the doctor standing there. You won't even know his name

Watching Marcus Welby on television, you'd see people dying in hospital beds. But Marcus Welby gave them the will to live. How can you have the will to live unless someone cares about you?

We don't just have Marcus Welby salespeople. At Leegin Leather, we assign every customer to one of our home office people. If Robbie is your contact at Leegin Leather and you have a question about damaged goods, you talk to Robbie. If the salesperson who handles your account has a question, he talks to Robbie. If there's a question about billing, credit, or inventory, the customer calls Robbie. And when Robbie talks to a customer, she knows the person she's talking to. It's not unusual for our account specialists to ask about a customer's child. For better or worse, our people are attached at the hip to their customers. They develop a relationship together.

These one-to-one relationships with account specialists work not only for Leegin's customers, but for my customers — our salespeople — as well. When you have salespeople out in the field, it's only natural that a wall goes up between the customer service people at the home office and your outside salespeople. We've established these one-to-one relationships to bring that wall down. Or never let it go up.

Our approach to customer service is valid for any business that has repeat sales. If you sell vacuum cleaners door to door, you probably don't need to worry about customer service, but if you ever plan to talk to a customer a second time, it matters to the customer that you know and care about him. You might think this approach could only work in small companies and to some extent that's true. But in many companies, top executives allow walls of bureaucracy to come up between themselves and their customers.

I'll give you an example. I own a BMW. It's the fourth BMW I've owned and I don't know a soul at BMW. How many cars does BMW sell? Not that many. Yet no one at that company has ever called or written to me to thank me for buying a BMW. Someone there should call and say, "Mr. Kohl, I want to thank you personally for your loyalty to BMW. This is the fourth BMW you've purchased from us and we're delighted. I'd like to give you my home phone number for you to call if you have any problem whatsoever with your car. Thank you again."

Executives don't have time? Well, I think they can't afford not to have time. Tom Peters recently made a few phone calls to test a commitment to customer service. He called Nordstrom to complain about a lousy shoe he bought there. He asked to speak to the president of the company. Well, 30 seconds later Mr. Nordstrom was on the phone with him.

I travel all the time. I fly on planes. I stay in hotels. We host parties and functions all the time. Do you know that in all my years of traveling, I have never had someone thank me for flying on an airplane or staying at a hotel. Except for a salesperson who wanted to get another sale, no one has ever called or written to thank me for my business.

Since we're on the subject of airlines, another example. I fly a lot and occasionally I'll get paged. The agent will tell me that my platinum card entitles me to an upgrade to First Class. I'll say thanks and go sit down. Now I'm happy to move up to First Class, but I never feel particularly good about this exchange. When I reach the counter, the attendant always hands me my upgrade as if it's just part of her job to do so. It doesn't cost anymore to have someone say "We're delighted that you've flown with us so often in the past. Could we invite you to move up into First Class? If there's anything we can do to make your flight more comfortable, please don't hesitate to ask, because you're a very valuable customer."

We figure we can teach people our business. But we can't teach them to be nice people. So we take a

lot of time and effort to try to hire the right people from the start. And we do a good job, because we don't have much turnover. What we look for in employees is not a superstar, but someone with his feet on the ground. We look for a good credit history and a good work history. In other words, we look for people who are responsible.

When we interview people, we ask if we can tape the phone interview, which lasts about 30 minutes. By recording the interview, we can give the prospect our full attention. We can listen instead of worrying about taking notes. This also allows us to sit down later and listen carefully to a prospective employee's answers to a series of preset questions we've developed. But the real secret to our hiring is that I don't hire employees. We all do. How often have you heard someone complain that his boss hired a dolt for them to work with? At Leegin Leather, the team that is going to work with this person interviews the prospect in person and all the team members have to sign off. This all may sound like a lot of work, but the people we hire are here to stay. I'm sure we lose some good people, but we want people who are compatible with our way of doing business.

Technology is part of our customer service story, because technology has enabled us to eliminate much of the paperwork our salespeople used to have to do. And that has freed them up to be more customer service oriented. I don't know any good company that isn't passionate about technology. I called Pizza Hut the other day and the girl rattled off my address and asked me if it was current. When I said yes, she asked me if I'd like another pepper and onion pizza like the last one I ordered. When I said yes, she said, "OK, it'll be right along!" Now that made me feel good. Now how many businesses make you feel good about giving them money? Not many. Pizza Hut is using technology to help me, but it's also helping them. I think anyone who isn't passionate about technology is a moron. ∎

2

How to Develop
"Relationship Marketing"

by Don Peppers and Martha Rogers, Ph.D.

Wat the Leegin Creative Leather story illustrates so powerfully is that relationship marketing — planning for share of customer rather than share of market — can yield astonishing results. By working to increase its share of each customer's market, rather than market share, Leegin broke through the ceiling that had stifled its growth for years. Let's examine what it means to shift from market share to share-of-customer strategic thinking.

For most of the 1980s, Leegin was a company that was knocking on the glass ceiling of $10 million per year in volume. But between 1987 and 1994, Leegin grew from $10 million to $70 million. In the mid-80s, owner Jerry Kohl realized that Leegin was a belt company just like every other belt company. What he did next reflects very cutting-edge strategic thinking. Without using the terminology, Kohl became a relationship marketer and restructured his business to manage customers, not products.

Most American businesses have made something of a science of product or brand management. The product manager's job is to find customers for his products. His compensation and bonuses are tied to sales increases or fluctuations in market share. It doesn't matter to a product manager who buys the product. Each buyer is treated as a newly-acquired customer, even though some may be loyal users. The same offers, ads, and coupons go out to everybody, or at least to everybody in a certain targeted segment.

The net result of this system is that products have champions looking out for them, but customers don't. The reason is simple: Until now, it hasn't been feasible to keep track of individual customers. But because of the rapidly declining cost curve of information-processing technology,

Don Peppers is president of marketing 1:1 in Weston, Conn. Martha Rogers, Ph.D., a founding partner in marketing 1:1, is associate professor of telecommunications at Bowling Green State University in Bowling Green, Ohio.

it is now possible — and therefore competitively necessary — to keep track of and remember every contact with every customer. In other words, marketers will need to remember their relationships with customers, the same way customers have always remembered their relationships with us.

The way to do this is to turn the organizational chart sideways. Instead of product managers, 1:1 marketers will rely on *customer managers*, who will manage portfolios of customers, one customer at a time. They will use computer memory to remember their relationship with each, and will constantly poll the statistically-projected lifetime value of each to measure their success.

Like many companies, Leegin was a victim of sales-quititis. Whenever a salesperson quit, Kohl lost dozens of accounts. By going on-line, he is now able to track customer relationships in a way that tran-

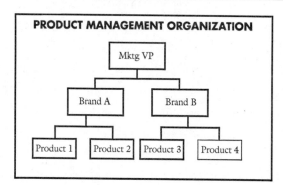

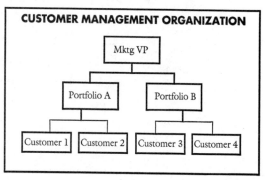

scends the individual salesperson, while making that person's job more productive. His next step will be to calculate share of customer and customer lifetime value to help guide the company and the salesperson who manages each customer account, and to use those measurements as a guide to intelligent investment in time, energy, resources, and collaboration with each.

Kohl's goal is very logical, though it isn't practiced by most mass marketers: He wants to make sure no customer has any conceivable reason to go to a competitor. Retention requires strategies that differ from the traditional acquisition orientation of most mass marketing firms. Jerry Kohl put customer management into practice the day he eliminated functional departments (order-processing, customer service, credit, collection) and folded all the functions into the job of the "account specialist," who is responsible for everything that customers, or salespeople for those customers, might need from the office.

The transition from product management to customer management is not a simple process, but it is not impossible either. Generally, we advise clients to use a best-customer transition strategy. Simply stated, it works like this:

In most product-management companies, the "chimney" or "silo" structure effectively blocks any ability on the part of the company at large to track all the available data about a customer, since bits and pieces of the relationship are held in different silos. So, although the customer may have a complete picture of the company, the company never has a complete picture of the customer. Or, worse, the company treats the customer as several different customers. (How many times have you had to fill out an address form for your bank as you applied for a new loan or account?)

However, in the customer-management organization, the strategic focus is on linking the data about each customer across divisions or product lines, the better to serve a greater number of each customer's needs, in order to get as great a share as possible of each customer's business (see Exercise on "Organizational Inventory," p. 69).

To begin the transition, we suggest starting with two or three top salespeople, or two or three top product managers, and give them a new title: Customer Manager. These will need to be upbeat, energetic people who enjoy breaking the box on traditional thinking and are not afraid of the opportunities created by a positive change. Next, identify the dozen or hundred most valuable customers, and make each of these customers the direct line responsibility of one of the Customer Managers. After the new strategy has had a chance to succeed (and we find that top company people combined with top customers make a great recipe for success), other product managers will want to climb on board and the company can change gradually, without wholesale disruption. We call it "moving the picket fence."

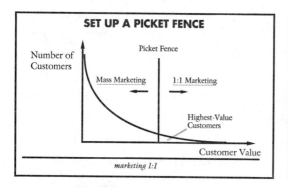

SET UP A PICKET FENCE

Number of Customers

Picket Fence

Mass Marketing ← | → 1:1 Marketing

Highest-Value Customers

Customer Value

marketing 1:1

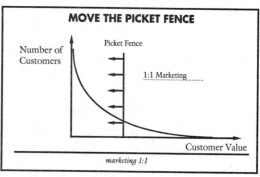

MOVE THE PICKET FENCE

Number of Customers

Picket Fence

1:1 Marketing

Customer Value

marketing 1:1

It should be noted that the picket fence will probably never hit the left axis. In other words, there will probably always be somebody in charge of mass marketing and acquisition. The customers against the left axis will have the least value to the company, and will be the most likely to defect to a competitor. But somebody will have to mine this skimpy lode for the occasional customer who can be moved to the right of the picket fence, where 1:1 marketing will be practiced.

The customer manager's primary responsibilities are:

- Manage all *addressable* communications to each customer under his/her management
- Find products and services for the customers in his/her portfolio
- Define sub-groups within the portfolios
- Serve as a "customer advocate" within the company.

Over time, as information-processing technology improves, data will become more detailed, analysis will become more and more useful, and portfolios can be increasingly fine-tuned and managed more and more efficiently on an individual basis.

Brand managers try to increase brand equity, but customer managers try to increase customer equity. Jerry Kohl's seven-fold increase in revenues — with increased profitability — over a seven-year period provides just one successful example of the switch from product to customer management

In the 1:1 future, economies of scale will yield to economies of scope. Companies will grapple with the structural impediments to managing customers rather than products, and will focus on new and streamlined ways of distributing products to customers.

Marketing in the 1:1 paradigm can be called "miniaturized marketing" because, in fact, marketing has been shrunk to the level of the individual consumer. The entire discipline is being miniaturized by advances in information and communications technology in the same way that the Sony Walkman miniaturized the music-listening experience or the remote control device miniaturized the television-viewing experience.

Many of the principles that apply to 1:1 marketing are a direct inversion of similar principles applied to mass marketing. Mass marketing requires product managers who concentrate on maximizing awareness and sales of one product at a time, and selling it to as many consumers as possible, whereas 1:1 marketing requires customer managers who work to sell as many products as possible to individual customers, one at a time. A mass marketer tries to differentiate products, while a 1:1 marketer seeks to differentiate customers. A mass marketer tries to acquire a constant stream of new customers, while a 1:1 marketer first tries to get a constant stream of new business from current customers.

This is the fundamental change that is beginning to occur in large and small marketing companies around the world. They are moving from mass marketing to 1:1 marketing, from product management to customer management. Marketers are re-thinking the task of selling, visualizing it in terms of "share of customer," rather than "share of market." Concentrating on one customer at a time, instead of on one product at a time, is generating new marketing strategies, new businesses, and new insights. Just ask Jerry Kohl at Leegin Creative Leather Products.

EXERCISE

Taking an Organizational Inventory

Choose the answer that best describes the way your company works, and then check your score (see next page).

1. **If a customer calls to complain,**
    A. the customer's call is routed through several people until someone tells the customer to go back to the nearest retailer or distributor.
    B. the customer's call or letter is forwarded directly to the nearest retailer or distributor.
    C. the complaint becomes the responsibility of a particular customer manager, who sees it as an opportunity to build a relationship with that customer.

2. **Everybody knows that market research is imperative. In order to best understand what customers want, we should**
    A. conduct mall intercepts.
    B. conduct statistically valid sampling and measurement procedures and project to the population of prospects.
    C. do research by experiment with each individual prospect.

3. **At your company, the corporate structure**
    A. emphasizes product management in order to produce a high quality product for the dealers to sell.
    B. recognizes that since customers are the heart of the business, the company must focus on product management that will constantly improve the quality of the product.
    C. implements customer management because the company knows that to remain competitive, it must develop products for their customers, not customers for its products.

4. **How does your company spend its promotional budget?**
    A. mass media advertising, especially newspaper, magazine, and television.
    B. a combination of mass media ads, direct mail, customer rebates, and trade incentives and promotions.
    C. explicit bargains with consumers to see or hear messages, interactive radio, or other ambush advertising, and putting best customers in touch with prospects.

5. What happens if prospects call your company's toll-free number?

A. Two weeks later, they receive a brochure with a form letter.

B. They are referred to their nearest outlet, based on their zip code.

C. After qualification, they receive a packet of material by overnight delivery, with a personal note. A week later, they get a follow-up dealer contact.

ORGANIZATIONAL INVENTORY SCORE SHEET

Add up your answers. If you find your answers are mostly A's, you should probably polish up your resumé and start looking for employment with a company that will survive the Information Revolution. If your answers are mostly B's, your company has made a lot of progress toward share-of-customer thinking, but still has a lot of work to do in terms of trust-building with customers, corporate culture, and individualizing your market efforts. If your answers were mostly C's, then marketing 1:1 wants to use you as our next example of a successful 1:1 strategy.

SHARE-OF-CUSTOMER WORKSHEET

A	B	C	D	E	F	G	H
1							
2							
3							
4							
5							
6							
7							
8							
9							
10							

COLUMN A

Write the names of your company's 10 most valuable customers — or the first 10 customers who come to mind.

COLUMN B

For each customer listed, estimate the approximate revenue your company generates each month, based on the past two or three years of experience with that customer.

COLUMN C

Check column C if there are any additional services or products you could be selling this customer. You should count products or services the customer is not using at all now, as well as products and services this customer is now getting from a competitor.

COLUMN D

If you checked Column C, then in Column D enter your best guess as to the total amount of additional services or products you could be selling to this customer, in dollars per month.

COLUMN E

Add Columns B and D.

COLUMN F

Divide Column B by Column E to calculate approximate share of customer in percentage.

COLUMN G

Consider customers' non-monetary value: Write down in the appropriate spaces the number of customer references you get from each customer in a year.

COLUMN H

1:1 marketing is collaborative. How well do you collaborate with your customers? Check here if you have ever referred a customer to this customer.

CUSTOMER MANAGEMENT QUESTIONNAIRE

1. **Based on your judgment, and without resorting to tables of information and research, how might you categorize some of your key consumer sub-groups that have similar characteristics, needs, and attitudes toward the kind of product or service you provide — groups that might be constituted into portfolios of customers?**

   A. New parents
   B. Repeat purchasers
   C. Respondents to a fax response program
   D. Female heads of household
   E. _____
   F. _____
   G. _____
   H. _____
   I. _____
   J. _____
   K. _____
   L _____

2. **If your company were to try to establish a portfolio of its "best" customers, what would these customers look like? What unique demands do they make on you, and what opportunities do they present?**

_____

_____

_____

_____

_____

3. **When a customer has characteristics that qualify him/her for two or more portfolios, should she/he be assigned to each of them?**

_____

_____

4. **What line responsibility should a customer portfolio manager have?**

_____

_____

_____

_____

_____

5. **How might a customer portfolio manager interact with retailers or distributors?**

_____

_____

_____

_____

_____

6. **How should customer portfolio managers be rewarded for doing a good job, and what information is necessary to evaluate them?**

_____

_____

_____

_____

_____

Summary

Although mass production made mass marketing possible 80 years ago, it was mass media — the ability to send a uniform message to a wide audience simultaneously —that mandated mass marketing. The current fractionalization of media and the rise of individualized media, enhanced by the plummeting cost of computational power, will likewise mandate a new 1:1 approach to marketing.

Share-of-customer analysis is not about a new way of doing business that will cause a paradigm shift. It is about a technology-based paradigm shift that will mandate a new way of doing business. Companies that do not begin now to plan back from the 1:1 future will watch their competitors — even very small competitors — pick off their very best customers, one customer at a time.■

Creating
Customer-Focused Teams

by Bruce Hodes

Jerry Kohl's success at Leegin Leather grew out of his strategic use of laptop computers and the empowerment of his employees. But there was another key element in the turnaround at Leegin: the creation of teams of employees centered passionately on serving their retail outlets.

In a business world that has undergone massive alteration as a result of the globalization of the marketplace, the continuing computer/information revolution, and the collapse of the marketplace into niches, how can small and mid-size companies survive, much less thrive? In the new and shifting business environment of the 1990s, customer-focused, high performance work teams will be the cornerstone of success.

Teams are emerging as a key element in organizations. No longer a radical idea, teams are widely accepted in business as a key to thriving in a competitive and fast-paced environment. With a loyal customer base, defining service for your company and delivering it consistently in a way that the customer defines as special is the challenge of the 1990s.

Traditional business environments as far back as the 1950s considered it sufficient to deliver mediocre customer service. As long as each person did his or her own job, the customer was properly served. Service education and relationships were not seen as vital to the task of doing business. In the 1950s, being polite and nice pretty much defined customer service. The following bureaucratic hierarchical model and rules combined to make service and customer focus afterthoughts.

Bruce Hodes is president of CMI in Oak Park, Ill.

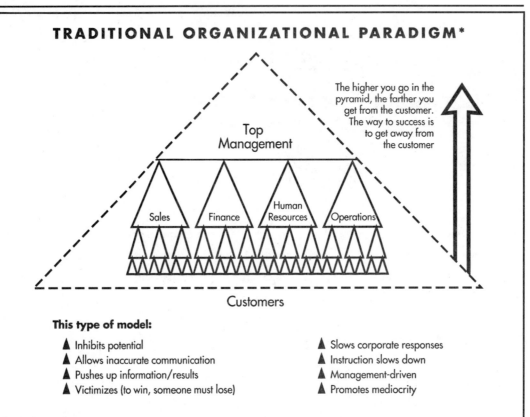

TRADITIONAL ORGANIZATIONAL PARADIGM*

Top Management

Sales   Finance   Human Resources   Operations

The higher you go in the pyramid, the farther you get from the customer. The way to success is to get away from the customer

Customers

This type of model:

▲ Inhibits potential
▲ Allows inaccurate communication
▲ Pushes up information/results
▲ Victimizes (to win, someone must lose)

▲ Slows corporate responses
▲ Instruction slows down
▲ Management-driven
▲ Promotes mediocrity

▶ Most companies want to promote interaction and exchange but are unwilling to give up control.

▶ As a company succeeds, it often invests profits into another layer of management. While this elevates some, it places greater stress on the lower layers.

▶ Upper layers dangle carrots to encourage those below to perform, in hopes of climbing the ladder.

▶ Creates a self-serving environment.

▶ Stepping out of assigned roles to problem solve is discouraged.

▶ Cautious organizational movement is favored over risk taking.

▶ Customers are at the bottom of the pyramid.

Adapted with permission from material developed by Mike Murphy, CEO, Comfortex, Winona, Minn.

Compare your company's organization chart with this one. If you seem to be getting too far away from your customers, you may want to restructure as shown on p. 79.

The Old Rules of Organizational Customer Service

- The company determines the level of customer service. Profit and efficiency have a lot to do with this determination.

- Business is product and task-driven. Customer service means being polite. Work is about getting the task done according to company standards.

- Everyone has a specific job. It is not necessary to step out of that job description to assist a customer. ("That's not my job.")

- Suppliers and customers sometimes operate at cross purposes. Special requests are viewed as interruptions and inconveniences.

- Marketing and customer service are separate functions, performed by different departments.

- Good enough is good enough. If traditional expectations have been met, then the customer is being properly served.

- Extra attention paid to the customer may be unacceptable to the company and viewed as an unnecessary expense.

- Errors discovered in manufacturing are routinely passed on to the customer in the hope that they won't be noticed.

- Added value means taking customers to lunch or sending them gifts

Although most business people immediately recognize how out-of-date such a mindset is today, the extent to which these antiquated rules continue to define business behavior is surprising. Habits are hard to break, and change is an unfamiliar road. Also, many business people do not know what new rules to substitute for the old ones. For leaders searching for an edge in today's competitive market, a different paradigm of customer service is emerging, bringing with it a new set of rules and assumptions.

The New Rules of Organizational Customer Service

- A quality product — as determined by the customer — is essential just to get into the game.

- Products are sold today by overwhelming the consumer with service Service is the differentiation that makes you "special." Service is defined as all the conveniences that accompany the product.

- Involve employees in everything. Information and education are critical to keeping employees focused.

- Since time is valuable to customers, they will remain loyal if you can save them time and make their lives simpler.

- Make technology your friend and use technology to add value to your customer relationships.

- You don't make a product, you make customers. If you wish to stay in business, you had better keep making them.

- Product and service must be value-priced so that the customer perceives great value for money spent.

- If you don't get close to your customer, your competition will.

- Create compensation programs based primarily on performance results and skill acquisition, not on hierarchy and position. Reward employees for customer service-oriented behavior.

- Get better or go broke — learn from mistakes.

- Continuously improve the quality of your processes so that you can eliminate waste and improve profit margins.

In reviewing the story of Leegin Creative Leather Products, can you list the new rules that Kohl used to transform his business (jot them down below)?

1. _____

   _____

2. _____

   _____

3 _____

   _____

4 _____

   _____

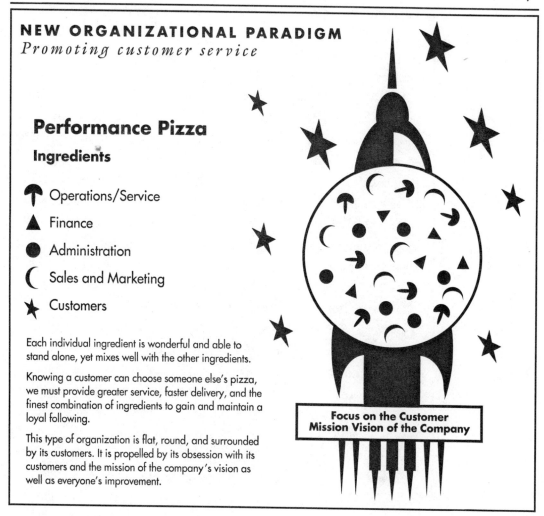

NEW ORGANIZATIONAL PARADIGM
Promoting customer service

Performance Pizza

Ingredients

↑ Operations/Service

▲ Finance

● Administration

☾ Sales and Marketing

★ Customers

Each individual ingredient is wonderful and able to stand alone, yet mixes well with the other ingredients.

Knowing a customer can choose someone else's pizza, we must provide greater service, faster delivery, and the finest combination of ingredients to gain and maintain a loyal following.

This type of organization is flat, round, and surrounded by its customers. It is propelled by its obsession with its customers and the mission of the company's vision as well as everyone's improvement.

**Focus on the Customer
Mission Vision of the Company**

OUR ANALYSIS: Buying laptop computers for the sales force enabled sales people to focus on their relationships with stores. Clearly, Leegin realized that it had to make its customers its number one product.

By revamping the office and support systems, Kohl enabled Leegin to overwhelm its customers with service. Service is all the conveniences that come with Leegin's belts. Service is what makes Leegin special. As a member of their account services team said, "I love what I'm doing. I know the customers, and they know me."

By introducing Leegin Express, the company is recognizing the value of time to its customers. Much of the change in production at Leegin helped drive waste out of the system. And Kohl aggressively used classes, workshops, and seminars to keep his employees focused and informed.

The following worksheets will help you create customer-focused teams in your business. Before you begin those exercises, however, terms should be defined. What, for example, is a team? Team has become a business catchword for any group in a work setting. What most business people call a team, we do not. The following definition, from *The Wisdom of Teams* by Jon R. Katzenbach and Douglas K. Smith, is one we prefer: "A team is a small number of people with complementary skills who are committed to a common purpose, performance goals, and approach for which they hold themselves mutually accountable."

The crucial words are *common purpose* and *mutually accountable*. All members hold themselves accountable for the results of the group.

For a team to exist there has to be adversity and tension between the team and the attainment of the common purpose. No adversity = no team. You do not need teams for easy tasks. High performance standards and teams go together. Performance standards are supportive, permitting a team to coalesce. At Leegin, Kohl was the catalyst who drew people together and focused their energy on serving the customer.

Customer Focus, Feedback, and Service Strategy

The front line (people who directly impact the customer or directly impact a process or product that impacts the customer) has to get feedback so that it can

1. know what it is doing right.
2. know what it is doing that is not working.
3. coordinate and fix problems with other departments.
4. be sure that the customer consistently perceives great value.

One challenge is getting the voice of the customer clearly delivered to the line regarding their service or product. It is important to create forums and opportunities for the front line to listen to the customer.

Another challenge is to make sure everyone understands that "great" is the standard and "extraordinary" is the goal.

Performance Standards

A team literally cannot exist without agreed-upon high performance standards. Standards are what give the group focus, challenge, and a focal point. Time after time, we have seen business groups that are teams in name only. Each team member has his own agenda. There is no "formal" mutual accountability or focus.

When setting the performance standards, the team must reach unanimity on the following issues:

1. focus and purpose of the group — general directions.
2. measurement standards — qualitative numbers that tell the group where it is.
3. goals — specific and time-oriented.

WORKSHEET
Agenda for a customer-focused work team

1. **Write a simple and clear purpose statement, i.e. what is the point and object of the team?**

   _____

   _____

   _____

   _____

   _____

2. **Address the broad directions and key result areas that the team must address. Example: Increase the level of customer service satisfaction. (You should list no more than four to five items in this section.)**

   _____

   _____

_____

_____

_____

3. Decide what measurements the team will use to determine whether or not it is going in the desired direction and attaining key results.

_____

_____

_____

_____

4. Create goals and milestones for the team. These are specific, measurable, and time-related results which the team is committed to accomplish.

_____

_____

_____

_____

_____

5. Generate the strategies by which the team will reach its goals. These should be written in the form of an action plan.

_____

_____

_____

_____

_____

_____

_____

Stages of Development

Customer-focused, high performance teams are like individuals. They need to grow and develop. That makes sense, given that teams are made up of people. Theorists have postulated for years that there are several major steps in a team's development. In our work with teams, we have also found this to be true.

Teams pass through phases. A two-year-old is very different from a 16-year-old in every area of development. A team that has been together two months is different from a team that has been together 16 months. The five principal stages of development for customer-focused teams are:

TEAM STAGE 1 — Getting to Know You
TEAM STAGE 2 — The Dysfunctional Stage
TEAM STAGE 3 — Creating and Getting Behind the Game
TEAM STAGE 4 — High Performance
TEAM STAGE 5 — The Times They Are a-Changing

Here are the characteristic highlights of the five developmental stages.

In Stage 1, or the Getting to Know You stage, the major characteristics are:

- A feeling that this could be fun, combined with some anxiety about how to do it

- More or less excitement about the concept of team

- Figuring out who is in charge here

- Questions: what really are the rules?

- Need to develop standards

- Dependence on the coach/leader

- Coach uses a directive approach

In Stage 2, or the Dysfunctional Stage, the major characteristics are:

- Feeling that this is definitely not fun
- Leadership and/or members confused
- Feeling that "something is definitely wrong here"
- Feeling uncertain and incapable
- Performance standards not being met, lots of finger-pointing
- Little agreement among team members regarding standards
- Customer focus rhetoric only
- Lots of individual agendas
- Internal strife — political concerns high
- No sense of mutual accountability
- Task-driven

In Stage 3, or the Getting Behind the Game stage, the characteristics are:

- Clearer definition of performance standards
- Increasing ownership of performance standards
- Decreasing hostility as the team works out personal differences
- Focus on the customer
- Mutual accountability starting to feel comfortable
- Positive feedback from customers starting to come in
- More honesty among team members
- Failing forward — learning and improving from trial/error — recovery rapid
- Enthusiasm and energy levels increasing
- Support for each other evident
- Small wins bring large smiles

In Stage 4, or the High Performance stage, the characteristics are:

- Customers consistently overwhelmed by service and product
- Team standards met and moved outwardly by the team

- Members feeling good about consistency

- Shared leadership

- Open and honest communication

- Meetings are cooperative and productive

- Results are recognized by customers as high performance

- Members feel deep concern for one another's personal growth and success

- Team outperforms all reasonable expectations

- Team members are having a lot of fun

In Stage 5, or the Times They Are A-Changing stage, the characteristics are:

- Major change occurs: members joining or leaving, a new coach, new performance standards, etc.

- Confusion

- Uncertainty regarding the implications of change

Developmental Stage Movement

Teams will most often get stuck in Stage 2. Setting and attaining performance standards are critical steps in moving a team to stage 3. Also, in stage 2, team members must find a way to integrate their personal agendas with team goals, which must take precedence.

In Stage 3 the team starts to take on a life of its own and begins to move aggressively in the direction of its performance standards and goals.

As teams come into their own in Stage 4, they have the capability to create intense customer loyalty. Stage 4 is where high performance is attained. When your organization becomes relentless in providing superior products and anticipates the changing needs of its customers, it becomes indispensable to its customers. This is a win-win stage of development because customer focus yields high performance, which, in turn, generates increased earnings, which, in turn, directly benefits employees and shareholders.

Stage 5 can occur at any time during the development of the team. It will be triggered by any change that significantly alters the team.

Examples include gaining or losing a member, altering performance standards, or the arrival of a new coach. A major change in the internal or external environment, such as a new product or service, new customers, or a change in rules and regulations will similarly alter the team's progress.

It is important to understand that each stage is a stepping-stone in the process leading to high performance. No stage is undesirable and all must be passed through.

1. What stage is your team in and why? What is your evidence?

———————————————————————————

———————————————————————————

———————————————————————————

———————————————————————————

———————————————————————————

2. What are you going to do to get it to the next stage? Please list the steps.

a.———————————————————————

———————————————————————————

———————————————————————————

b.———————————————————————

———————————————————————————

———————————————————————————

d.———————————————————————

———————————————————————————

———————————————————————————

d. _____

_____

_____

High Performance, Customer-Focused Teams:
Points to Remember

Members must want to make the team successful. Members must share a common basic respect and regard for one another. Members need not love each other; they just have to be willing to try to work out problems. Neither victims nor enemies fit in customer-focused teams.

Conflict is to be expected. Because standards are high, members will differ on how to achieve them. Dialogue and discussion are useful in moving things forward. Team members should not lose sight of the team's goal: to serve the customer in an extraordinary fashion.

Experiment! Customer service strategies need to be planned; however, be flexible and try new ideas that will make your organization indispensable to the customers it serves.

Customer-focused, high performing teams are intensely engaged in their work. Team members love the game of service and look forward to focusing on the customer.

Use the following scorecard to build your customer-focused teams.

On a scale of 1-5 (low to high), how would your team rank? (Rate each category as a whole.)

Purpose

_____ Members committed to common purpose, performance goals

_____ Goals are specific and relevant to purpose

_____ Strategies for achieving goals are clear

_____ Members are clear on their roles

Approach

_____ Members use their skills to complement one another.

_____ Leadership is shared.

_____ Constructive conflict is taking place.

_____ Various ideas are explored.

Product

_____ Output is high.

_____ Quality is excellent.

_____ Decision making is effective.

_____ Customer's expectations have been exceeded.

Interpersonal

_____ Members feel good about the team.

_____ Members are charged and motivated.

_____ Members feel pride and confidence.

_____ Commitment and trust exist between members.

Customer Service

_____ Customers are kept informed on task progress.

_____ Customer service strategy in place and operating.

_____ Relationship with customer being developed.

_____ Customer is overwhelmed with service.

How did you do? What would you need to do to raise your scores by one point? Use the Team Audit to pinpoint exactly what you would need to do to improve your score.

TEAM AUDIT

Think about each of these six basic elements when you assess your team:

1. Are you small enough in number?

a. Can you convene easily and frequently?

b. Can you communicate with all members easily and frequently?

c. Are your discussions open and interactive for all members?

d. Does each member understand the others' roles and skills?

e. Do you need more people to achieve your ends?

f Are sub-teams possible or necessary?

2. **Do you have adequate levels of complementary skills and skill potential in all three categories necessary for team performance (functional/technical, problem-solving/decision-making, and interpersonal)?**

   a. Are all three categories of skills either actually or potentially represented across the membership ?

   b. Does each member have the potential in all three categories to advance his or her skills to the level required by the team's purpose and goals?

   c. Are any skill areas that are critical to team performance missing or under-represented?

   d. Are the members, individually and collectively, willing to spend the time to help themselves and others learn and develop skills?

   e. Can you introduce new or supplemental skills as needed?

3. **Do you have a broader, meaningful purpose to which all members aspire?**

   a. Does it constitute a broader, deeper aspiration than just short-term goals?

   b. Is it a team purpose as opposed to a broader organizational purpose or just one individual's purpose (e.g., the leader's)?

   c. Do all members understand and articulate it the same way? Do they do so without relying on ambiguous abstractions?

   d. Do members define it vigorously in discussions with outsiders?

   e. Do members frequently refer to it and explore its implications?

   f. Do members feel it is important, if not exciting?

4. **Do you have a specific set of performance goals agreed upon by all?**

   a. Are they team goals versus broader organizational goals or just one individual's goals (e.g., the leader's)?

   b. Are they clear, simple, and measurable? If not measurable, can their achievement be determined?

   c. Are they realistic as well as ambitious? Do they allow small wins along the way?

d. Do they call for a concrete set of team work-products?

e. Is their relative importance and priority clear to all members?

f. Do all members agree with the goals, their relative importance, and the way in which their achievement will be measured?

g. Do all members articulate the goals the same way?

5. **Is your working approach clearly understood and commonly agreed upon?**

a. Is the approach concrete, clear, and really understood and agreed to by everybody? Will it result in achievement of the objectives?

b. Will it capitalize on and enhance the skills of all members? Is it consistent with other demands on the members?

c. Does it require all members to contribute equivalent amounts of real work?

d. Does it provide for open interaction, fact-based problem solving, and results-based evaluation?

e. Do all members articulate the approach the same way?

f. Does it provide for modification and improvement over time?

g. Are fresh input and perspectives systematically sought and added, for example, through information and analysis, new members, and senior sponsors?

6. **Do you hold yourselves individually and mutually accountable for the group's results?**

a. Are you individually and jointly accountable for the team's purpose, goals, approach, and work-products?

b. Can you and do you measure progress against specific goals?

c. Do all members feel responsible for all measures?

d. Are the members clear on what they are individually responsible for and what they are jointly responsible for?

e. Is there a sense that "only the team can fail"?

Answers to the preceding questions can establish the degree to which your group functions as a real team. By focusing efforts on improving weak areas, your team will reach its potential. (From *The Wisdom of Teams* by Jon Katzenbach & Douglas Smith.)

Now, what are the next steps that you are prepared to take in creating customer-focused high performance work teams?

1. _____

_____

_____

_____

2. _____

_____

_____

_____

3. _____

_____

_____

_____

4. _____

_____

_____

_____

5. _____

_____

_____

_____

CONCLUSION

Business is a complicated matter, and customer-focused teams are not the whole story. We know that teams are not called for in every instance. They are useful when serving the customer requires a lot of interdependence within the company. We do believe that teams of employees focused on the customer are a key to customer service in the 1990s. We also believe that if you use the information in this chapter, it will actively promote the formation, implementation, and success of customer-focused teams in your workplace. ■

Notes

2

How're We Doing?

Like Leegin Leather Products, Granite Rock Co., of Watsonville, Calif., barters in basic goods. There's nothing high tech about this 100-year-old family-owned company with operations in a dozen locations between San Francisco and Monterey. The company quarries granite and produces concrete, asphalt, sand, and gravel. It also buys and resells such materials as brick, cinder block, and drywall, as well as masonry tools. With 1990 sales of $90 million, it is one of the smaller construction-materials companies around. But it is an industry leader, attracting a steady stream of international visitors interested in learning more about what it does.

Granite Rock's fame is based largely on its reputation as the high-end producer in an industry that all but defines the term commodity business. Construction-materials companies habitually compete on price. Customers are conditioned to seize the low bid, assuming — wrongly — that if you've seen one load of stone, you've seen them all. But Granite Rock has always opted to turn out high-quality rock and back it up with high-quality customer service. On average, Granite Rock customers pay up to 6% more than they would be charged by the competition. "Our competitors tend to see price as the main wedge," says Wes Clark, division general manager of the company's three northern concrete plants. "We are not low price, but we are high value."

Charging a premium and touting itself as providing the best value in a commodity-based business puts an obvious burden on Granite Rock. It must work hard to prove to cus-

Granite Rock Co.'s annual report card from customers, and what's done with the grades

tomers that its products and services are worth the extra cost — which means making sure that employees strive to provide the kind of value customers are willing to pay for. How can the company accomplish this? First, it must understand clearly how its customers define quality and service. Second, it must regularly monitor customers' opinions about Granite Rock's performance relative to that of its competitors. Third, it must communicate all this information to its work force.

Granite Rock handles the first step of the process in the traditional manner. Every three or four years, each division conducts an extensive survey of its customers, probing their wants and needs as they relate to each of the company's product lines. Among other things, the survey asks customers to rank the most important factors in choosing a supplier. Clark's division conducted such a survey in 1987. Another is being done this spring. It is in the second and third steps that Granite Rock breaks new ground. To compare its own performance with that of its competitors, every year the company conducts an opinion survey that amounts to an annual report card from the customers. All customers receive a short survey form on which they are asked to grade their top three suppliers in terms of product quality and customer service.

Granite Rock then combines the long-survey data on customer priorities with the short-survey data on competitive performance to produce graphs that are posted on bulletin boards around the company. The graphs show employees at each plant how they measure up in the eyes of their customers.

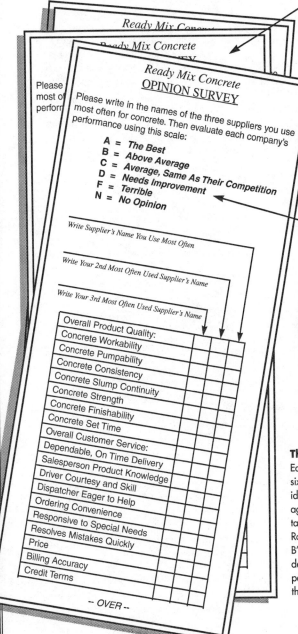

Ready Mix Concrete
OPINION SURVEY

Please write in the names of the three suppliers you use most often for concrete. Then evaluate each company's performance using this scale:

A = *The Best*
B = *Above Average*
C = *Average, Same As Their Competition*
D = *Needs Improvement*
F = *Terrible*
N = *No Opinion*

Write Supplier's Name You Use Most Often

Write Your 2nd Most Often Used Supplier's Name

Write Your 3rd Most Often Used Supplier's Name

Overall Product Quality:			
Concrete Workability			
Concrete Pumpability			
Concrete Consistency			
Concrete Slump Continuity			
Concrete Strength			
Concrete Finishability			
Concrete Set Time			
Overall Customer Service:			
Dependable, On Time Delivery			
Salesperson Product Knowledge			
Driver Courtesy and Skill			
Dispatcher Eager to Help			
Ordering Convenience			
Responsive to Special Needs			
Resolves Mistakes Quickly			
Price			
Billing Accuracy			
Credit Terms			

-- OVER --

The Annual Report Card

Once a year, each of Granite Rock's 12 plants sends out forms like the one above to all its customers. The specific questions vary slightly from plant to plant, each of which is responsible for a different product, but the format is the same. Some divisions use color-coded survey forms to distinguish between types of contractors. (Blue forms go to landscapers. Masons receive orange forms.) All the completed forms are addressed to the divisional headquarters, where the results are compiled and forwarded to the rest of the division.

The Grading System

The form asks the customer to grade its top three suppliers — one of which is presumably Granite Rock — on their performance in terms of product quality and customer service. Although there are six grades in the scale, the company bases its charts on the total number of A's and B's a supplier gets in a given category. "A C is neutral," says Wes Clark. "If they give you a C, they feel there's no difference between you and everybody else. If they give you a D or an F, they are just punishing you." But A's and B's amount to fairly uniform positive votes, he reasons. A is for a job well done. B is a similar response from a tougher grader.

The Customer Service Graph

Each of Granite Rock's 12 operations generates about six of these graphs a year, one for each competitor. The idea is to show employees how the operation stacks up against the competitor on the matters of greatest importance to the customers. Triangles indicate Granite Rock's performance rating — that is, its total of A's and B's on the issue in question — plotted against the degree of importance customers have assigned that particular issue. Circles designate the performance of the competitor on the issues.

GOOD FORMS

The Importance Axis

The graph's vertical axis is derived from the extensive customer survey conducted by the divisions. One section of the survey asks customers to rank the most important factors in choosing a supplier. Granite Rock concluded that those factors were, in descending order of importance: on-time delivery, product quality, scheduling (ability to deliver products on short notice), problem resolution, price, credit terms, and personnel's selling skills.

It came as little surprise that customers put on-time delivery at the top of the list. Granite Rock's typical customer is a general contractor engaged in coordinating complex construction projects involving many suppliers. A delay in one step of the project can throw the whole schedule off. What was a surprise — and a pleasant one — was the relative unimportance of price. It affirmed the company's strategy of emphasizing quality and customer service.

This April Wes Clark's division of Granite Rock is again sending out the long customer survey to probe for shifts in the market. "We do this every three or four years, or if there's a significant market change," says Clark. "We're in a recession now. Does that mean customers are suddenly going to be more price sensitive?"

The Performance Axis

The results of the opinion survey — the annual report card — are plotted along the graph's horizontal axis. The grades on the axis are determined by adding up the number of A's and B's that the Granite Rock operation or its competitor has received from customers in any given category. An A+ indicates all A's and B's; an F means none. In addition, Granite Rock calculates the group norm, that is, the average number of A's and B's received by companies mentioned in a particular product survey. The goal of each Granite Rock operation is to outperform the group average (that is, garner more A's and B's) by at least 33%. Last year, for instance, customers rated Granite Rock's San Jose concrete operation 59% above the norm for on-time delivery, 69% better for quality, and 76% better for scheduling.

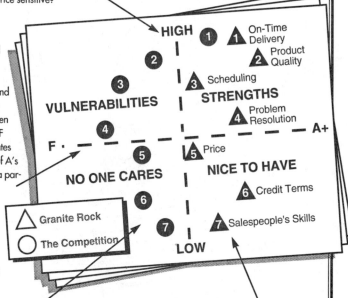

The Quadrants

The intersecting axes create four quadrants, which provide a rough guide to the results. A marker in the upper-right quadrant, for example, indicates that the company (whether Granite Rock or the competitor) performs well in an area of importance to the customers. A marker in the upper-left quadrant means the company has a vulnerability: It has scored relatively poorly on one of the customers' priority issues. A Granite Rock vulnerability is clearly of greater concern than a "No One Cares" (poor performance on a relatively unimportant issue) or a "Nice to Have" (good performance on same).

The Lessons of the Graph

Granite Rock places greatest emphasis on the distance between its markers and those of the competitor. A Granite Rock triangle in the upper-right corner of the graph is something to celebrate only if it is safely removed from the competitor's circle. "No matter how well we're doing," notes Wes Clark, "if they can't differentiate us from a competitor, it's a cause for concern."

The graphs thus serve to remind everyone — managers as well as employees — of the areas in which the company can improve. They also point to issues that ought to be explored in customer focus groups and serve as tools for the sales staff.

Motivating Employees to Serve Customers

The community bank may well be the institution that coined the concept of customer service. Yet, over the years, something happened. If bankers showed a folksy concern and attentiveness toward their depositors and borrowers a century ago, any such solicitousness has long since fossilized. And if clichés are nothing more than distilled truths, then that dreaded certainty we all seem to feel about inevitably choosing the longest bank teller line says mountains about the depths to which customer service in the banking industry has sunk today. So it is reassuring to find a county bank among the companies we have selected to showcase for excellence in customer service.

That most sacrosanct of banking traditions — banker's hours — has been modified at Phelps County Bank, an early indication that this is no ordinary bank. PCB, as it is known, opens at five minutes before 9 a.m. and closes at five minutes past 3 p.m. Not an onerous burden for employees, this small favor has enormous psychological impact on customers. What's more, PCB has none of the stuffiness of ordinary banks, thanks largely to its CEO, Emma Lou Brent. PCB may appear warm and fuzzy, but it's as professional and conservative as other well-run banks. It is simply no slave to convention.

Brent's secret is her ability to enthuse her employees with a commitment to deliver "more than customers expect" of a bank. She has instilled in employees a sense of customer service excellence that has become routine. And she has sustained that fervor by reinforcing the bank's customer service creed each and every day.

At Phelps County Bank, Brent has earned the trust of her employees by trusting them. She has delighted and empowered employees. She lets employees make mistakes. Moreover, she has rewarded them by giving them ownership stakes in the bank. Employees of PCB carry business cards that do not bear their titles but, rather, identify them as employee-owners of the bank.

Linda Miller (see p. 123), of Development Dimensions International, believes that quality customer service depends to a great degree on establishing the kind of trust that Brent has developed at PCB. Miller poses tough questions here for business people willing to undergo self-scrutiny.

What Margo Chevers (see p. 117) emphasizes about Brent's success at PCB is her uncanny ability to get everyone moving in the same direction. Through ESOPs, training, empowerment, employee involvement in creating a creed and setting goals, Brent has created a well-oiled machine that consistently delivers a level of service that exceeds customer expectations.

Turning Employees Into Problem Solvers

*Phelps County Bank's prices are high,
its product line is not the most extensive, and yet it
dominates its market. The secret? Turning each
employee into a problem solver for customers — and
into a keen observer of the bottom line.*

Banks are where one of the most precious of personal possessions moves from hand to hand. In such institutions, trust is critical. And customer service is critical in building that trust.

But somewhere along the line, banks began to offer more lip service than customer service. Somewhere along the line, banks began to take their customers for granted. There was probably some truth to that even at Phelps County Bank of Rolla, Mo. before Emma Lou Brent came on the scene. But if Phelps ever took its customers for granted, it does so no longer. Today, it's just about the friendliest, most service-oriented bank you could imagine. And if there is any question about the value of customer service, consider what taking care of customers has done for Phelps County Bank. Since Emma Lou Brent took the helm at PCB, as it's known, her brand of customer service has brought the little bank startling growth and prosperity. Indeed, PCB's two chief competitors, both affiliated with big bank holding companies and bearing those holding companies' well-known names, have dropped to number two and number three in town while PCB has taken over as top banana.

As they say, there's a lesson here. Maybe a lot of lessons, because it turns out that PCB chief executive Emma Lou Brent had to build a different kind of company before her bank was capable of delivering the level of service that has made it so successful.

Pure Middle America

Rolla, Mo., sits in the foothills of the Ozarks, a two-hour drive from St. Louis southwest along Interstate 44. It's a modest-size community, pure middle America, set apart from a thousand similar towns only by its lovely surroundings and a University of Missouri campus. Its economy isn't exactly booming, but neither is it depressed. There's a little farming. The university generates some business, as does a modest stream of tourists and retirees. The bank's market area — including Rolla, the neighboring town of St. James, and the surrounding countryside — is home to some 35,000. PCB's main office sits on the corner of Eighth and Pine streets, downtown. The building was once a hotel, though by the time the bank was founded, in 1963, it had degenerated into a flophouse. Today it has been reborn, with plush carpets and dark wooden paneling, as befits a thriving financial institution. Thirty-six of PCB's 55 employees work here. The rest staff three other facilities: a branch in St. James, a drive-in bank on the outskirts of Rolla, and a tiny office on the university campus.

The service on which the bank stakes both its reputation and its bottom line makes itself felt in a dozen different ways, routine and not so routine.

The lobby opens five minutes before 9 a.m. and closes five minutes after 3 p.m. — there are no disgruntled customers peering in and looking angrily at their watches. If people knock on the door after closing, customer-service reps have been trained to invite them into a secure room and ask how they can help. Reps have the authority to resolve most customers' complaints on the spot. Mr. Jones is upset because he lost track of his checkbook balance and now doesn't want to pay the overdraft charge? A rep like Patti Douglas might refund the amount if she thinks it was an honest mistake. Or she might propose splitting it with him

At the windows, tellers learn basics that escape tellers at most other banks, such as: When you hear the door open, look up. If you see somebody looking around, lost, offer help. Acknowledge customers. Let them know you know they're there. Tellers, too, can resolve many customer complaints — unless there's a line, in which case they refer them to a customer-service rep. PCB's customer-service creed, displayed on easels in the lobbies and the loan department, reminds tellers (and everyone else) of their commitments. No keeping customers waiting while you finish paperwork. No using "the computer" or "policy" as a reason for not doing something.

House Calls

In the loan department, lending officers typically sit down with prospective borrowers for most of an hour, just to get to know them, before even beginning on the loan application. The bank's newspaper ads carry lending officers' home phone numbers, as do the officers' business cards. Customers are encouraged to call nights or weekends on urgent matters. House calls of that sort go in both directions. One day recently, Adolph Mueller at the St. James branch reported closing a $150,000 loan — in the evening, at the customers' home. "They both work, and they have three children," explains Mueller matter-of-factly. "So it's a convenience for them."

Service is partly a matter of systems, and PCB monitors its service by sending surveys to new borrowers (after three months) and customers opening new accounts (after six). The surveys alert the bank to bottlenecks ("Would you say that the waiting time, if any, at the bank is acceptable?") and to unmet customer needs (an automated teller machine at the drive-in facility). Service is also a matter of innovation, and PCB employees are forever coming up with new ideas. Patti Douglas, the customer-service rep, has developed a detailed proposal for a program aimed at seniors. Peggy Laun, an assistant in the loan department, has been investigating the possibility of offering electronic tax filing.

But service is also a matter of day-in-and-day-out culture, of people going out of their way to be helpful. Managers know that and make it a point to reinforce behavior that reflects the culture. "Remember when Mary tracked down that guy's Veterans' Administration check that hadn't come in yet?" asks Bonita Prock, senior vice-president in charge of operations, as she and three other managers sit around reminiscing. "She called around and got everything straightened out for him. She even called the telephone company because they were going to cut him off. And Patti helped a customer who had been duped by somebody over the phone. Before she was done she had talked to the Better Business Bureau in California and gotten those people their money."

Last spring the bank sponsored a promotion dubbed the "You Bet We Can Can-can," with graphics complete with caricatures of staffers doing the cancan, and advertised it all over Rolla. Tell us a story of employees who went out of their way to help you, the bank asked customers. Each month, we'll pick one. The winners — customer and employee — will each get dinner for two.

Dinner on the Bank

At most banks, such a request would be a joke. When PCB tried it, literally hundreds of responses poured in. A flower-shop owner, short of cash to pay for the repair of a critical piece of cooling equipment, called the bank while the angry repairman waited; Jody Sanders, a PCB loan officer, hand-delivered a small loan to cover the expense. At church one Sunday, an apparel retailer mentioned to Alice Malone, a customer-service rep, that she was having trouble with her credit-card imprinter. "When I got to the bank Monday, there was a new imprinter waiting for me," the retailer reported. A professor at the university got his mortgage approved by PCB before he had even moved to Rolla. Later, he wrote, the bank went to bat for him against an insurance company that had canceled his policy but tried to get its automatic monthly payment anyway.

PCB builds its very mission around that kind of service — "Always give customers more than they expect," preaches CEO Brent — and spares no expense in the pursuit of it. But the business logic is unassailable because service is the one essential ingredient of PCB's profitability. The bank's prices are high. Its interest rate on residential mortgages, for example, may be as much as a full percentage point above the competition's. And its product line isn't the most extensive in town. (Other banks offer items such as mutual funds.) So top-quality service is the only way PCB can keep customers coming in the door.

As for how you build a company capable of delivering that level of service — well, that's something it took Emma Lou Brent several years to learn.

Brent, known to all as Emmy, was born in 1938 on an Arkansas cotton farm. College wasn't in the cards. She married a man who became a high school chemistry teacher; they had two children. As the kids reached school age, in the late 1960s, she looked around for work — something that would allow her time for Scouts and other after-school activities. Phelps County Bank hired her as a part-time relief teller. Soon she was filling in for a variety of employees, staying after work when necessary, learning on the job during the day, studying banking manuals at night. When her children reached junior high she went full-time, taking on more responsibility every year. In 1976 the principal owner, Don Castleman, asked her to become executive vice-president. Six years later he named her CEO.

Aggressive, Self-Taught, and Gutsy

Maybe because of that up-from-the-bottom history, Brent is an unusual, almost paradoxical, figure. On the one hand, she exhibits confidence bordering on fearlessness, leading her employees to regard her with something close to awe. "She's an aggressive, self-taught, gutsy woman," says one, "and she has led this bank to success." On the other hand, she has a healthy respect for what she doesn't know. She'll tell you of the time she forgot to pay the bank's tax bill, just because she assumed it was due the same day as individual taxes. She remembers learning to say, "I'll get back to you," when the Federal Reserve called with a question she couldn't answer. She felt she'd never succeed unless she attracted smart people to work with her.

In the early 1980s, of course, running a small bank was a daunting enough prospect for anyone. "I kept hearing that community banks were not going to be a thing of the future," Brent recalls, the clipped syllables and soft twang of her speech reflecting her roots in the region. "By the year 1995 or 2000, people said, we'd have a banking system like the Canadians' — seven or eight large banks. Banks in places like Rolla would be franchises." She doesn't add, though she might have, that a version of that prediction came true for Rolla's two other commercial banks. Both changed hands during the decade. Both now carry the names of huge statewide bank holding companies, Boatmen's and Mercantile.

Characteristically, Brent had a plan. "I visualized what I thought the community bank of the future would need to look like. It would need to have a whole staff of knowledgeable, intelligent bankers to work with people." Banking wasn't just taking money and making loans — big banks could do that well enough. It was helping people manage their lives, their assets, their businesses. It was providing hands-on personal service, the kind that would let a customer speak proudly of "my banker." Granted, that would be a tall order. The bank would need to attract, keep, and motivate first-rate, customer-oriented people, and somehow build up that culture of service. A second tall order: making money with the plan. Good people don't come cheap. Personal service is costly because it's time-consuming. The bank's prices could be a little higher than the competition's — but in Rolla, Mo., they couldn't be a whole lot higher. To make money with its costly approach, PCB would have to operate with unparalleled bottom-line efficiency.

Spring Cleaning

Brent began with some straightforward moves, the stuff of sound banking and good management. She cleaned up the loan portfolio, taking some losses and tightening up on delinquency. She revamped lending procedures, emphasizing the ability to repay a loan more than the collateral behind it. ("It never did make sense to me to lend $50,000 on a $200,000 farm if the customer couldn't pay back the $50,000.") She let go a couple of people who didn't share her outlook; she hired people who did. She continually updated the bank's computer system. And Brent brought in new lending personnel, including Bill Marshall, who helped clean up the loan portfolio.

But she also took three less conventional steps, not so much

> **HOT TIP**

Some people, it seems, you just can't please. But Neil Cannon will die trying. Cannon, CEO of Schmidt-Cannon International, a distributor of promotional items headquartered in Ontario, Calif., has developed a problem-customer order tracking system. Cannon is convinced that customers most prone to complaining are those who have done so already. So anytime the company receives a complaint, that customer's next order gets placed in a red file folder. As the folder is passed through departments, each manager personally signs off on it. If a problem arises, the manager responsible speaks directly with the customer. Since the system was introduced, there has been a noticeable drop in repeat complaints.

because she had a grand strategy in mind as because they seemed, intu-itively, like good ideas. As it turned out, they were the seeds of a compa-ny that could realize her vision.

- While looking for some sort of profit-sharing or retirement plan — "to let people know their work was appreciated," she says, and to encourage them to stay with PCB — she heard about employee stock ownership plans, or ESOPs. An ESOP was an appealing device: It could provide employees with a retirement benefit, and it could give Castleman, who owned most of the stock, some liquidi-ty. Brent established a small plan, and the plan bought a little stock. Over time she began to see other possibilities in the ESOP. Maybe ownership would give employees a reason for taking that extra step with customers. And in an industry in which companies were changing hands regularly, employee ownership offered a degree of job security that would surely attract the best people. Bit by bit, the ESOP began buying Castleman out (although he remains chairman).

- Figuring her employees would need training if they were to be "knowledgeable, intelligent bankers," Brent arranged for the American Institute of Banking to offer them classes in banking principles. She knew some employees had good ideas but were struggling to express them, so she brought in Dale Carnegie instructors to help them communicate. She set up seminars in sales techniques and in problem solving. To make sure everyone was familiar with the services PCB offered, she designed a yearlong in-house training program, in which each department prepared a ses-sion for the others. The program culminated in a mock *Jeopardy* game with six employee teams competing and an electric score-board tallying the answers.

- Remembering her own days as a teller — and her frustration when management ignored her ideas — Brent began involving the bank's employees in decisions. At first it was mostly informal. But in 1987, when she mapped out PCB's first formal goal-setting meeting, she invited not just managers or the board but the whole staff. ("I said, 'You've gotta be kidding!'" recalls an employee who had recently joined PCB from another bank. "At the other place, the executives would get their computers and leave. Then they'd come back and say, 'This is our plan.'") The goal-setting meetings became regular annual events. Meanwhile, Brent created an ideas program she called the ESOP Challenge. Employees with ideas for improvements of any sort — new products, process improvements, whatever — could write them up and present them to top management. The best idea each month would win its author $100. The best of the year brought a trip for two worth $1,500.

By 1991 — nine years after she took over as CEO — those seeds were taking root, and Brent figured it was time to take notice of the "new" PCB. So that fall the bank threw itself a banquet dubbed the Old Settlers Dinner. The managers put on a skit — Brent played Thomas Jefferson, others played Ben Franklin and John Adams — celebrating PCB's independence and declaring war on "megabank" competitors. The upstart's weapon: its commitment to service. The revolutionaries unveiled a "customer-service creed" drafted earlier by a committee of employees and hand-lettered on parchment-like paper. Everyone signed it. "Each of us has the authority and the responsibility to do what we feel necessary to solve a customer's problem," read one of the document's many declarations. "We are owners of our bank, and customers expect owners to solve problems."

It was a symbolic statement, of course. But there was a distinct reality behind it. Gradually, almost without anyone's realizing the extent of the change, PCB was becoming an unusual kind of company. What made the difference was how Brent's three initiatives evolved over time — and how they turned out to fit so neatly, hand in well-matched glove, with her vision of a service-oriented business.

Making the E$OP Count

Where ownership was concerned, Brent's problem was making it real — not just words on paper but something that employees felt and acted on. Thousands of companies have ESOPs, after all, thanks in part to the tax breaks the plans offer. But a retirement plan with a few shares of stock doesn't magically transform employees into owners, and it doesn't keep them on the payroll when another company offers $50 more a week. For Brent's strategy to work, people had to stay at PCB, building up relationships with customers. And they had to care about the level of service the bank offered those customers.

For a while, PCB's ESOP fell into the who-cares category. "The attitude was, it's just a piece of paper and it doesn't mean anything," says operations senior vice president Prock. Even Brent got tired of trying to persuade her staff members that they were really part owners of the bank. "There was a short period of time when I just let it die," she admits. "It was too hard to convince people."

What overcame everyone's skepticism was — no surprise — money.

Buying Out the Bank

An ESOP is actually a trust, legally separate from the bank itself. PCB's ESOP, a so-called leveraged plan, works like this: The ESOP borrows money to buy stock from Castleman. PCB contributes so much to the ESOP each year, and the ESOP pays down its debt. As it does so, it allocates shares to individuals' accounts.

One way to make this one-step-removed ownership seem real, Brent had read, was to contribute sizable amounts to the ESOP, thus hurrying along the process of debt reduction and stock allocation. In 1986 the bank contributed $50,000 to the ESOP. By 1989, however, the yearly contribution was up to $250,000, and in the past couple of years it has been higher still. Soon big numbers were appearing on individual employee's statements. When a couple of long-timers retired, taking their cash with them, the skeptics watched in amazement. "They saw a couple hundred thousand dollars going out — and they knew only two people had left," says Prock. "It made them realize it's real money."

Real indeed. Right now the ESOP owns virtually all the bank's stock. Eighteen people had ESOP balances in six figures as of the end of 1993. Many more have balances between $50,000 and $100,000. In another eight years, the ESOP will have paid for and allocated all its shares — and the bank, presumably, will have continued to grow, thus boosting share value. At that point an account worth $50,000 today — about the average — should be worth close to $200,000. That goes a long way where in Rolla a typical three-bedroom home sells for perhaps $65,000.

PCB enthusiastically broadcasts its employee ownership. Ads and other marketing materials trumpet it. Business cards announce "employee owner" instead of the employee's title. Employees elect a seven-person ESOP committee and send representatives to national employee-ownership conferences. The committee publishes a newsletter called "PCB ESOP Pride."

What lends substance to all the hoopla, however, are the economic underpinnings. Every spring the bank holds a shareholders' dinner. There's entertainment, good food, maybe a speech or two. But the highlight of the evening, by common consent, is when Brent passes out the sealed envelopes showing individual ESOP balances and projections for the future.

It's a family affair, with spouses as interested as employees. "I barely got to look at mine," says Patti Douglas, grinning as she thinks back on her first dinner. "My husband had ripped it out of my hand!" When they both looked at the numbers, it hit them. "That's when it really came home to me, full-fledged," she adds. "Gee whiz. I'm an owner of that bank."

Asked to elaborate, Douglas turns reflective. "If you're just an employee, you know no matter how hard you beat your head against the wall, they may or may not notice. You may or may not get a raise. You may or may not get a promotion. Here, all that gets put aside. Anything that I can do for this bank to improve it, to bring in new customers, to increase the bottom line, I benefit from."

Douglas isn't thinking of leaving anytime soon. Aside from the occasional employee who leaves to start a family or accompany a spouse on a move, turnover at the bank is virtually zero.

How Does a Bank Make Money?

Training presented Brent with a different kind of problem. On the one hand, delivering first-rate service requires no more than a positive attitude and job-specific skills, like knowing what to do when a customer wants to deposit English pounds. Ownership, combined with the banking and business-skill training employees were receiving, thus went far toward producing those intelligent, knowledgeable bankers. On the other hand, service is costly, by definition. And unless all the employees were paying as much attention to the bottom line as they were to customers, PCB would service itself right out of existence.

So about a year ago Brent embarked on a program to teach all employees how their bank makes money, and hence what they can do to boost profits and control costs.

New employees get what amounts to basic training — a chart titled "How We Make Each Dollar and How It Is Spent," complete with real figures for the last seven years. Brent walks them through it as part of their orientation, pointing out essential figures. ("It's easy to see that your biggest income producer is your loan portfolio.")

Others have begun more advanced training in the financials. PCB's seven customer-service reps, for example, recently spent part of every Thursday's meeting calculating by hand item after item on the bank's so-called monitoring report. "We could pull them off the computer, but this way we really understand where the numbers come from," one rep explains. The report, a compilation of nearly two dozen ratios used in the industry, provides a detailed snapshot of the bank's performance as a business.

Focusing on Crucial Variables

An incentive-compensation plan pays annual bonuses based on six or eight key numbers. The purpose isn't so much to reward or retain people; the ESOP does that, as do salary levels that are about 20% above market rates. Rather, it's to focus attention month by month on crucial variables such as loan delinquency. (A nice touch: The plan was introduced late in 1992, ostensibly for implementation — and first bonus — in 1993. Then management surprised the employees by paying 1992 bonuses anyway.)

Thanks to all the training, people learn to keep a hawk eye on key figures — and to take action if they're headed the wrong way. "We watch deposit totals," says Melanie Boyda, a teller. "If they're down, maybe we need to cross-sell a little more." Tellers also watch their overtime hours, knowing that too much overtime cuts into earnings. Customer-service reps, such as Douglas, get monthly reports detailing the accounts they have opened and closed and how much those accounts earned the bank. "If I see that one of my customers has closed an account," she says, "I'll get on the phone and ask if there was anything wrong. We don't want to lose a customer due to dissatisfaction."

PCB makes money by attending to a hundred such details. Traveler's checks and other reimbursables go out for payment immediately. If they don't, says Bonita Prock, someone's likely to holler. ("Do you realize that the $30,000 you could have shipped cost us x dollars a day?") Customer-service reps learn to be generous in refunding service charges to disgruntled customers — but not too generous, because the refunds will reduce the "noninterest income" line of the income statement. "We've gone to the point of breaking down the loans by facility, breaking down the vaults by facility, so each facility can track itself, see where it is and how it compares," explains Prock.

The signs of PCB's success show up in the reports, provided throughout the banking industry, that compare an individual bank with banks of a similar size and situation. In a recent one, PCB's so-called peer banks had per capita personnel costs of $27,810. That was 21% lower than PCB's costs of $34,540, which included payments to the ESOP. Yet PCB's return on assets was 17% higher than that of its peers.

Turn $uggestion$ into Involvement

Brent began her experiments with employee involvement in modest-enough fashion, through steps such as inviting everyone to the annual planning meetings. But corporate culture is a dynamic entity — and when fundamentals such as ownership and employees' understanding of the business change, so too does the nature of involvement. Consider PCB's main suggestion program.

Last July Patti Douglas's entry in the monthly competition was her proposal for a seniors' program. Hire a program director, she recommended, and develop a comprehensive marketing program to appeal to elderly customers. Offer special checking and savings accounts. Sponsor meetings and seminars to help seniors with financial planning. Set up an advisory board of over-65 people to serve as "ambassadors" in the community. Behind the 12-page proposal lay nearly two years' worth of research. Douglas had dug up demographic statistics. She had compiled information about what every other financial institution in the area offered seniors. She tracked PCB's experience with its existing elderly customers. She costed out her proposal and projected its impact on the bank's bottom line. The week before it was due, she estimates, she spent 27 off-the-clock hours getting it ready (see CEO's Insight: "Buzz Off with the PC-Bees," p. 116).

Douglas's proposal — it won both a monthly and an annual award — was unusual in its level of detail. It was not so unusual in its level of sophistication. Sandy Karr (in loans) and Stella Ravenscraft (in bookkeeping) researched and designed the customer survey that the bank uses to evaluate its service levels. Peggy Laun investigated whether the bank should offer its customers electronic tax filing with the IRS.

Brent and other managers, of course, make the decisions about whether to and when to implement the ideas. That doesn't mean the suggestions disappear into a managerial black hole. Proposals often come back to their originators for more research or for modification. The originators often become point people for research and development in the areas they've carved out. Laun, for instance, recommended against offering electronic filing with the IRS in her original proposal. The software, she had learned, was still pretty iffy. But she has since become the bank's clearinghouse for information on the subject and plans now to look at the possibilities once more.

The mechanisms of involvement have undergone an evolution of their own. For a while, PCB had an active committee known as the Problem Busters, charged with untangling bottlenecks and dealing with employee grievances. Over time Brent noticed a funny thing: The committee had less and less to do. Employees were learning to solve problems on their own. They let everyone else know what they had done

> **HOT TIP**

Valid or not, a complaint is tangible. You can take action to correct a problem or appease a customer. But what of those non-confrontational customers who would rather flee than complain? Clarke Otten, president of Professional Swedish Car Repair in Atlanta, doesn't want dissatisfied customers to quietly switch companies, so he ferrets out Milquetoasts by telephoning all his customers one week after they visit one of his four locations. He sets aside an hour or two to make 20 to 50 phone calls. When customers receive a call from the president of the company, they are impressed, to say the least. And Otten is in a position to do something — on the spot — if they have a complaint.

through the bank's electronic-mail system. Today the Problem Busters mostly track the E-mail messages, watching for recurring issues and occasionally offering a helping hand.

It's hard to quantify exactly how all the innovations proposed and implemented by bank employees have paid off. But Brent keeps a little productivity chart that she likes to look at periodically. It measures the bank's costs and earnings per million dollars of assets per day.

In 1989 PCB's total overhead — a figure that includes all personnel expenses — came to $93 per million dollars of assets per day. Net income was $34. In fiscal year 1993, overhead fell to $91.50 (with bonuses). Net income was up to $45.

The drawbacks of PCB's approach are few in number but not zero. Since the bank's employees are human, not every transaction results in a happy customer. ("There was a lady who was pretty unfriendly," reports a college-student customer contacted by *Inc.*) Yet the bank's very emphasis on service leads customers to expect near perfection. "The better we are in service, the better we constantly have to get," says Brent, shaking her head. "When a customer has been referred by someone, they're expecting first-class service from the minute they walk in." Like a manufacturer aiming for zero defects, PCB has little margin for error.

Then, too, not every employee is as gung-ho about the ESOP and participatory management as, say, Patti Douglas or Peggy Laun is. Indeed, the system tends to squeeze out people who prefer a job that begins at 9 a.m. and ends at 5 p.m. and doesn't take too much thinking in between. That process isn't bloodless. Says Brent, "We had situations where employees wouldn't want to do something — but wouldn't want the person next to them to do it, either, for fear they'd look bad." Only a couple of senior people were asked to leave, but many others did: Brent says the bank had a 40% turnover in the two and a half years between early 1986 and late 1988. Even today, she adds, new employees can quickly feel lost or left behind. That's why the bank has recently implemented a "buddy system" to shepherd them along.

And yet, what is striking on a visit to PCB is how much fun people seem to be having. Several employees mentioned getting together for pizza after work — and racking up a video on the machine down in the lunch-room. The bank's newsletter reads like a high-spirited gossip sheet. ("EMMY BRENT had her whole family with her for her birthday & some birthday it was — she ended up cooking. Haven't they heard of eating out?...The big news for SANDY KING concerns her son, Derik, who grad-uates in May with his M.D. degree....") And Bill Marshall, senior vice-pres-ident in charge of loans, explained how his staff gently informed him he'd have to answer the phones for half an hour every Thursday.

"One of the employees came to me and said, 'I've noticed we're all under a lot of stress. Everybody's up to here, and we're going as hard as we can go.' I had been up there saying how great things were — our growth last month was great — and here were these people saying, You're killing us.

"Anyway, they went out and bought a game. It's like charades, and what they decided was that they were going to play it for half an hour every week. They didn't come to me and say, Would you mind? They said, 'On Thursday mornings, do you have appointments?' And I said no. They said, 'That's great — because you need to answer the phones while we play our game.'"

It was only for a little while, and it was early in the morning, when calls would be few. Even so, there aren't many companies in which the support staff would decide to take time out for a game, then inform the boss he had to play receptionist. "People are always pushing," says Marshall. "They correct their own problems before they get to us — the petty problems just don't appear. People are way past that and are cre-ative. It's difficult to keep up with."

Ultimately, the key to PCB's success may be as simple as that: People are always pushing to do a little more, a little better, stress or no. All of them.

"I always have higher hopes for us than where we are now," says Emma Lou Brent, who set the bank on its present course. "I'm always saying there are so many things I still want to do."

Evidently, she's not the only one who feels that way. ■

CEO'S INSIGHT

BUZZ OFF WITH THE PC-BEES

Patti Douglas's proposal for a seniors' program at Phelps County Bank was not immediately pursued by the bank. There were other projects that had to be attended to first. But early in 1994, PCB turned its attention to the idea of creating a seniors' club of some sort.

There was nothing new about senior citizen bank programs. And Emma Lou Brent was not about to simply duplicate what was already on the market. "One thing we've learned over the years," says Brent, "is that if you're going to do something for a customer, go out and ask that customer what he wants. We always used to just follow the crowd. If a bank introduced a checking account, we'd create the same program and then spend thousands of dollars selling it. We don't do that anymore. When we come up with a good idea, we test it first to see if it will fly."

Brent asked employees for the names of senior citizen customers who might be interested in a bank club. Then the bank sent out invitations to a focus luncheon to the 80 seniors whose names were proposed, hoping for a group of 20 to 25. Sixty seniors accepted the invitation. So PCB broke the group into three focus groups and hosted three luncheons. "It cost us some money," says Brent, "but it was money well spent."

The seniors expressed interest in a seniors' bank club, but were put off by the names most such clubs are given. "They were not at all interested in being part of a club with 'Golden Years' or 'Prime of Life' as part of the name. They wanted a name that reflected the way they felt, which was active. They also wanted to be affiliated with the bank. We let them name the club and they decided to call it the PC-Bees, with a bee as the mascot. They wanted to convey the idea of a beehive of activity." One elderly gentleman designed an ad that the bank ran in the newspaper to publicize the club. It read: "Buzz off... with us."

"They really got into it," says Brent. And, as a result, so did the bank. The seniors very much wanted their club to be a win-win situation for themselves and the bank. They wanted to understand how the bank earned a profit (how deposits are turned into loans for a profit) and how they fit into that equation. The bank began promoting the club on April 1 with a membership goal of 100 by May 15. By May 12, 200 seniors had signed up, by May 15, 235, and by mid-June, the PC-Bees had over 300 members.

Now there's talk of taking the club farther. "There's always a certain amount of resentment toward older customers because of the discounts they receive," says Brent. "With that in mind, the PC-Bees are talking about adding a service function to the club. Although we haven't done anything about it yet, we're exploring the idea of making the PC-Bees both a bank club and a service club."

The idea is to create a community-based program for the PC-Bees to champion. Whether a foster grandparent program or a community hospice, the PC-Bees are interested in giving something back to their community. And the bank is exploring with them how this might be accomplished, perhaps through matching funds.

Phelps County Bank continues to explore new avenues of customer service, but never without the feedback and input of the very customers they seek to serve. At PCB, Brent looks to her owner employees for ideas which she then floats to the bank's customers who design the program. Then, when the program is brought back into the bank and implemented, it's virtually guaranteed to succeed. ∎

3

Getting Everyone Moving in the Same Direction

by Margo Chevers

Exceptional customer service is the reason Phelps County Bank is a strong contender in its marketplace, but without the underpinnings created by the president, there would be no motivation to deliver that service. Let's take a look at how you can develop in your company the same atmosphere that Phelps County Bank has created.

Imagine you bought an automobile and it was just delivered to your house. As the proud owner, you park it in front of your house so you can admire it. You look at it from all angles and fantasize about the type of ride you'll have when you get in it and drive away.

While you've been admiring your car, unbeknownst to you the four wheels are assessing the situation. The right front wheel can see the meadow to the side of your house and dreams of the fun the car will have when it finally gets into motion. It imagines the coolness of the grass as well as the way the car will have a bumpy ride over the uneven terrain. At the same time, the left rear wheel is observing the dirt road in its line of sight, and it imagines the scenery down around the bend. Perhaps there's a bubbling stream where it would be enjoyable to park the car and have a picnic.

Meanwhile, the left front wheel is looking excitedly at the super highway that runs by the house and calculates how quickly the car can accelerate to 90 miles per hour, imagining the excitement and challenge of traveling on a congested thoroughfare. However, the right rear wheel is eyeing the garage and reflecting on the safety and security of parking the car out of the danger of the elements. The sun won't be able to fade

Margo Chevers is president of Northeast Leadership Enterprise, in Plainville, Mass.

the paint, no snow or rain to dirty up the shine, and no passing motorists to avoid hitting.

With these four conflicting motives, when you get in the car, start it up and accelerate, you'll find that all you'll get are spinning wheels. The more fuel you give it, the faster the wheels will spin, but you won't go anywhere. If you insist on attempting to drive your car, you'll end up ruining it or at best, spending a lot of money on repairs.

Now think about your own company with its many departments. Too often, their efforts are not aligned but are pulling in opposite directions. This leads to multiple assumptions about the priorities of the company and the needs of the customers. Consequently, much unnecessary effort is expended, not because employees are trying to sabotage the company or their co-workers but because they haven't been given the big picture. They aren't encouraged to communicate with each other, share information, or work in tandem. Each department works in a semi-vacuum of information.

Salespeople interact with the customer on a daily basis and, because of what they see and hear, pull the company in the direction the customer is telling them on that particular day.

At the same time, operations is responding to the requests not only of the sales department but of the employees, as well as to the limitations of machines, materials, time, and money. Their viewpoint on what needs to be done can differ vastly from that of sales.

Meanwhile, the finance department is looking at the cost of doing business, the credit of the customers, and overhead. Therefore, finance draws the company in the direction that makes sense on the basis of this information. All the other departments, involved in their own struggles, try to influence the company according to their needs and priorities.

How do we get the company aligned? With a car, it is easy. Take it into the repair shop and put it up on lifts, align the wheels, and the problem is solved. Once all four wheels of the car are aligned, you could jump into it and drive away. In fact, if you were to use the same amount of acceleration you did when the wheels were pointed in opposite directions, you'd get a speeding ticket.

With a company, it is more complicated than that. Phelps County Bank has been able to bring everyone under the same assumptions, so everyone's efforts are pointed in the same direction.

Let's take a look at how they did this.

PCB started with a customer service creed. All employees had a part in creating it. When employees get involved in determining the direction in which the company will head, there is an implied ownership of ideas. If it is their idea, they will work to make it come true.

This creed (or mission statement) is the reason your company exists. In every mission statement, the customer and the employee must both play a prominent part. A mission statement answers the questions: What does your company do? Why does it do it? How does it affect your customers and employees?

For example, I recently saw a tour bus with part of the company's mission printed on the side. It stated, *"We help you create memories."* You can see how, with this phrase as the stated mission, everything the company does is geared toward making every customer's trip a positive experience.

With a statement prominently displayed, not only for the customer but for the employee as well, everyone's efforts are directed toward accomplishing the mission. At PCB, the creed is posted in the lobby.

My company's customer service creed:

_____

_____

_____

_____

_____

_____

Where will you post this creed? Will all the members of your team sign it?

The next step in getting the company in alignment is to set corporate goals that help the company to attain its mission. Everyone must be involved in the development of these goals, since everyone is responsible for accomplishing them. Again, the feeling of ownership and commitment will be higher if everyone is involved in setting goals.

What are the mechanics of setting goals?

STEP 1: Goals must be specific and measurable so there is no confusion as to what is expected.

For example, if you told an employee to drive a vehicle from Phoenix to the East Coast, the driver would have many options. The employee could drive to Bangor, Philadelphia, or Miami, or any other city on the East Coast, and would have accomplished the goal according to the information given. However, if you want the vehicle to end up in Boston, you had better be specific. Likewise, your goals need to be specific, so that all employees will have a clear understanding of the outcome expected.

My company's number one goal is:

_____

_____

_____

_____

_____

STEP 2: Your goals must also be realistic.

If you sent your employee across country in an old car in need of repair, with no air conditioning and bald tires, and you gave no cash or credit cards to the driver, the chances of accomplishing the drive would be slim.

Your company needs to have the experience, resources, talented personnel, and capacity to accomplish your goals, or you are setting yourself up for failure.

We can accomplish our goal with these resources:

_____

_____

_____

_____

_____

STEP 3: Deadlines are important when setting your goals, so that employees feel it is urgent to complete them.

Unless the deadlines are communicated to your cross-country driver, your employee could very well spend extra days on the road, not realizing the urgency of delivering the vehicle.

Our deadline for accomplishment is: _____

STEP 4: There are always obstacles to accomplishing goals.

You must identify any obstacles that exist so that you can prepare a plan to overcome them. Not identifying them does not make them disappear. Not planning for roadblocks simply adds time and effort when you bump into them.

Take the cross-country trip you've sent your employee on. If a bridge is washed out, the driver will have to re-route up or down the river, taking extra time and money.

The obstacles we'll encounter along the way are:

_____

_____

_____

_____

_____

STEP 5: Prepare a plan of action. What must you do to accomplish your goals?

This is where the departments and the individuals in the departments become invaluable. They should have a big say in the "how" of accomplishing goals. They are the ones who will be executing the plan. Their buy-in is important, otherwise the plan may not be successfully completed.

Success in business is the result of effective planning and goal setting with the cooperation of the individuals responsible for serving the customer. As in any journey, you're more likely to reach your destination if you involve your driver. ■

Building Trust with
Employees and Customers

by Linda Miller

As a leader, have you ever been guilty of the following:

- Making assumptions?
- Covering yourself?
- Breaking promises?
- Shooting the messenger?
- Mixing messages?
- Sugar-coating?

If the answer is "yes" to any or all of these questions, you have fallen into the most common of "Trust Traps." These actions erode and often demolish any bridge of trust that might exist between you and your workers. Once destroyed, trust is difficult to rebuild. But it is possible.

To establish a high level of trust in today's cynical work world, leaders must first exhibit superior business competence — a combination of leadership skills and action orientation. Leaders do not have to be technical experts, but they do have to be leadership experts. And once a skilled leader takes over, he or she must be able and willing to take action. When employees know their boss is a competent business leader who is action oriented, trust is enhanced

No matter how strong the leader's business competence, however, he or she will still have difficulty establishing trust without incorporating a strong people orientation. Leaders must look at their people not as commodities but as individuals who have a desire to do a good job, who are trusted, who deserve to be treated with respect, and who know their

Linda Miller is manager of strategies for high-involvement leadership at Development Dimensions International (DDI), in Pittsburgh, Pa.

jobs better than anyone else. For leaders to accept this view, they must be willing to empower their people.

Lack of trust destroys initiative, creates unrest, and erodes team spirit. Managers who fail to establish a strong culture of trust can unknowingly foster all of these morale problems. Conversely, once a deep level of trust is established, amazing success can result.

No one knows this better than Emma Lou Brent, CEO of Phelps County Bank (PCB) in Rolla, Mo. When Brent took over in 1982, PCB was following the path of many community banks: losing customers and losing money. But she had a vision: a bank filled with employees who really cared about their customers. Today, 12 years later, not only has this vision become a reality but PCB has surged ahead of two much larger banks in town to become number one.

FIVE CRUCIAL WAYS LEADERS MUST BEHAVE TO BUILD TRUST

- Be positive
- Seek others' ideas
- Listen
- Disclose
- Don't shoot the messenger

Back in the early days, Brent made the same assumptions about her staff as other banking CEOs in town: People know enough about their jobs to do them adequately. But she began to wonder what might happen if her staff knew their jobs and customer service so well that they not only met but exceeded customers' expectations? Total Quality had not yet become an industry buzzword, so Brent was clearly ahead of her time.

After taking some gutsy steps to clean up PCB's portfolio and tighten up on delinquency, she began to concentrate on customer service. There had to be a way, she thought, to make her bank the "friendliest, most service-oriented bank" in town. To enhance her associates' self-esteem, Brent brought in Dale Carnegie instructors. To teach them banking principles, she hired people from the American Institute of Banking. She, herself, spent an entire year educating every employee in banking products and administration and building their customer service skills.

This training was successful because Brent took steps at the outset to instill trust: She was open and honest with people, rewarded innovation, and gave constructive feedback. These are all critical factors in establishing trust, according to Robert W. Rogers, chief operating officer of Development Dimensions International (DDI), a company that specializes in value-driven culture change and research into trust issues.

Rogers says that the first step toward inspiring trust is accentuating the positive. "Leaders need to develop the analytical skills to be able to distinguish the 'good' behaviors from the 'bad'," he says. "Then they must learn to focus on the positive while providing constructive feedback about areas needing improvement." By focusing on her associates' successes and using mistakes as learning experiences, Brent took the first important step toward building trust.

Seeking the ideas of others — a somewhat revolutionary idea in the early days of PCB's new growth — proved invaluable in building trust. Brent had learned in the "old school," where leaders were the problem solvers, idea producers, and decision makers, but she began to imagine what could happen if she got valuable input from others. She soon learned that giving credence to associates' ideas inspired them to increasing levels of creativity, and she used this to its best advantage. Employees with ideas for improvements of any sort — new products, process improvements — could write them up and present them to top management.

Not only did Brent reward innovation financially, she and her executives acknowledged and acted on the ideas. She communicated to each person that his or her ideas were valuable and would not fall into a black hole. Suggestions abounded and continue to do so. In many organizations today, trust is built even further when the idea person is given responsibility and authority to take the idea all the way to fruition.

Brent had to learn to really listen when people talked because listening is one of the simplest ways to inspire trust. Rogers underlines the need for empathetic listening: "It doesn't take many empathetic responses for leaders to begin seeing people's trust level rise."

Brent not only listens to her staff; she also listens to the bank's customers. Recently, in a promotion called "You Bet We Can Can-can," she urged PCB's customers to "tell us a story of employees who went out of their way to help you." She was overwhelmed by the hundreds of responses, and she read and evaluated each one. "Always give customers more than they expect" has become PCB's mission. Such a mission would have been impossible if Brent had not taken the time to build a bridge of trust. Staff members were also given authority to solve customer complaints on the spot. This empowerment to take action independently showed trust on Brent's part and trust on the employees' part — they were not afraid to act.

Brent realized early on that she needed to be open and honest with associates in order to involve them in the operation and make them feel a part of it. Her willingness to disclose her vision has gone a long way toward building trust. In 1987, when she planned PCB's first formal goal-setting meeting, she invited not only managers and the board but the entire staff. They were astounded, knowing that at goal-setting time, the norm for executives was to go off-site and come back with a final plan that they might or might not share with line staff. Historically, this is one of the fundamental reasons employees have low trust: They do not know what their leaders think or believe.

Creating a high-trust vision means:
- You are confident that others' actions are consistent with their words.
- People with whom you work are concerned about your welfare and interests apart from what you can do for them.
- Skills you have developed are respected and valued by your co-workers and the larger organization.
- Who you are and what you believe truly matter in the workplace.

Finally, trust can be taught, although many leaders still refuse to believe so. Leaders need to create a high-trust vision, know themselves, model their beliefs, and encourage team trust. Front-line leaders constantly must build strong bridges of communication with employees and with other departments, and they need to make it easy for others to cross those bridges. Honest, open, and straightforward communication is the key to open dialogue among team members and across organizational boundaries — on a personal and professional level. One of the best ways to teach trust is to empower people. Emma Brent's customer service creed has taught her associates that she trusts them implicitly: "Each of us has the authority and the responsibility to do what we feel necessary to solve a customer's problem." Showing this level of trust has caused such growth and success at PCB that her competitors can only scratch their heads in amazement.

If you are committed to building a deep level of trust in your organization, you need to learn to accentuate the positive, seek others' ideas, listen with empathy, disclose vision and plans, and use mistakes as learning experiences. Might it be possible for your organization to develop a trust so strong that you will reach levels of growth and success that you never dreamed possible?

Ask Emmy Brent.

CREATE TRUST THROUGH LEADERSHIP

- Create a high-trust vision.
- Know yourself.
- Build bridges of communication.
- Model your beliefs.
- Encourage team trust.

EXERCISE: TAKING STOCK

The first step in strengthening trust, often a difficult one, is to examine the level of trust within your own work group, and your own ability to trust and be trusted. This can help you identify where you need to start and what you will need to do to strengthen trust.

Putting yourself under a microscope takes courage. Being honest with yourself is the first step in deciding whether to change and what to change. The surveys that follow are designed to help you become more aware of how the actions or words you use affect trust between you and others. Pay attention to the items where you answer "Sometimes" or "Never" because these will be important indicators of where your behavior is inconsistent. Consistent behavior is critical to building trust.

Think about these questions and answer them honestly; then consider what you can do to change the way you look at trust.

DO YOU INSPIRE TRUST?

Respond to each of the following statements with:

A = Almost Always   **S = Sometimes**   **N = Never**

1. I follow through on the things I commit myself to do.

2. I say what I believe rather than what I think people want to hear.

3. Others can rely on me to keep confidence.

4. I share information — good and bad — with the people who need to have it.

5. I listen to people and take time to ask for their opinions.

6. I acknowledge people's accomplishments and make sure they get credit for their ideas.

7 I give honest, constructive feedback rather than avoiding the truth when it needs to be told

8. I practice what I preach — what I say is what I do.

9. I show respect for others regardless of their positions or what they can do for me

10 I delegate sensibly and don't abdicate responsibility.

11. I focus on solving problems rather than finding someone to blame.

12. I make sure my personal goals and opinions don't interfere with team or organizational objectives.

13. I accept responsibility for my mistakes.

14. I behave consistently regardless of the person or situation and my level of stress.

15. I champion my team members when I talk with people outside the team.

Do You Trust Others?

Respond to each of the following statements with:

A = Almost Always   **S = Sometimes**   **N = Never**

1. I avoid looking over people's shoulders while they do their jobs.

2. I check on facts before making assumptions or jumping to conclusions.

3. I share information — good and bad — with the people who need to have it.

4. I share decision-making authority and then support my group's decisions whenever appropriate.

5. I say what I think in a way that shows respect for others' opinions.

6 I support the feasible ideas, decisions, and actions of others.

7. I ask for and accept feedback about my performance.

8 I consider mistakes to be opportunities for learning, and I admit my mistakes and problems.

10. I promote innovative thinking and risk-taking.

11. I provide opportunities for people to develop their talents.

12. I listen openly to people's concerns, ideas, and feelings.

13. I address problems with the people directly involved and seek solutions that benefit everyone.

14. I disclose my thoughts, feelings, and rationale when appropriate.

15. I accept that there are ways besides my own to accomplish tasks and achieve goals. ■

Notes

The Open-Book Travel Analysis

At Phelps County Bank, CEO Emma Lou Brent took employees into her confidence when she opened up the books to educate them about how the bank earned a profit.

At Cleveland-based Meridian Travel, founder and CEO Cyndie Bender took what some would consider an even bigger leap of faith when she decided to apply open-book-management techniques to manage her customer relationships. Instead of educating her employees about how to earn a profit, she decided to educate her customers about how to earn savings. As a result Bender now gets the kind of customer cooperation, loyalty, and referrals — not to mention profit margins — most CEOs only dream about. What gave Bender the idea? Well, the success of Meridian Travel depends heavily on how well its major corporate customers follow their travel policies. When a customer doesn't follow policy, not only do the big savings Meridian had promised evaporate, but so do Meridian's own profit margins, souring the agency's relationship with airlines in the process. Bender conducted in-house profitability studies on her biggest accounts and decided to share them with those customers to get them more involved in managing their travel expenses and enforcing travel policy. That was the origin of the quarterly travel analysis, which spells out exactly how the travel policy can save the client money and how closely the client is following it.

Compared with the thick reports customers formerly received and ignored, the analysis is a user-friendly document that makes enforcing travel pol-

Cyndie Bender, CEO of Meridian Travel, fattens her bottom line by showing her customers how to buy her services more efficiently.

icy a cinch by breaking out critical data such as frequently used routes, average ticket price, and types of fares booked.

"When people see these graphs, it makes them view travel expenditures with the same eye for the bottom line they use when purchasing raw materials," says Bender, who gives the report free of charge to her top 25 accounts and charges others $35. "That kind of information makes it easier for me to persuade prospective clients to go with us."

Clients' purchasing agents are expected to generate that kind of tally of their companies' travel-and-entertainment expenses for the year. But since Meridian can quickly and easily generate graphs conveying that information, why not provide a customer service to purchasing agents, Meridian's real customers? "It helps them keep on top of this with very little effort and makes them look smart with their bosses," says Bender.

A less courageous salesperson might cringe to see a report spelling out how a client could spend less with her company, but not Bender. For example, after receiving a few reports, one Cleveland client noticed that its employees were taking 70 trips a month to Louisville and decided teleconferencing would be cheaper. Although Meridian lost the air travel to Louisville, it gained the trust — and the business — of that client's entire corporation. Bender's open-book approach to customer service has contributed to Meridian's 30% annual growth rate in an extremely price-sensitive market. The agency Bender founded in 1984 topped $25 million in 1991 revenues.

3 GOOD FORMS

Special Requests/Frequent-Flier Conflict

"We can negotiate a low rate using a group travel fare, but that requires clients to fly with the carrier we negotiated with. That can cut into travelers' frequent-flier plans — a touchy topic. But savings are obtained by using the carrier that provides the best discounts for the traveler's company. Frequent-flier perks shouldn't be a priority when deciding how to book a ticket."

Savings Require Planning

"Booking late happens frequently, but the more careful people are about planning trips and managing their schedules, the more money is saved. Meridian defines savings as the difference between the cost of a Meridian ticket and one bought three to five days before departure. The biggest single source of savings is booking excursion fares. Excursion fares involve 21-to 7-day advance purchase with a Saturday-night stay, often with day and time restrictions. Nine out of 10 business travelers don't want to stay the night. But sometimes the savings can be dramatic. For instance, fares from Chicago to Cleveland range from $78 for the excursion fare to $646 for a three-day advance ticket. A pie chart can show a travel manager if the company's travel budget is being met, where the savings are coming from, and what he or she can do to increase them."

Fare-Code Analysis

"Fare-code analysis tells clients what types of tickets their travelers booked. Did a traveler book too late, after our lowest fare was sold out [Code B]? Did someone request a special airline instead of the one we had designated for a specific route [Code A]? Did someone travel first-class unnecessarily [Code F]? Some expenditures are unavoidable. For instance, business travelers at times need their routes changed because something comes up [Code C]. But often it's simply poor planning that incurs the expense."

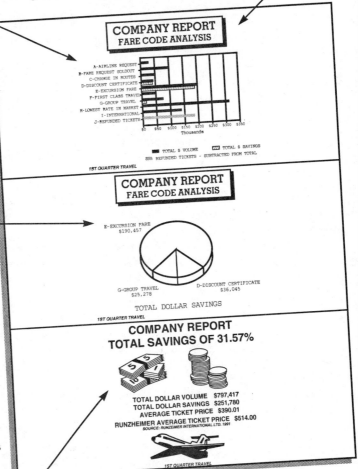

Dollars, Coins, and Airplanes

"There is an average ticket price that Runzheimer, an air-travel market analyst, lists — currently it's around $514. We always try to get below that. At an average ticket price of $390.01, this client is well below the average. This is the real bottom line for the customer, a way for us to demonstrate that we are keeping our original sales promise. If the savings aren't on target, clients can look at the fare-code analysis and see where they might not be keeping up their end of the bargain."

Anyone Can Do This

This type of report can be adapted for many other kinds of businesses. Think about how your company buys its raw materials and prices finished products or services to customers. What kinds of terms do you get from vendors? What kinds of terms do you offer customers? What's the cost of rush orders? What are the charges for customization? The point is to figure out how your customers can purchase from you in the most efficient manner, allowing you to negotiate the best possible rates on their behalf and provide them with maximum savings.

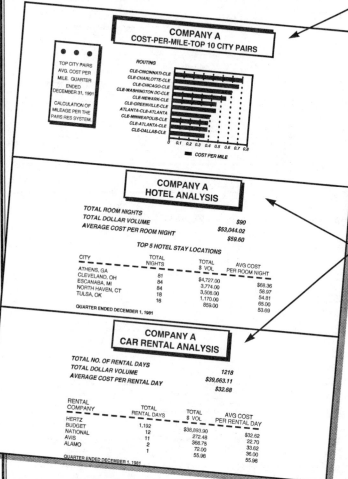

Top 10 City Pairs Cost Per Mile

"Many of our larger clients have frequent meetings at the same destinations. An agency can negotiate a discounted fare based on heavy traffic to the specific destination. Those typically range up to 50% off coach. A chart of the cost-per-mile to various common destinations is a very useful tool because it shows companies where it's most expensive to conduct business and makes it easier for them to allocate their other resources most efficiently."

Nonprofit Centers Can Make Money for You

"If a company is traveling a lot to certain destinations because it has an office or a branch there, we comparison shop and pick the three hotels that meet the client's standards and have the best rates. We'll negotiate a rate for each, but the one with the best rate becomes the primary vendor at that destination. Also, as a service to our clients, we research car-rental companies and show the client the rates offered. Sometimes this business is commissionable for us, and sometimes it's not, depending on the contract a company signs. That's just part of being in this industry. Booking hotel rooms and car rentals is not a profit center for us. We do it as a customer service. If our clients see an overall T&E savings, they're more likely to stay with us or recommend us. Our overall goal is to get new customers and consolidate the accounts of current customers. We might start with a branch and eventually get an entire corporation on board. Then we really make our money through booking air travel." ■

Your Business Is My Business

"This is how a travel agent sees a customer's business. Take the category 'group travel.' If we promise an airline a certain amount of traffic on a route and then our customer doesn't make everyone take that airline, the customer won't be saving money, and we won't be meeting our volume targets with the airline. Those departures from a company's travel policy eat away at the profitability of an account for us. By sharing this information, we insulate ourselves somewhat from another agency coming in to bid on the business."

Notes

_____

_____

_____

_____

_____

_____

_____

_____

_____

_____

_____

_____

_____

_____

_____

_____

_____

_____

_____

_____

_____

_____

CHAPTER

4

Outserving the Competition

Barry Steinberg learned about customer service from his father, Meyer, who ran a clothing store. Meyer taught Barry how a gesture that most businesses would chalk up in the debit column can in fact prove to be the most valuable of credits to a firm's bottom line.

What Barry Steinberg learned so well from his father is the value of repeat business. The greatest return on investment, Steinberg knows, is the investment that brings a customer back through the door, time and again. And Steinberg will spare no expense, he will spare no effort to achieve this goal. On any given day, 75% of Direct Tire Sales' customers are repeat customers.

As Lori Laub notes (see p. 166), Direct Tire empowers its employees through technology. While it has always been critical to hire good people, Laub says that is no longer sufficient. In today's competitive environment, success equals people plus systems. Systems support often comes in the form of technology that is designed to both increase knowledge and hike productivity. That Barry Steinberg understands that equation is clear from his insistence on investing in the best equipment available for his mechanics and technicians.

While technology is important, Howard Hyden (see p. 158) believes that people are the critical investment for repeat business. You must hire top-notch employees and then invest in their training to attain superior customer service.

Susan Clarke (see p. 149) agrees with both Laub and Hyden. But even with technology and good people, a business must understand its customers. What customers say they want is not always what they need. Direct Tire's success, argues Clarke, reflects the company's uncanny accuracy in determining what customers need. Steinberg understands that customers need to feel informed They need service that accommodates their busy schedules. They need a clean and inviting waiting room. They need to receive quality products and service

Steinberg understands all this. And Direct Tire delivers it

We'll Brake, Shock, and Exhaust You with Customer Service!

As a result of Direct Tire's fanatical attention to customers, its margins are twice the industry average. Here's how owner Barry Steinberg calculates the return on his investment.

These words — "We'll brake, shock, and exhaust you!" — are on a hanging sign at Direct Tire Sales in Watertown, Mass. The sign should go on to read: "We'll brake, shock, and exhaust you with Customer Service!" For that is what Direct Tire has done for the past 20 years. It's why Barry Steinberg, the president and owner of this very unusual tire retailer/total undercar service shop, was voted the first Tire Dealer of the Year last year by *Modern Tire Dealer* magazine.

Steinberg's secret? He doesn't sell to consumers, he sells to customers. "Consumers have no loyalty," he says. "Consumers go out of their way to find what they want at the lowest possible price. And when they need something else, they'll do it all over again. A customer finds a store he likes and keeps going back."

Steinberg's secret is also his strategy. He wants to turn everyone who enters his store into a repeat customer. Virtually everything that happens at Direct Tire is done with that single objective in mind. It works too: on any given day, 75% of Direct Tire's customers are repeat customers.

It's not very difficult to fathom Steinberg's logic or motives here.

Anyone who's ever run a lemonade stand knows that loyal customers are the best kind. To some extent, their value is quantifiable. You don't have to be Albert Einstein to figure out that if your average sale is $100, a onetime customer represents $100 in revenues for your company, whereas someone who comes back 100 times represents $10,000.

Barry Steinberg learned a lesson from his father. As a boy working in his father's children's clothing store, Barry was folding boxes one day after school when a pregnant woman walked into the store with two small children. She held out a pair of stained and worn pajamas and told Meyer Steinberg she couldn't get them clean. Meyer Steinberg took the pajamas from her and dropped them into a wastebasket. He handed the woman a new pair of pajamas and apologized for any inconvenience she might have suffered.

The Best $17 I Ever Spent

Years later, Meyer Steinberg's son stood listening to a customer complain that he'd called ahead to make sure there would be no trouble getting a ride to work after leaving his car off to be serviced at Direct Tire. His car was on the lift, but Steinberg's driver, who ferries passengers to and from work, had just called to say that his car wouldn't start and he'd be late to work himself. Steinberg would have been more than happy to hand over the keys to one of the company's loaners, but those cars had already been borrowed. Steinberg reached for the phone. Five minutes later, a cab driver arrived and drove Steinberg's customer to his job in a neighboring town. The cab fare cost Steinberg $17.

"It was the best $17 I ever spent," says Steinberg, echoing the words his father spoke when he was a boy. "Can you imagine how many people he told that story to?"

This kind of customer service is anything but typical in the automotive business or, for that matter, in any other business. Equally atypical is Direct Tire's 3% net margins — twice the industry average — on sales of $6 million for the fiscal year ended March 31. And that's the point: In the coming years, providing atypical customer service will become typical. Attention to customer service will be the key to survival.

"I see lots of small retailers, travel agencies, hardware stores that are being smothered by giants like Kmart and Home Depot," says Steinberg. "The trouble is they panic and all make the same mistake. They start to lower their prices. That, of course, is just what Kmart and Home Depot want you to do. And you can't win. You can't compete with giants on price."

Direct Tire doesn't compete on price. Steinberg doesn't offer his customers bargains. "On average, we are consistently 10% or 12% higher than just about everybody," he says. But then, his customers don't come to Direct Tire for bargains. "If you keep your promises," says Steinberg, "customers are more than willing to pay for value, service, and convenience." And Barry Steinberg loves to make promises.

Guaranteed, Unconditionally — Forever

One of those promises is an unconditional guarantee on any tire he sells and any work his shop does — forever. Another? How about Steinberg's promise that if you buy a set of premium Toyo tires from Direct Tire and have them aligned at least once a year, he will replace them free as often as necessary (vandalism and traffic accidents excepted) for as long as you own your car? Steinberg came up with that idea when he began carrying the hitherto unknown Toyo brand. Toyo is no longer unknown. Customers ask for Toyos by name. And Steinberg is making a new promise. Buy a set of Toyo snow tires and he'll replace them free for as long as you own your car.

It's one thing to make a promise. It's quite another to keep it. Especially if you're operating on a tight budget. After all, there is a cost to extraordinary customer service, isn't there? Sooner or later, customer service comes down to decisions about how to spend money. Should you go all out decorating your waiting room, or would you be wiser to send your employees to a training course? Is it more important to buy a new piece of testing equipment or to carry enough inventory to meet your customers' every need? Can you afford to do it all? How do you know if the investment is paying off? Are we talking about taking a leap of faith here, or are there ways to measure the costs and the returns?

This is the great gray area of customer service, the part you haven't read about in Tom Peters' books — or in *Inc.* magazine, for that matter. By now you've heard a lot about the virtues of staying close to customers. You may even have bought the argument that service is the best way companies can differentiate themselves. But if customer service is such good business, shouldn't the benefits eventually show up in the numbers? And, if so, which numbers should you be looking at? How, in effect, can you calculate the return on your customer service investment?

Management gurus seldom talk about that, but Barry Steinberg does. He can tell you exactly what his brand of customer service costs him and how the investment pays off for Direct Tire. For Steinberg, service is not just a way to distinguish his shop from other tire stores. It's the most profitable way to run his business.

And he can prove it.

GQ to *Vogue*

When you enter Direct Tire, you step inside a waiting room that is immaculate. The magazines on the rack are current, with titles ranging from *Sports Illustrated* and *GQ* to *Vogue*. Beside a cooler full of complimentary sodas sits an open box of doughnut holes. A Filterfresh system offers a variety of freshly brewed coffee selections. There are windows in every wall, allowing you to watch Direct Tire's technicians as they work. Looking around, you notice that everyone is in uniform. Store manager Douglas Smith and the salespeople wear shirts and ties with a baseball-style jacket that carries the company logo; everyone else has on dark blue work pants and T-shirts with the company name and slogan. Even the way people address you is different. "I've never heard so many yes ma'ams and no ma'ams in my life," says one 40-year-old customer who has been going to Direct Tire for years.

It's been like this from the beginning. Steinberg says he always intended to have a store that would cater to people who take driving seriously, but he had no interest in owning a typical speed shop, with tires strewn about and pictures of healthy young ladies clad in next to nothing on the walls. Partly that was a matter of personal taste: Spending time in

> **HOT TIP**
> Customer service has a cost. And for Karmak Software Inc., in Carlinville, Ill., that cost was wrecking the company's bottom line. Under Karmak's old service plan a fixed customer service charge was automatically tacked onto every sale. With that kind of plan, customers would call at the drop of a hat with the most minor problems. They didn't bother to master the system or even read the manual. Now things are different. Under the new plan, customers must sign up in advance for the level of service they desire — a set number of calls per month and a surcharge for calls that exceed that limit. Today, customer service at Karmak has become a profit center. Says CEO Richard Schein, "We've had to double the size of the department."

a speed shop was not his idea of fun. But he also realized early on that he could use the environment of his shop to differentiate it from competitors. Indeed, he has done just that. The mere fact that women — and today 50% of his customers are female — feel comfortable visiting Direct Tire sets it apart.

The ambiance of the store is just one component of a much broader strategy. Simply put, Steinberg's goal is to turn everyone who enters his store into a repeat customer. Virtually everything that happens at Direct Tire is done with that objective in mind.

The trick, of course, is to generate the kind of loyalty that keeps customers coming back. This is, in fact, the whole purpose — and the true meaning — of customer service. It goes well beyond smile schools, where employees learn to deal with aggrieved customers and to say please and thank you a lot. "Those warm, fuzzy things are certainly part of providing good service, but if customer service were a cake, they'd just be the icing," says Dallas car dealer Carl Sewell, who's been selling through service since 1966. "The real cake would be the systems that allow you to do the job right the first time."

Customers think about service in similar terms, says Leonard L. Berry, professor of retailing and marketing studies at Texas A&M University. From an exhaustive study of consumer expectations, he concluded that customers want companies to do what they say they are going to do — to keep the service promise.

This is something Steinberg has understood all along, and he has built his business accordingly. And, by viewing customer service in this light, Steinberg has found he's able to identify and measure exactly what he's spending on it and what Direct Tire is getting in return. In the process, he often winds up including costs that, on the surface, don't seem to be related to customer service at all.

Consider Recruitment.

Steinberg knows that to keep his service promise he needs the best mechanics and alignment specialists around. He doesn't even bother to advertise for them. "Want ads tend to attract people who are unemployed," he says. "I want people who already have a job." To find them, Steinberg did something virtually unheard-of in his industry: He used headhunters. Or he used to. Today, Steinberg rarely resorts to headhunters, because Direct Tire's reputation and high profile bring good people knocking.

His requirements were precise. He would tell the recruiter he wanted people with a minimum of two to three years' experience, so they would know what they were doing, and he expected them to be certified in their specialty. "They can't have had five jobs in the last five years. I want people who are reliable. Ideally, they'll be married with a couple of kids. People with responsibilities are more dependable. And they have to be able to get along with both customers and their fellow employees."

It's not easy to find candidates who meet every condition on the checklist, but then again, the headhunters are fairly compensated for their efforts. They earn a commission equal to 10% to 15% of the employee's first-year salary for placing a candidate. In most cases, that salary is substantially higher than it was at the employee's last job. As a rule, Steinberg pays his 40 employees 15% to 25% over scale. Simply by paying the industry standard and taking the usual approach to hiring, Steinberg figures he could cut his expenses by $235,000. But he is committed to having reliable, well-qualified technicians.

Hiring Smarts

Steinberg considers the money well spent. For one thing, good people make fewer mistakes, and mistakes cost money. For another, good people are more self-reliant, so he needs fewer supervisors. Beyond that, he credits his approach with helping him build a reputation for doing the job right the first time. And besides, he notes, who would you rather have dealing with your customers? Someone who's smart and who understands what he's doing or someone who isn't? From that perspective, the $235,000 represents an investment in customer service, and Steinberg regards it as such.

He has a similar attitude toward equipment. Before he invested $24,000 in a Hunter Brake Analyzer, Steinberg's mechanics would need about 10 minutes to conduct a visual inspection of a car's brake system.

➤ **HOT TIP**

About nine years ago, a food service director in the San Diego school system approached Cres-Cor with an idea for a mobile serving table for the schoolyard, offering students an alternative to their usual fast-food diet. Cres-Cor, a food service equipment maker and distributor in Cleveland, went on to produce the table, which is among the top 25 sellers in the company's line of more than 800 products. Cres-Cor president George E. Baggott knew an opportunity when he saw one. He presented the food service director with a plaque and publicized her contribution in the company newsletter and the trade press. Since then, the company has received a number of ideas for new products from customers.

But all a visual inspection and road tests reveal are worn brake pads and shoes. The new machine does that, plus it identifies alignment and hydraulic problems and prints out the diagnosis within 90 seconds. Steinberg says he wants the best equipment available. Not only does it allow him to improve the level of service Direct Tire offers, but it helps him attract the best technicians. His customers benefit both ways.

"I am the only independent tire dealer in the country with five wheel alignment machines," says Steinberg. "I just bought my fifth. It cost me $36,000. They are very expensive machines, but they make us very efficient."

This approach even extends to inventory. Sitting in his office, Steinberg proudly shows off his customized software package that can tell him immediately what's in stock. That $48,000 system also allows Direct Tire to take full advantage of its large inventory of uncommon tires. "See this," Steinberg says, pointing to the screen, "that's the code for a rear tire on a '94 Porsche Turbo. Call around. You'll find nobody has them in stock. I have 12. That one's for a Mercedes 500 SL. I have 60 in six different brands — nobody has that many." Steinberg says he could get by with $320,000 worth of inventory, but that would mean occasionally disappointing a customer. By increasing his inventory 20%, he almost always has what customers want. At 8% interest, the annual cost on the extra inventory is $5,120.

Clothes, Coffee, and Cars

Like the software system, the testing and alignment equipment, the headhunter commissions, and the pay scale, inventory, too, represents an investment in customer service. It's part of Steinberg's effort to keep the service promise by making sure customers get what they come for. In Direct Tire's case, the service promise goes beyond tires and beyond brake and alignment work. Steinberg has also promised customers an extraordinary level of convenience and comfort, and he is determined to keep that promise, too. For example, he wants all his people to look professional, so he buys the clothes they wear at work, to the tune of $25,000 per year. He also spends $900 per year on magazines for the waiting room, and another $3,600 per year on fresh coffee ("I put in the Filterfresh system," he says. "It's fabulous.") and half-and-half.

Then there are the loaner cars. One of Steinberg's employees had suggested that Direct Tire do what car dealerships used to do: provide customers with loaners to get to and from work while their cars were being serviced. ("Ninety percent of the ideas here weren't mine," says Steinberg, "they're from one of my guys.") The employee with that bright idea knew his brother-in-law had a car he wanted to sell. So Steinberg bought the 1986 Chevy Nova. The car almost immediately broke down, but it launched what has become Steinberg's most valuable and visible customer service tool.

Today, Direct Tire's logo is emblazoned on 15 loaners — Chevy Geo Prisms ("They're great little cars," says Steinberg). By the time Steinberg adds up the monthly payments, maintenance, insurance, and the like, he figures those "great little cars" cost him $90,000 per year. And that's in addition to the $8 per hour he spends having an employee drive customers home while their cars are in the shop.

Tire Dealer of the Year

It's a lot of money, but the effort does not go unappreciated or unnoticed. *Modern Tire Dealer* magazine selected Steinberg Tire Dealer of the Year from among 25,000 tire dealers in the country. Steinberg, for his part, does all he can to make sure customers notice. By having windows in his waiting room, for example, he lets customers see how his highly qualified technicians go about their jobs. Similarly, he does more than leave postage-paid customer comment cards in each car on which work has been completed; he personally calls every single person who complains. Nor is he content to have salespeople apologize to a customer who has been kept waiting for a repair that has taken longer than promised. Each of them is also empowered to knock a few bucks off the bill, which makes the apology seem more sincere.

But giving away money is the last thing Steinberg wants to do. This is, after all, a business he's running. The real secret of his success is to make customers pay for the service they receive, and he makes no bones about doing it. Sure, he'll keep that uncommon Porsche tire around, the one no other dealer has in stock, but you'll pay more to get it. On average, Steinberg makes a gross profit of 41%. The harder the tire is to find, the greater his profit. So while his gross margin on an everyday tire is 33.3%, it's 47.4% on the one for that high-performance Porsche.

Still, if Direct Tire charges more for its tires and service than its competitors, it offers better value. Steinberg is always looking for ways to add value to the service he offers customers. For example, Steinberg heard a common complaint from his apartment-dwelling customers: They had no place to store their snow tires during the summer. "We finally figured out that letting them keep the tires here was a good idea," Steinberg says. So he rented a trailer and announced that Direct Tire was launching a storage service. "In addition to storing the tires, we'll change them over twice a year and mount and balance them each time. We charge $100 a year for the service."

When he needed to expand his service operations (he's up to 14 bays in the main store and has added another seven service bays at his Alignment Annex up the street), Steinberg got rid of the trailer and rented the 11,000 square-foot warehouse behind the store. That enabled him to move his entire inventory of tires into one location. He also stores 280 sets of snow tires in the warehouse (280 sets times $100 per years = $28,000 a year for storing tires).

Walkie-talkies and Mini-Computers

To be sure his tire inventory did not become inaccessible, he hired two warehousemen, fitted them out with walkie-talkies, and gave them portable Casio mini-computers. He then punched into the Casios his entire inventory of tires (some 2,500 models) by code number. When a tire is needed, someone from the main store can call the warehouse by walkie-talkie and order an 1177 for a Lexus, rather than risk miscommunication by ordering a 20565 VR15 Dunlop.

While Direct Tire offers its customers superior service by carrying a larger tire inventory and storing snow tires, it's easy to see that those services are profitable. It's harder to see how Steinberg generates a return on his other services. But the profit is there as well. Take the lifetime guarantee. Its appeal can't be denied. "It tells customers we fully stand behind what we sell," says Steinberg. Doesn't that get expensive? After all, people get flats and run over curbs all the time. "True, but if you actually sit down and figure out the number of people who damage their tires, it comes to less than 1% of sales. So we build that premium into the price of each tire. That way, the guarantee doesn't cost us anything."

But what about the loaner cars, which — as we have seen — cost plenty? "Before I had the loaners, I was doing $50,000 to $55,000 a month in service work. Three years and seven loaners later, I was averaging $120,000 a month. Today, with 15 loaners, I'm doing $200,000 a month in brakes, shocks, exhaust, alignment, and batteries. And the gross margins on service work are 25% higher than on tires. People will call up and say, 'I understand you have a free car I can use while you work on mine.' We'll say, 'Yes, that's right,' and they'll schedule an appointment right then. A lot of them don't even bother to ask what the work will cost. I'm going to add more cars."

It is this kind of reasoning that has allowed Steinberg to maintain his high net margin, even as he has increased his investment in customer service. But he measures his return on that investment with another set of numbers — the ones that show how effective he has been in turning onetime buyers into regular customers.

On any given day, Steinberg notes, Direct Tire handles about 105 transactions. About three-quarters of those purchases are made by people who have done business with him before. What does that mean? Big bucks.

Three times a year, Direct Tire does a mailing to people who live nearby, offering them a special deal on, say, shock absorbers — buy three and get one free. The average revenue from that type of promotion is $130. But a customer who has been to Direct Tire before spends $200 during an average visit, and new customers who have been referred by someone else will spend $250. Steinberg says that these big spenders have usually been putting off a major repair or purchase until they could find a repair shop they could trust. Once they hear about Direct Tire's service, they come in — and spend.

And so it goes. Steinberg invests in customer service, and that wins over customers, who bring in their friends, who spend even more money and are won over and tell their friends, and on and on. Small wonder that Direct Tire's revenues continue to increase steadily, as they have every year since its founding in 1974, despite generally flat sales for the industry as a whole.

It is numbers like these, the steady expansion of his Watertown shop, and the hunger for a new challenge that has convinced Barry Steinberg to attempt to replicate his Watertown monument to Automotive Customer Service. And he's going to do it on the Auto Mile, a stretch of car dealerships, automotive repair shops, and service stations just off Route 128 southwest of Boston in Norwood. (New customer service features for the Norwood store: a phone room with free outgoing calls, a playroom with toys, and a television room.)

"It'll be 20 years this November that I started this business," says Steinberg. "It seems like the right time to open a second store. I have the people who can do it. In fact, without a second store, some of my people will feel stifled. It's a way of permitting employees to grow to their potential. We have credibility in the market. Our name is a household word in the area because of our radio advertising. All my employees are psyched about it. All my vendors are dying for me to open another store. The bank says go ahead. It's a financial risk, but I think I can pull it off."

Do you have any doubts he will? ■

What You Want
is Not Necessarily
What You Need

Susan Clarke

Recently, I became the proud owner of a computer, laser printer, copy machine, fax machine, and cellular telephone. Everyone had been telling me I couldn't live without all this technology, that it would make my life immeasurably easier. Well, now that I have it, I admit I can no longer live without it. But I beg to differ on the second count. My life has become vastly more complicated, not simpler.

What has all this to do with customer service?

In an age when personal and professional lives are becoming more and more demanding, here's some advice for you: Keep your customer service personal, simple, and basic. Don't make customer service technical and don't make it difficult. Your systems can be technical, but customer contact should be smooth as silk.

A recent study by Management Horizons, a division of Price Waterhouse, concludes, "By the end of the decade more than half of today's retailers will be out of business. There are simply too many stores that are too much alike." We keep hearing, "competition is fiercer today that it's ever been before." If that is true and if customer service is to be the business battleground of the 1990s, then companies providing atypical service will succeed.

The problem is, how do you define great customer service? Superior customer service means many different things to many different people.

However you define it, customer service is the competitive edge.

Susan Clarke runs her own consulting and training company, Motivation Unlimited, in San Diego, Calif.

After all, a hotel is a place to sleep. A restaurant is a place to eat. A store is a place to buy goods. What makes one different from the other? The level of service you receive, the way you're treated, whether or not you feel good about spending your money, whether or not you want to return.

Everyone who deals directly with customers on a day-to-day basis is in the people business. Without customers, you would have no business. Your staff must create an environment that makes the customer feel special and appreciated. Coming into contact with another human being and making that moment of contact meaningful is the simplest definition of customer service. What separates those in the people business from those who work in other professions is also simple: making a difference in the lives of customers.

EXERCISE
Interacting with People

1. How much do I like interacting with others?

_____

_____

2. What ways do our services make a difference to our customers? Fill in the statement, *when they come to me they need:*

a. _____

b. _____

c. _____

3. Why are you in this business? Why do you have the job you have?
(Be honest here: Are you primarily interested in earning a living? Learning a new skill? Getting started on your career path?)

_____

_____

_____

_____

_____

4. If you were your own customer, what would most please you about the service you would receive from someone like yourself?

_____

_____

_____

_____

5. If you were your own customer, what would most annoy you about the service you would receive from someone like yourself?

_____

_____

_____

_____

In the theme song from the television show *Cheers*, people want to go to places where everybody knows their name. Part of great customer service is making your customers feel as though they are guests and not strangers in your place of business. In an oft-quoted study, customers listed their reasons for quitting a product or service:

- 1% die,
- 3% move away,
- 5% change their habits or interests,
- 9% quit because they're attracted to a competitor,
- 14% leave because they're unhappy with a product,
- 68% leave because they encounter an attitude of indifference from employees.

More and more I'm finding that customers want to be seen and heard. They want to feel that they are valued and appreciated. Frankly, isn't that what we all want in our personal and professional relationships? This translates into three basic desires. Customers want:

- their needs satisfied;
- to receive value;
- to have their egos fed.

What do customers really need? Well, many things, depending on what they're shopping for or where they are. But what they need is often not what they want. Basically, everybody needs the same things:

- food and protection from the elements;
- safety, security, comfort;
- to feel good about themselves, to feel that they are important and have worth;
- to enjoy themselves (to have their lives made easier).

On the surface, customers want a product or a service. But underneath, where it really counts, they are buying something to satisfy one or more of their needs. In the case of Direct Tire Sales, customers want name brand tires for two reasons: They need to feel safe, secure and comfortable, and they need to feel that they are important and have worth.

When it comes to value, customers want quality. They want better than average, something beyond the normal. To put it another way, customers walk into a place of business with certain expectations. They expect the place to look clean, they expect a certain amount of attention, and they expect whatever they buy to work. When these expectations are met, the customer has received a good experience or good value. But when these expectations are exceeded, quality has been added to the experience. Quality can be found in:

Product: Not only does Direct Tire carry a wide assortment of brand-name tires, the store also stocks a large inventory of uncommon tires. By doing that, they exceed customers' expectations. Barry Steinberg knows this will attract customers and keep them coming back

Quality Service: Quality service satisfies more than surface needs. Direct Tire exceeds expectations in several ways. You can schedule an appointment to be in and out in about an hour. If you can't wait, you will be handed the keys to a loaner car to use until your car has been serviced. If your new tires blow out after 30,000 miles or if you decide after a month that you just don't like them, no problem — Steinberg guarantees the tires, as well as any service work his shop does, forever. Once again, he exceeds expectations by backing everything that he sells.

Quality Atmosphere: Atmosphere is more than pretty flowers and plants or pictures on the wall. Those things are important. But quality atmosphere is created company-wide. It is a positive energy flow. It is the feeling generated by people who enjoy their jobs. When the atmosphere is right, customers sense it. Barry Steinberg understood that a quality atmosphere demanded an immaculate waiting room stocked with current magazine titles and fresh brewed coffee. He put windows in every wall, permitting customers to watch mechanics at work, which fosters a sense of trust. Everyone in the company is in uniform. As one customer put it: "I've never heard so many yes ma'ams and no ma'ams in my life."

People: Steinberg only hires the best mechanics and alignment specialists. They must have a minimum of two to three years of experience and be certified in their field. He wants people who are reliable. He also pays his employees 20% over scale. He believes it is money well spent. Good people make fewer mistakes and mistakes cost money. Good people are more self-reliant, so fewer supervisors are necessary. Steinberg credits his approach with building a reputation for doing the job right the first time

How your customers perceive value is by how much they pay. It takes a quality product consistently delivered with quality service in a quality atmosphere that sets one company apart from the competition. Customers will pay to have their needs met. And the more needs you meet, the more they will be willing to pay. Direct Tire charges, on average,

10% to 12% more than the competition, because the company meets so many customer needs. If you keep your promises, says Steinberg, customers are more than willing to pay for value and convenience. And he is constantly looking for new ways to keep his promises.

EXERCISE
You and Your Staff

1. **When customers come to you, what do you think they:**
   - *want:*

   _____

   _____

   - *need:*

   _____

   _____

2. **How can you create more value in your products?**

   _____

   _____

   _____

   _____

3. **How can you create more value in your service?**

   _____

   _____

   _____

4. **How can you create more value in your atmosphere?**

   _____

   _____

   _____

5. Concerning the service you provide:

- *When customers come to my business, they probably expect:*

_____

_____

_____

- *I can exceed my customers' expectations in the following ways:*

_____

_____

_____

CARE AND FEEDING OF CUSTOMERS

1. Customers like to feel good about spending their money.

People like to feel that they are important, that they have value, and that other people respect them. Spending money often reflects a degree of success, a level of status, a sense of control over one's life.

2. Customers don't want to appear stupid or uninformed, or have their intelligence insulted.

Be sure that you communicate with customers in terms and language they will understand. Use technical vocabulary only when you know they will understand it. Successful customer service is knowing how to ask leading questions, how to listen to a customer, how to point out the advantages of a product in simple terms. At the same time, the customer should not be made to feel that the burden of the decision is his or hers alone.

3. Customers also want guidance in making a purchase.

Buying is fun but often stressful, especially when your customers are making important decisions. They are concerned about buying an inferior product or one that doesn't fit all of their needs. They're concerned about paying too much or about getting poor follow-up service.

The customer doesn't want to appear stupid, but he or she also doesn't want to make a mistake. Customers look to professionals to supply them with information and choices, and to help them make decisions.

4. Customers don't like to lose arguments.

You will never win an argument with a customer, which brings us to the most important aspect of egos. Leave yours at home! When you bring your ego to work, it gets in the way, and that's usually what starts an argument. Remember that it's up to you and your staff to make your customers feel good about spending their money. Steinberg says you have to be willing to do whatever it takes to make the customer happy.

EXERCISE
Feeding Customer Ego

1. **In what ways can you help your customers feel good about spending their money?**

   _____

   _____

   _____

2. **What questions can you ask to determine a customer's level of sophistication?**

   _____

   _____

   _____

3. **How can you feed your customer's ego?**

   _____

   _____

   _____

To come full circle, keep it simple. Many of the points I've made are basic. At its heart, so is customer service. Keep your staff focused on customer needs. Constantly challenge your staff to exceed the expectations of customers. By reinvesting in customer service, Barry Steinberg wins over customers who come back time and again, spending more money and regaling their friends with stories of his superior customer service. ■

Bodacious
Customer Service

by Howard E. Hyden

The focus on quality in the 1980s made it increasingly difficult to differentiate yourself on product alone. In the 1990s, the critical difference between companies is clearly the quality of their customer service. And since service cannot be delivered without people, the challenge for business tomorrow will be to motivate employees to deliver extraordinary customer service.

There are four steps to extraordinary customer service:

STEP 1 • COMMUNICATIONS: Let's think about the mission statements of various organizations that espouse excellent customer service. When Barry Steinberg of Direct Tire Sales hung a sign that reads: "We'll brake, shock, and exhaust you," his vision extended beyond replacing tires and mufflers. He had a vision of extraordinary customer service. Today, it's common for organizations to craft mission statements. The problem is, most employees can't relate to their company's mission statement. Why? For one of two reasons: Either it does not reflect the true mission of the company, or the mission of the company has not been properly communicated.

Too many mission statements are vague or abstract. An effective mission statement must be understood by every employee. For it to be understood — and accepted — an employee must understand what the company's mission means at the department level. How does manufacturing contribute to the mission? What does it mean for sales? for shipping? for the accounting department or the finance department? Unless

Howard E. Hyden is president of Hyden & Hyden, a Minneapolis-based marketing consulting firm.

management has crisply articulated what that mission statement means for each department, the employees can't relate to it and the mission won't be realized.

EXERCISE:
Mission, Training, and Empowerment

Write in your company's Mission Statement

_____

_____

_____

_____

Write in the percentage of your company's employees who could write out your company's Mission Statement unaided. _____%

On the following scale, rate your company's effectiveness at communicating the Mission Statement at the employee level.

Employee understanding:

NO CLUE   WELL UNDERSTOOD

0   1   2   3   4   5   6   7   8   9   10

Let me give you an example of a Mission Statement that employees can relate to. The mission of Tuffy Auto Centers is "To Provide the Best Automotive Service in the Industry through a Continuous Commitment to Quality and Customer Service." To give that statement meaning, Tuffy's president, Keenan Moran, brought the "Customers for Life" message right into the shops to the people who interacted directly with the customer. Then Tuffy held a series of specially designed weekend workshops for its technicians.

During the holiday season, Art Rott, a Detroit-area Tuffy franchisee, was visited by a single parent who needed work done on her car. Burdened with substantial medical bills for one of her two sons, she could not afford the repairs. Rott offered to extend her terms, but she managed to borrow the money she needed. When she arrived to pick up her car, she asked how much she owed. Rott simply handed her the warranty and wished her a Merry Christmas. When Rott refused her repeated attempts to pay the bill, she called the *Detroit Free Press*. The paper came out to Rott's shop, interviewed him, and ran a photo story.

Rott did not refuse his customer's money as a publicity stunt. He did it "because I wanted to." What he did fit Tuffy's mission statement.

STEP 2 • TRAINING: In most companies today, training is viewed as an expense. It should be viewed as an investment. Malcolm Baldrige Award winner Motorola conducted a study to determine the impact of training. For every dollar invested in training, the study found a $30 increase in productivity.

According to the American Productivity Center, "Human Resource development is the number one key to improving this nation's economy."

A study conducted by the American Society of Training & Development compared percentage of payroll allocated to training in American, Japanese, and European companies. The study found that American companies spent 1.5% to 2% of gross payroll on training, while in Japan and Europe, companies spent 4% to 6% of gross payroll on training.

Calculate the training investment for your organization:

$$\frac{\text{Training}}{\text{Investment}} = \frac{\$ \ Invested \ in \ training/yr.}{Gross \ payroll \ \$/yr.} = \frac{x}{y} = z\%$$

GM's Saturn division sets a training goal of 92 hours a year for all employees. As a training incentive, the company places a percentage of employee pay "at risk." If an employee does not meet his training goal, he forfeits his "at risk" income.

Calculate how many hours of training your employees received in the last year:

Last 12-month period	_____	*hours*
Target next 12-month period	_____	*hours*

Organizations that are pursuing quality understand that continuous improvement must be a way of life. My philosophy is "Continuous Improvement comes from continuous learning."

STEP 3 • EMPOWERMENT: Arriving recently at a Ritz Carlton Hotel, I was greeted by the bellman: "Hello, Mr. Hyden. Welcome to the Ritz Carlton." I realized he had noticed the luggage tag on my attaché case. Then he directed me to the front desk. I thanked him and went in, turned right and was approaching the registration desk when a receptionist stepped out from behind the desk to say, "Good morning, Mr. Hyden. Welcome back to the Ritz Carlton."

I was not wearing a name badge. When I asked how she knew who I was, she explained: "The bellman told me. Before he loaded the luggage cart, he called us on his walkie-talkie. He told me a gentleman was coming in. He said you were about six feet tall with a reddish beard and that your name was Mr. Hyden. Then I simply typed your name into the computer which told me you last stayed with us two years ago." That receptionist also knows whether I read the *Wall Street Journal* or *USA Today*, and whether I prefer decaf or regular coffee. Once captured on computer, that information is accessible to any employee across the Ritz network.

Ritz Carlton not only trains its employees, it empowers them. One way the Ritz empowers its employees is to grant each employee $2,000 a year in discretionary funds to do whatever it takes to knock the socks off customers or solve customer problems. When I asked about the fund, I learned that most employees don't even come close to spending the $2,000. But by taking the handcuffs off employees, the Ritz Carlton gives them the means to make a difference in the life of a customer.

It has been my experience that most organizations fail to delegate responsibility to their employees. Most employees indicate they could — and wish to — make more decisions.

Estimate how *your employees* would rate the level of empowerment for your organization.

NOT EVEN CLOSE					ADEQUATE					ALL I NEED
0	1	2	3	4	5	6	7	8	9	10

STEP 4 • CUSTOMER PROBLEMS: Frank, an entrepreneur with no experience in the travel industry, bought a travel agency called Quality Travel in central Wisconsin. Shortly thereafter, he called me. He wanted to create a "Wow!" experience for his customers.

We began to train his employees. Some time later, Frank got a new corporate account. He plugged the company's employee travel preferences into the computer. Its first order, however, was not a business flight. It was a vacation. The president of the company, his wife, and their two dogs were traveling to Boston. Everything was fine on the way out. But when it was time to fly home, the president had to remain in the East on business, while his wife and the dogs returned to Wisconsin.

On this particular day, Boston set a record for heat and humidity, and the airline wouldn't take the dogs because their safety could not be guaranteed. In frustration the woman called Quality Travel and explained the scenario to a young travel agent. The agent said, "I don't know what I'm going to do, but I'll do something." After several phone calls, she convinced Northwest to take the dogs, so long as the owner traveled on the same flight and signed a release.

That got the woman and her dogs as far as Minneapolis, but dogs can't travel on commuter flights because the baggage compartment is not pressurized. So what did the agent do? She ran down the hall to brainstorm with several other employees, one of whom suggested calling a town car service the agency had used. Although the town car service didn't usually transport animals, they made an exception The young travel agent called the customer, who was elated.

When the woman reached Minneapolis, the general manager of the town car service was there to greet her with two bowls of fresh water for the dogs Reaching into a brown paper bag, he pulled out some dog biscuits. And, in case the dogs felt cramped from the flight and the upcoming three-hour drive, the general manager handed the woman two leashes he picked up at a pet store on the way to the airport.

That's a Quality Travel "Wow!" experience, and it creates a lifetime customer.

In seminar after seminar that I present to management, managers unanimously agree that the creativity and innovation of our employees is a tremendous competitive advantage. Yet a majority also agree that employee creativity and innovation are effectively dormant in their companies. Why? Because we don't ask our employees for ideas. And when we do, there is too much negative feedback.

EXERCISE

Creating Lifetime Customers

A. List examples of behaviors, policies, systems, or attitudes in your organization that either inhibit or enable innovation.

Inhibit   *Enable*

_____   _____

_____   _____

_____   _____

_____   _____

_____   _____

_____   _____

_____   _____

_____   _____

_____   _____

_____   _____

_____   _____

_____   _____

B. Does your organization operate with a Customer for Life philosophy or are you short-term oriented?

Circle one:

Mostly Short Term   Mostly Long Term

C. Lifetime Value of a Customer

_____	*Average dollars/week customer spends*
X	*52 weeks/year*
X	*Number of years the customer could potentially buy from you*
= _____	*Lifetime value*

If a customer spends $200/week, their lifetime value could easily surpass $250,000. However, it doesn't stop there. Consider the impact of word of mouth. There are two kinds of word of mouth (W.O.M.): Positive word of mouth (+ W.O.M.) — the number of people the customer will tell when he/she is delighted; and negative word of mouth (– W.O.M.), the number of people who hear about it if the customer is upset.

– W.O.M. =	*# of people customer could tell*
X	*% that you could lose*
X	*Lifetime value of a customer*
= _____	*Total Lost Opportunities*

Now we will calculate the revenue that was lost due to the missed opportunity of creating + W.O.M.

+ W.O.M. =	*# of people customer could have told*
X	*% that could become customers*
X	*Lifetime value of a customer*
= _____	*Total Missed Opportunities*

EXERCISE
Indifference is the single biggest killer of customers.

List the top 10 examples of indifference in your organization. In other words, what do employees do that translates into indifference to the customer?

1. _____

2. _____

3. _____

4. _____

5. _____

6. _____

7. _____

8. _____

9. _____

10. _____

Empowering People with Technology

by Lori Laub

People continue to be our greatest asset in companies today. People *are* the company. They're the nucleus, the brains, the energy, the creative source. They're what allows companies to continue to compete in the future…so long as they are well-managed, well-supported, and well-treated.

Until recently, people were not often thought of as needing support systems in order to provide value efficiently to the company. Employees lucky enough to receive support often got it in the form of assistants (who are also people), or tools which increase productivity but not necessarily knowledge (such as telephones, typewriters, and photocopy machines).

The formula for success in today's marketplace requires people and the systems they need to support themselves (Success = People + Systems). This support often comes in the form of technology designed to increase knowledge as well as increase productivity. In today's increasingly competitive environment, empowering people with knowledge and increased capability is a requirement for future survival, let alone success.

Barry Steinberg is the kind of boss who understands this truth. Direct Tire Sales, Steinberg's company, boasts of having the best equipment and the most of it. Direct Tire also has a more extensive inventory of tires than the competition.

Pursuing success in this competitive environment has caused many companies to invest in technology. Wise investments often bring solid positive returns through increased productivity, improved intra-company processes, reduced operating costs, increased quality, and a bottom line

Lori Laub is principal of Excellence by Design, Woodside, Calif.

of increased customer satisfaction. This leads to increased revenues and an improved competitive position in the market. A clear example of this is the computer software industry. In a recent study completed by Price Waterhouse, the most frequently cited concern of software companies is customer satisfaction, with profitability and cost-effective marketing tied for a distant second place.

In the 1980s, companies developed their understanding that customer satisfaction was key to achieving and maintaining market leadership and long-term success. The challenge in the 1990s is knowing what technologies to invest in and how to persuade people to use chosen technologies to achieve the greatest gain possible.

In the service segment, technology is no longer considered a luxury but, rather, a necessity. U.S. corporate expenditures in service-related information technologies amounted to $1.4 trillion between 1983 and 1993. In a study completed for the period 1991 to 1992, 53% of companies were utilizing voicemail technology, 52% fax technology, 51% problem management systems, 49% telephone headsets, and 34% Automatic Call Distributors [ACDs]. The study goes on to show that the greatest investments in technology in 1993 and 1994 were expected in expert systems (up 22% to 31%), problem management systems (up 12% to 63%), interactive voice response [IVR] (up 12% to 19%), ACDs (up 9% to 43%) and telephone headsets (up 7% to 56%). Other technologies often used include computers and workstations, pagers, bulletin boards, teleconferencing, and remote monitoring systems. Direct Tire Sales is clearly one of the companies using technology to stay in the forefront of the customer service evolution.

Blueprint for Success

It is very easy to overdo technology in our dealings with employees and customers. As a result, it is essential to consider the human factor when designing and implementing a new system. If that system is intended to increase customer satisfaction and employee productivity, taking the human factor into account will be the key to ensuring that your investments have a solid payback

1. Managing the Customer Buy-In

Customers must accept and adapt to the new technology if it is to prove beneficial to the company. This can be achieved by keeping the requirements for customers using the new system very simple. Often this requires changes to internal procedures, as well as thoughtful and innovative designs within the technology itself.

It is important to inform customers of upcoming changes before they are implemented. Few people like or appreciate surprises in business, or life for that matter, so by informing your customers ahead of time, you'll be preparing them for the change. Keeping the old process in place for a period of time allows your customers to adapt to the new system.

Explain the benefits of the new process to your customers through the mail, fax, newsletter, "music on hold," or other methods of communication. Don't assume they will automatically understand and support the change. You've probably invested quite a bit of time convincing yourself and others in your organization that this is a wise technology investment. By sharing a little of that thinking with the people you want to use the new system, you'll increase their support and speed of adaptation.

Always ask your users for feedback. Regardless of how well thought through your design or implementation is, the people who actually use the system will know best what's working and what's not. And because most businesses need to move fast to stay competitive today, what's right today may not be right tomorrow.

2. Employee Training

It is essential that employees accept and adapt to the new technology. They're the ones who will either make the system work or cause it to fail. Employees have a tremendous influence over customers and their willingness to adapt to a new system.

To obtain their support, take the time to explain its value to employees. Focus on how it will make their jobs better and why it will benefit them personally. It's fine to include how use of this technology will benefit the company, but emphasize the direct employee benefit of becoming more knowledgeable. More knowledgeable employees impress customers with their skills in tracking items down, for example. Or perhaps the new system will cut down repetitive tasks, hiking productivity and allowing employees more time to work on projects of greater impact and interest. The new technology might improve employee efficiency, which translates into bigger profit-sharing checks.

Discuss the customer benefits of the new system. This gives employees a better understanding of how the change will improve customer satisfaction, while also giving them the data necessary to reassure customers about the new systems.

Take the time to teach employees how the tool works. This enables them to provide feedback on ways to improve the tool and identify new ways to use it. Empowering employees in this manner will help them see that technology is not just another way for management to assert control; rather, it encourages them to take ownership of the new system.

Winning employee support is accomplished by making the technology their tool to use to achieve well-defined and communicated objectives. Human nature fears the unknown, so gaining employee support is often the most challenging aspect of empowering people with technology. By sending a clear message that the tool is designed to help employees achieve both personal and corporate objectives, management can get employees to support the investment.

3. Integrate Technology into the Corporate Culture

Another critical component to a successful introduction of technology is to ensure that users are part of the "technology process." Involving employees in the design and implementation of a new system goes a long way toward gaining their support. This can be done rather easily by holding a suggestion contest, turning a department meeting into a brainstorm session, and asking employees to volunteer to serve on project task forces.

Hold ongoing review sessions or technology "rap sessions" to identify new and improved uses for technology. This keeps everyone involved and aware that they are empowered and responsible for making these technology investments work for them and for your customers. Creating this culture requires the leader of the meeting to make sure all ideas are given consideration and that all contributors are recognized and appreciated.

Publicizing early successes internally and externally will make people realize their efforts are appreciated and provide encouragement in similar opportunities going forward. Formally recognizing and rewarding early employee adapters helps other employees visualize what behavior is rewarded by the company, so they know more clearly what they need to advance in the company.

4. Re-think Business Processes and Goals

The quickest way for a technology project to fail is to give the impression, either real or perceived, that technology is in charge of the users rather than vice versa. To assure that users are in charge of technology in your organization, be sure that employees remain customer- rather than activity- focused. Employees must be responsible for an entire situation, not just a part of it. Employees need to know they are expected to stay in touch with a customer until the situation is resolved.

Use your technology investment to empower users to be responsible for helping to develop a problem-solving process. This can be done through cross-company issue resolution teams, involving users in designing the new technology's interface they or customers use, or involving users in setting goals and strategies for improvement.

Assure that your new technology has the capability not only of capturing data but also of providing you with information you can use to monitor the current situation and make decisions. Analyzing this information to encourage, not intimidate, employees will also help assure the success of your investment. Such data can be used to improve processes, identify training and career opportunities for employees, and provide measurable feedback in a very intangible customer service environment. Tying information gained from these systems to well-defined, positive employee compensation programs provides employees with greater incentive to achieve their career goals and the company's objectives.

Achieving success by empowering people with technology requires you to:

- Develop your technology philosophy
- Choose the right technologies
- Provide support and tools
- Assess your progress
- Market your successes
- Modify as needed

A company strategy that utilizes technology to support people results in multiple benefits by capturing and analyzing productivity information, tracking product and service feedback, segmenting customers for marketing and sales purposes, and tracking inventory levels and shipping status. These and other benefits help differentiate companies so they can attain greater market share.

Companies that use information gathered via technology to improve the business for customers and employees, that communicate their philosophy to employees and customers, and that involve employees and customers in the design and implementation of chosen technologies will reap the benefits of loyal, repeat, satisfied customers, happier, more productive employees, and increased profitability. These benefits are being realized in greater degrees as companies invest more in streamlining processes to improve customer satisfaction and the bottom line. ◼

Notes

_____

_____

_____

_____

_____

_____

_____

_____

_____

_____

_____

_____

_____

_____

_____

_____

_____

_____

_____

_____

_____

The Mystery Shopper Questionnaire

4

At Direct Tire Sales, Barry Steinberg is fanatical about the way his employees treat customers. He's right there to observe his employees himself. At its many restaurants, Au Bon Pain has to rely on the mystery shopper.

That phrase may call to mind the kind of comic television commercial in which persnickety houseguests surreptitiously examine their friends' homes for dusty tabletops or water-spotted dishes. But Au Bon Pain's mystery shoppers are nothing like those caricatures — they are part of an ongoing, extensive program to measure whether the company's quality and service standards are being met.

The program emphasizes improving performance by rewarding employees for excellence. With 1,600 people on its payroll (another 400 are employed by franchisees) and systemwide sales of $70 million in 1990, Au Bon Pain uses its mystery-shopper program — in which anonymous customers not affiliated with the company buy a meal and fill out a questionnaire about the restaurant, the food, and the service — as a key element in its compensation system. Bonuses for everyone from line employees to vice-presidents are based in large part on how well they treat the chain's average customer, i.e., the hundreds of mystery shoppers who get paid to check on customer service.

Here's how the program

How Au Bon Pain boosts customer service by rewarding employees who keep on their toes

works: The corporate office compiles the questionnaires so managers can track trends and the long-term performance of the units. Individual servers and shift managers who have scored high are rewarded with certificates that can be traded in for gifts. Managers at all levels also receive cash profit-sharing bonuses based in part on their mystery-shopper evaluations.

In the three years that the 10-year-old company has been systematically mystery shopping, the number of questions has been whittled down from a high of 200 to the current 60, which span a four-page questionnaire. "We're still doing some rewording," says Joy Pomeroy, the company's first store manager and current head of Retail Quality Control, "to get shoppers to pay attention to the things we want."

The program appears to be improving customer service. An average of 20 people from the 69 company-owned restaurants and express units receive rave reviews each week. That "win rate" of 25% to 30% is about double what it was when the program was launched. Overall site performance scores also have risen, from an average of 72%, to 80%.

Here, Ron Shaich, Au Bon Pain's co-chief executive, and Pomeroy explain the questionnaire and the program, and what the company gets out of them.

4 GOOD FORMS

Where the Shoppers Come From

For the 40 Boston-area locations, Pomeroy recruits shoppers through newspaper advertisements and word of mouth, employing about 30 people at a time on the team. "I look for constant turnover," she says, to help guarantee the "mystery" part of the program. A national in-store research firm, Acker, Capozzi & Petersen Inc., based in Lyndhurst, N.J., monitors the out-of-state sites.

The Boston shoppers are paid $10 a visit; Acker gets $30 for each visit. All shoppers receive a two-to-three-hour training session on the company's customer service philosophy and are given samples of the food as it should be prepared. Shoppers are then expected to spend at least 20 minutes (30 is average) during their visits.

Overall, counting internal administration, the program costs more than $150,000. Shaich says it's worth it: "The results are as important as your profit-and-loss statement" for tracking the health of the company, he maintains.

Frequency of the Visits

Each company-owned store is visited three times over four weeks, during breakfast, lunch, and dinner shifts. There are more visits if a district manager is concerned about the service or cleanliness of a particular unit. "It's a battle, figuring out how much is enough," says Shaich. "Many other food companies seem to shop once a month, although some do it 30 times a week. The more information the better. The important part is that it be systematic and statistically significant."

SHOP DATES: From 2-3-91 To 2-9-91

#1057 Liberty
(Enter Mall on Market Street side.)
1625 Chestnut Street
Philadelphia, PA 19103
CONDUCT SHOP: M-F B/L/D to 6 PM   SA/SU 12-5 PM

Shopper ID: 38M-DI
Day: SUN Date: 2-3-91
Start Time: 1:24 AM/PM
End Time: 1:50 AM/PM
Food Purchase: $ 5.28
(Lunch/Dinner attach receipt)

PEGS SCORE
10 OUT OF 12
83.3 %

PRODUCT: ORDER THE CORRECT MEAL FOR THE HOURS OF THIS SHOP. For each menu category permitted for this meal, only order items listed on the MENU BOARD. REMEMBER— order ONE item, then WAIT a few seconds for the CSR to suggest additional items. Then order any other item specified for this meal occasion.

( ) 7 AM - 9 AM: BREAKFAST
• ANY Croissant or Muffin
• Coffee/Tea/Hot Chocolate
• Orange Juice

(✓) 12 - 1:30 PM (LUNCH)
• 1/2 Sandwich
• Cup of Soup
• Regular size bev - Coffee, Tea (hot/iced), Hot Choc, Soda, or Lemonade

( ) AFTER 3 PM: DINNER
• 1/2 Sandwich or Hot Croissant (Ham, Cheese, or Spinach)
• Cup of Soup
• Beverage (same as lunch)

(Check YES or NO)
1. All order items available. If NO, list items that were on MENU BOARD, but were not available: _____
*Circle: On Menu Board [Y / N]
2. All purchased products look like display. (If NO, explain: _____

YES   NO
 X   P1
 X   __

3. PRODUCT RECEIVED *(Specify in Detail)	4. TEMPERATURE (circle one) P3	5. TASTE/ FRESHNESS (circle one) P2	6. COMMENTS: If TASTE/FRESHNESS was n Very Good, what was lacking/wrong?
A. Breakfast - Croissant/Muffin	• Hot/Warm/Room • Other...	Very Good Good Fair Poor	burnt...dry...too hard...too crusty...too doughy...underbaked...not flaky...tastes like bread...soggy OTHER:_____
B. Dinner - Hot Croissant	• Hot/Warm Enough • Not Hot/Warm Enough	(Very Good) Good Fair Poor	LETTUCE...limp/spoiled...TOMATO...spoile ...BREAD...burnt...dry...too hard...too crusty...doughy...underba CHEESE/SA
C. 1/2 SANDWICH Filling: HAM + CHEESE Bread: BAGUETTE Condiments: L/T MAYO	*Filling Only* (At Standard) • Not At Standard		
D. SOUP/C			

Reading the Overall Rating

PEGS — Product, Environment, and Great Service — encompasses 12 specific criteria Au Bon Pain has chosen to focus on, from food availability to length of waiting time to restating the order when it's handed to the customer. They are scattered throughout the form and added up for an overall score.

Managers whose shifts score 100% receive on-the-spot bonuses of 20 "Club Excellence Dollars" — dubbed CDs — which can be traded like green stamps for items in a company catalog. Half of all items are in the $10-to-$70 range, from Au Bon Pain sunglasses to portable cassette players.

In addition, the PEGS scores received by shift and district managers help determine their eligibility for monthly profit-sharing cash bonuses. A score of less than 78% cancels out any bonus, while higher numbers mean more money. Shaich also uses PEGS to track performance of both individual stores and larger regions. "I'm not worried about whether one shift was good or bad," he says. "That happens to everybody. But I'm certainly interested in whether we have a systematic problem across a specific district or a store, whether it's service speed or product quality."

Choosing the Right Questions

Figuring out what to target in the areas of food, environment, and service wasn't easy, says Shaich. Some questions — such as, Does the rail in front of the counter have smudge marks on it? — were pulled in favor of those more critical to measuring quality and service.

Also, there are limits to how much mystery shoppers can observe. They can't evaluate "house standards" — for example, whether the chicken is being kept at 140 degrees — which district managers check up on. And they don't interact with bakers or prep people or clean-up people, who are monitored by in-house managers.

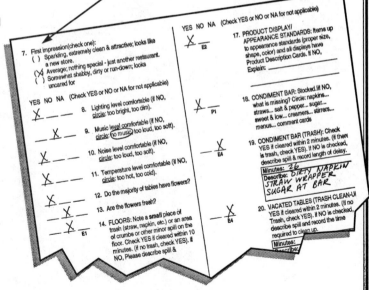

4 GOOD FORMS

Measuring Service Quality

Individual workers — the servers — get 10 CD points if they score 100% in six areas of customer interaction, such as an overall willingness to serve and greeting the shopper within three seconds.

Indeed, recognition for treating a mystery shopper well is a culmination of the constant reinforcement employees receive for good customer service. Winners' names are posted on each store's bulletin board next to a list of the judging criteria, and all winners get letters of congratula-

tion from Pomeroy and the vice-president of operations. Notices reminding employees about the service priorities are also periodically included in paychecks.

Shoppers are expected to fill out the forms surreptitiously, so the crew members won't give them special treatment; things like how long it takes to be served are supposed to be noted subtly and jotted down later. But employees look out for them. "We encourage people to wonder," says Pomeroy. "It's a good motivator."

Reading the General Comments

"I don't read every evaluation individually," says Shaich. "I'm mainly looking at the trend line on the scores by district, by the company overall, and in some cases, by the store. But I'll often pick up a bunch of them and read the food reviews and general comments. I'm looking for patterns.

"The biggest decision we've made from these? We fire people. Absolutely. The purpose of the program is still to reward people and find systematic trends, but if there are real problems, we'll go in and talk to that manager. I don't think we'd ever fire anybody over one bad review, but clearly if someone's consistently performing below par, they should be fired, shouldn't they?" ■

QUALITY OF SERVICE
Your server is a:
☒ CSR (Red Apron) — "you must go to a CSR; if not possible, explain why in the Overall Comment."

☐ Manager (Tie/Black Apron)

44. Name of server: TANYA S.
• Check: If ( ) no tag or ( ) not visible, describe server
• Circle: [M (F)]

45. Impression of server; check one & comment:
GS4 (☒) polite, friendly, genuinely pleased to wait on customer
( ) satisfactory, ok - "got the job done type of person"
( ) average, routine, mechanical, not warm
( ) rude, sarcastic, unfriendly

COMMENT REQUIRED: SHE WAS VERY PLEASANT, BUT SHE DIDN'T ASK ME IF I WANTED ANYTHING ELSE

YES NO NA
X___ GS2   46. Acknowledged within 3 seconds after reaching first place in line.

X___ GS2   47. Acknowledged pleasantly.

X___ GS2   48. Server's English adequate (does not slow down line).

YES NO NA
___ X   49. Server suggested additional item(s). If YES, circle: chips, soup dessert, drink, large drink, take home, other:

X___   50. Server requested payment prior to delivering order.

X___   51. Received receipt (For sandwich orders only).

X___   52. Received correct change.

X___ GS3   53. Shown sandwich # on receipt or told sandwich # (For sandwich orders only).

X___   54. Products served neatly (observe two other customer's orders).

X___ GS4   55. Server's parting said pleasantly (Thank you, smiled, etc.)

X___ GS3   56. Sandwich # and complete description called out by sandwich maker (For sandwich orders only).

X___ GS3   57. Correct order received. If NO, explain.

OVERALL RATING
(E) G F P   57. Overall Rating of Food Quality
E (G) F P   57. Overall Rating of Store Cleanliness
(E) G F P   57. Overall Rating of Service Quality

60. OVERALL COMMENT: Step back for a moment and comment on the overall experience. Use the space below to give detailed aspects- "paint a picture" - of the food, cleanliness and service. Also, give aspects of the experience that are not covered in the questionnai
[NOTE: Do not compare your visits; each shop should be conducted independently.]

THE SOUP WAS HOT AND UM-UM GOOD. THE HAM WAS FRESH WITH A NICE SMOKED FLAVOR. THE CAFE HAD 13 PEOPLE IN IT, SO EMPLOYEES HAD TIME TO CLEAN AND CH ALL THE AREAS BUT THEY DIDN'T FOR 14½ MINUTES AND WALKED PAST THE DIRTY CONDIMENT BAR LIKE THEY WERE BLIND.

CHAPTER

5

Designing for the Customer

As Mark Sanborn (see p. 190) so rightly notes in his analysis of Dell Computer Corp.'s explosive growth, customer service is but a piece of the business puzzle. Nonetheless, customer service is a key piece of that puzzle, one that can complete the puzzle and free a business to flourish. Or it can be the piece that's missing. For, as Sanborn says, all businesses have customer service strategies — whether by design or default. Companies interact with customers, says Sanborn, either intentionally or accidentally.

In Dell Computer's case, the interaction with customers has always been intentional. Customer service has been the centerpiece of Dell's business strategy. Whether through technical support or by customizing computers to suit a customer's needs, Dell has been as innovative as it has been aggressive in serving its customers. What is startling about Dell is that it has been able to sustain its connectedness to customers through its explosive growth. As the company has expanded, Michael Dell has kept the focus on the customer. That's not to say that customer service at Dell is delivered the same way today as it was 10 years ago. Still, the spirit and commitment that define Dell's brand of customer service has never wavered. Dell has managed to refine, adapt, and augment its customer service strategy to keep pace with its astonishing growth.

After reading the story of Dell Computer's first decade, spend a few minutes answering the 13 questions that Mark Sanborn poses. Your answers to these questions will help you modify and improve your own customer service strategy.

When you've come to grips with Sanborn's challenge, consider Nate Booth's analysis of rising levels of customer service (see p. 199). Booth sees in Dell Computer the paradigm of the service provider of the 1990s. If it was once sufficient to find a need and fill it, it has now become essential to deliver more than your customer expects. But Dell has broken new ground. Dell has vaulted to what Booth refers to as "Third-Level Service." Dell is "actively discovering a customer problem and then uniquely and quickly over-solving it."

Michael Dell succeeded in part because he managed to bring custom-tailoring to an assembly-line industry. At a time when computer manufacturers were pushing Model Ts off the line, Dell was custom-designing its vehicles. At Dell, computers are made to order and serviced at a level that matches the needs of the customer. As Michael Dell himself has said so many times, the one-size-fits-all mentality does not exist at Dell Computer.

Dell's Magnificent Obsession

The curtain rises on a large open room in an office tower. We are in Austin, Texas. The year is 1989. The room has the look and sound of a brokerage house on a busy day. Everyone in the room is young, most are under 30. Under fluorescent lights, amidst a clutter of Coke cans and order forms, about a hundred salespeople clutch telephones, begging, cajoling, and persuading customers to buy computers.

What you hear and see may look and sound like any other struggling young business. But it is not. In this large, open room, an extraordinary evolution is occurring. A corporate culture is being built, telephone call by telephone call. You are present at the creation of a culture of customer service, a commitment to customer satisfaction almost regardless of the cost.

The company is Dell Computer Corp. In less than four years, the company has grown into a $159-million business. Sales for 1989 will more than double to $388 million.

Dell Computer has succeeded without the benefit of face-to-face interaction with its customers. Dell salespeople work blind. They have no body language to read. All they have is a phone...and the vision of the founder of the company, a vision that places the customer on a pedestal. Customer satisfaction is the obsession at Dell Computer Corp. To work at Dell, you have to have an attitude. And that attitude is personified in Michael Dell.

As a student at the University of Texas in 1984, Michael Dell saw a personal-computer industry that was still full of promise. The 19-year-old pre-med student started a business selling microcomputer components to local computer enthusiasts. The next year Dell started assembling his own line of PCs. By the end of fiscal 1986 annual sales reached $33 million. "Everything was wrong — we didn't have the money, the people, the resources," Dell says. "But I had a gut feeling that drove me to start this company."

Dell's Niche Is the Phone

Direct marketing by phone is at the heart of Dell's success. When he entered the computer market, it was too late to challenge the technological standard that IBM had established with its PC. So Dell searched for a different niche, one that could be defined by a unique marketing and distribution strategy.

One potential approach — developing a strong dealers-only network for a PC clone — had already been worked to perfection by Compaq Computer, while Tandy Corp. enjoyed the benefit of its network of 6,500 Radio Shack stores. IBM, of course, exercised its traditional sway through both dealers and its own vaunted sales staff.

So Dell decided on telemarketing, selling PC compatibles. By side-stepping the dealers and their big markups, Dell was able to undersell such competitors as IBM and Compaq by as much as 40% while staying in roughly the same price league with the low-balling Korean and Taiwanese clone manufacturers

But Dell never fell into the trap of competing by price alone "Too many companies have concentrated simply on the mass market, on competing on price," notes Roberta Graves, president of Qualitative Marketing, a leading microcomputer marketing company in San Jose, Calif. "They have not realized that for many of the new users, the key is not price but service, support, and solutions."

While selling directly to customers made Dell competitive, the company recognized other, even more important benefits. By selling directly to customers, ranging from individuals to major corporations, Dell gains an instantaneous reading of the latest trends. "Direct sales," one sales manager notes, "give you fantastic market intelligence."

That intelligence, gleaned from more than 1,000 phone calls a day, coaxed Dell into a new product line. Despite all the hoopla about IBM's new PS/2 line, many customers still wanted upgraded versions of computers based on Intel Corp.'s popular 286 and 386 microprocessors. Rather than meekly following Big Blue's lead, the company developed a series of highly successful PCs based on the older technology.

90% of Problems Solved on the Phone

Equally important in terms of customer satisfaction is the support given by the company's service organization. A team of about 75 technicians deals daily with as many as 1,500 questions from customers. Dell estimates that 90% of the problems encountered by users are solved over the phone. Such responsiveness is particularly appealing to business customers — now accounting for up to 85% of sales — who must overcome glitches fast. For repair problems, Dell also offers, for $35 a year, a service contract with Honeywell-Bull, which fixes the machines on site.

The phone calls also enable Dell to identify defective parts quickly. "If we get more than a few complaints," notes Ronald Leonard, a marketing manager, "I go about 130 feet to the people who design the thing. Within five or six hours, engineering has fixed the design, and within two or three days, the factory's got that change incorporated on the line."

Dell's ability to respond quickly gives it a major competitive advantage, particularly over personal-computer makers in Asia. Cut off from their market by thousands of miles and huge cultural gaps, the Japanese have been overwhelmed by the rapid rate of change in the PC industry. Accustomed to large production runs of standardized products with two- to three-year life cycles and the use of mass-distribution channels like retail stores, they have shown only limited ability to adjust to a market

> **HOT TIP**
> *Prospective customers get their photo taken when they visit Eriez Magnetics, a $60 million manufacturer of magnetic laboratory and metal detection equipment in Erie, Pa. "It's our way of saying thank you," says president and CEO Chet Giermak, who sends the photos to visitors with a cover letter reminding them of the reason they came and the people they met. The photo comes in a cardboard frame with the company's mission statement on the back. Giermak says it takes just a minute to dictate the letter and that the complete package costs only $2, including the stamp.*

that absorbs new models quickly, sometimes every six months.

"To them, manufacturing is the lifeblood of the industry. Everything is manufacturing-driven," notes a top Dell marketing executive. "But that's not the way in computers. The ideal — direct marketing — is a totally customer-driven system."

The experience of the Japanese in the PC market shows the importance of the customer-driven approach. In the early 1980s, for instance, Japanese manufacturers were slow to adopt the MS-DOS operating standard used by IBM. This compatibility problem grew out of the Japanese experience at home, where each company produced PCs with its own standards, notes Yasuhiro Tsubota, president of Epson America Inc.

That mistake virtually doomed the first generation of Japanese machines. Even when they finally adopted MS-DOS, the Japanese ignored customer needs, as when they designed computers that couldn't run popular software, such as Lotus 1-2-3, or generate high-quality graphics.

Agility Becomes a Competitive Edge

Small companies such as Dell wield yet another strategic weapon against larger domestic and Asian competitors: their ability to move quickly. In the manufacturing of consumer electronic products, such as televisions and videocassette recorders, standardization and mass production work to the advantage of large companies. But the PC industry's quick-changing marketplace provides a unique opportunity for small companies — as long as they organize themselves to be fast and flexible.

Asian mass-production lines can provide PC clones at low cost, but they can't do what Dell does: build computers to order and build them fast. Dell's telemarketers take the customers' specs right off the phone. A number is assigned to each customer's request, specifying the kind of machine, the disk drive, memory size, and other components required. Each computer is then assembled and tested individually. Delivery is made within one to three weeks by United Parcel Service, whose trucks pull out of Dell's Austin factory three or four times a day. For an additional fee, the computer will be shipped even faster via Federal Express.

For the customer, there's no waiting for a cargo ship to arrive from Asia or for a retail store to receive its back order on memory boards.

Manufacturing to order has cost advantages, too. It keeps down inventory costs by enabling the company to build only what is required. "Each order is automatically entered as a computerized list of all the specs for manufacturing," explains Herschel Hochman, Dell's former vice-president of manufacturing and now vice-president for strategic planning. "At the same time, sales has access to the customers' complete sales histories. We can determine what equipment they already have and their complete repair history. This gives us the opportunity to ensure that customers are ordering equipment appropriate for their needs. You have a sort of inventory control that you never have reacting on the retail level. You can save yourself a bundle on building machines and buying parts nobody wants or needs."

Fast forward five years to 1994...

No longer the entrepreneurial operation it was in 1989, Dell has nonetheless managed to sustain its commitment to customer satisfaction as it has grown by orders of magnitude each year. In 1991, sales hit $546 million. In 1992, $890 million. In 1993, $2 billion. And in fiscal 1994, sales topped $2.9 billion. Dell today is one of the world's top five personal computer vendors.

Dell in 1994 is a souped-up version of the Dell of 1988. The one hundred salespeople of 1989 have multiplied to nearly 700. The technical support group alone numbers 350 individuals who handle more than 35,000 telephone calls each day. At a service call volume 35 times greater than it was six years before, Dell's technical support group has actually improved its problem-solving ratio. Today, nearly 95% of the problems encountered by users are solved over the telephone. And solving problems is what is important to users, particularly business users, who account for fully 90% of Dell's sales today.

Dell Computer employees occupy an array of building sites in and around Austin. But that changed in August 1994 when the company

➤ **HOT TIP**

Ed Loke understands the importance of setting reasonable, specific, measurable goals, with rewards for achieving them. When he instituted his "No Surprises Guarantee Program," shipping errors at Texcel, a $6 million Houston-based industrial rubber products wholesaler, fell by 75%. Loke promised that Texcel would ship goods within 24 hours, notify customers of back-ordered items prior to shipping, ship the correct goods, make no pricing errors, and provide error-free paperwork. Failing these, Texcel mails customers a "bonus check" gift certificate, good for 5% off their next order. Any balance in the fund set up to cover the guarantee goes to order-handling people. The result: Texcel has cut shipping errors from 10 to 3 a month, there are fewer dissatisfied customers, and employee morale has improved.

consolidated its offices in a low-rise campus of buildings in Round Rock, some four miles north of Austin. Yet Dell extends well beyond Austin and the United States. Today, Dell is an international firm employing 7,500 people worldwide.

For all the changes, Dell remains as close to and in touch with its customers as ever it was in the past. "Michael Dell is the spiritual leader here," says Roger Rydell, senior public relations manager. "Michael Dell is not a difficult read. For Michael, customers are gods. And most people who work in this organization emulate the values that Michael has instilled in this company."

In the current annual report, Michael Dell writes, "We plan to pursue customers who value customization and integration and who are willing to pay for flexible, relevant service and support, through high value-added solution providers who want to add Dell hardware and support to their solution mix."

Techno-Typing

Dell's commitment to customer service can be measured not just in quantitative terms, such as service calls handled, but in innovation as well. Consider Techno-Typing. Introduced in 1993, Techno-Typing classifies customers based on their PC usage patterns. Some customers are totally at ease with computers, while others are first-time buyers of home PCs. Dell's "Techno-Wizard," for example, is a sophisticated "power-user" who is interested in owning and using the fastest and highest-performing systems on the market. A "Techno-Critical user" is a corporate executive responsible for the establishment and maintenance of one or more local area networks, while "Techno-Teamers" are people working on PCs within a network.

Using the extensive customer database the company has developed over the years, researchers group customers according to their usage patterns. By comparing usage patterns to purchasing patterns (features and services), Dell believes it can design systems that are more specifically tailored to end-users.

Dell has always rejected the "one-size-fits-all" philosophy. Not only does it design systems for individuals, but it designs service and support to suit individuals as well. While competitors bundle services, Dell permits customers to select the services they need and to pay only for those services.

In 1993, Dell introduced SelectCare, a diverse menu of user-configurable service options. SelectCare lets users choose — and pay for — exactly the level of service and support that they require. For instance, SelectCare offers customers with advanced service needs three optional, customized programs:

• Dell Parts Only, which offers up to an additional four-year warranty on component parts within Dell PCs;

• the Dell Self-Maintainer program, designed for corporate customers who handle the primary service needs for their networks;

• the Dell Third-Party Maintenance program, offering complete training and certification in the service of Dell PCs for corporate customers who retain outside service vendors.

Other new, specialized programs introduced in fiscal 1994 include a broad array of service and support options tailored for advanced systems customers, as well as dedicated programs for mobile computing customers.

First in the Industry

Innovations like SelectCare come as no surprise in a company that pioneered the concept of direct contact between customers and the manufacturer via a toll-free phone line that operates 24 hours a day, 365 days a year. Dell was the first in the industry to recognize the benefits that manufacturer-direct support and next-day on-site service could bring to customers. Dell also was the first to offer guarantees for timely on-site service and for product compatibility.

This year, Dell enhanced its customers' ability to access its technical support team with a new program called OpenLine This new service provides around-the-clock, seven-day-per-week technical support by telephone for the life of all Dell products. Dell also enhanced the ability of its technical support experts to service customer needs by improving the proprietary software they use to trouble-shoot specific system issues for individual customers. The company's technical support responsiveness additionally benefited from improved embedded diagnostics that were introduced for a number of Dell PCs. These diagnostics allow technicians to zero in more efficiently on a specific system's performance problem.

As part of the restructuring of its European operations, Dell consolidated its sales and service capabilities into three locations. The customer support center (CSC) in Bray, Ireland handles all sales and service needs for customers in the United Kingdom and Ireland. The CSC in Montpellier, France manages the same functions for the majority of customers in the southern portion of the continent, while a smaller facility in Stockholm, Sweden has been established to handle the sales and support needs for the entire northern region of Europe.

The CSCs were made possible in part by an improved systems capability that helps Dell handle larger customer call volumes and better identify caller needs. This segmentation of incoming calls allows Dell to connect customers directly to technicians who speak their language.

Tops in Customer Satisfaction

Any lingering doubts about Dell's commitment to customers are dismissed by customers themselves. Dell has ranked highest in 19 large-scale, independent surveys of customers' satisfaction over the years. In the 1993 Desktop Personal Computer Satisfaction Study that J.D. Power and Associates conducted among business users, Dell was tops once again. But the clearest validation of Michael Dell's vision — his obsession with satisfying his customers — comes from another question on that survey. For the first time, respondents to the 1993 J.D. Power survey gave a higher weighting to service and support than they did to ease of use when rating their level of satisfaction with their computer purchases.

In 1994, Dell had to come to grips with three years of compounded annual revenue growth in excess of 79%. Management realized that in order for Dell to achieve profitable growth in the future, it needed to moderate the hypergrowth it had been experiencing in favor of managed growth, coupled with infrastructure improvements.

Part of that restructuring involved improving demand/supply forecasting capabilities in Dell's world-wide operations to avoid over- or underestimating the company's component needs in the future. That the company is doing a better job forecasting is evident in its 1994 inventory levels: less than five weeks, compared with an industry average of eight to eleven weeks. Lower inventory levels give Dell greater flexibility as well as relief from the costs associated with carrying extraneous components and accessory products on its books. And by tightening procedures for its sales and technical support functions, Dell managed to reduce the average number of parts sent out per service call by 16% during the second half of 1993.

As Dell restructures, the company is looking for ways to improve productivity and cut waste without lowering its customer service standards. For example, while better software capability in the technical support area has made Dell technicians' jobs easier, it has also made each customer call more efficient. And enhanced communication among Dell's procurement and product development organizations should result in shorter time to market for relevant technology required by Dell customers.

Dell's first ten years were marked by an entrepreneurial spirit that shaped the culture of the organization. Throughout the company's early development, it was this uncompromising commitment to growth and success that drove Dell's employees to do whatever it took, not only to serve but to delight their customers. A decade ago, as a new organization, Dell had to prove it was worthy of every sale it won from larger rivals. This often required the provision of extraordinary service. Today, the company still strives to maintain that same customer-driven focus as it sets its sights on the decade ahead.

Regardless of how people are buying their PCs or how they are operating them, Dell plans to remain a point of contact through the ownership life of its products. As much as Dell Computer has changed in its first decade of doing business, its corporate culture has remained fundamentally unaltered. Michael Dell has committed himself and his company to keeping the promises Dell makes to its customers.

In the words of the founder, "We are committed to helping deliver on technology's promise of a decade ago — to make people more productive."

5

13 Questions Every Service Provider Must Answer

by Mark Sanborn

As a key to Dell Computer's growth and success, customer service is a piece in the business puzzle — a very important piece — but the piece is not the puzzle. Dell innovated and integrated its customer service strategy into a larger business strategy. By combining low prices, made possible through sidestepping a dealer network and relying on telemarketing, with service support, Dell exploited an opportunity that was in its infancy in 1984. In the early years, Dell did lots of things right.

Beware seeing customer service as a panacea — it cannot and will not save or significantly improve a business if the other fundamentals are not in place. Actually, a lack of the fundamentals will prevent a truly effective service strategy from being implemented.

With that caveat in mind, how can you create or improve on a customer service strategy? Whether you realize it or not, your company already has a customer service strategy, by either design or default. Your current way of interacting with customers has evolved intentionally or accidentally. The way to make sure that future service efforts are effective is to keep asking the kinds of important questions that drive a customer service program by design.

It isn't enough to have the right answers; you've got to ask the right questions. The 13 questions that follow will guide you in your efforts to design a superior customer service strategy.

Mark Sanborn heads up Sanborn & Associates, in Denver, Colo.

THE 13 QUESTIONS

1. Who is our customer?

Who in the marketplace is choosing to do business with you? Customers are a moving target. Has your customer base changed over time? Has the type of customer you serve remained the same while the wants, needs, tastes, and preferences of that type of customer have changed? Service strategy must be dynamic. You must continually assess both who your customers are and who they are becoming.

When Michael Dell launched his startup in 1984, he didn't have customers yet. But he knew what kind of customers he wanted: the price-conscious, direct-mail buyer. Dell identified a profitable niche by analyzing the existing market then asking:

2. Who do we want our customers to be?

This is a truly strategic question. "Who is our customer?" gives you information about the present. "Who do we want our customer to be?" provides information that will allow you to shape your future.

You may find that you have acquired some customers with whom you really don't want to be doing business. Their needs distract you from your core competencies and the cost of providing them the kind of service they demand is excessive. Rather than reacting to those types of customers indefinitely, start to develop a service strategy that attracts the kind of customer you hope to be serving in the future.

Your service strategy needs to address both of the previous questions.

Deciding to do anything without taking into account the unique needs of customers is foolish, and yet many companies base their service strategy on what the company does (probably because they have always done it that way and/or do it quite well) rather than on what the customers want to have done.

Dell Computer exploited a marketplace advantage that their telemarketing and direct contact with customers provided: immediate feedback and market intelligence. This regular contact allowed them to answer the next question:

3. What are the important things we know about our customer?

Harvey Mackay isn't just a well-known author and business speaker. He runs a successful envelope company as well. The Mackay 66 questionnaire used by Mackay's salespeople is an excellent example of the lengths to which a customer-driven organization will go to gather information about its customers. Each of the 66 carefully constructed questions is designed to give Mackay's company the advantage of superior information. The questionnaire, which can be found in his book, *Swim with the Sharks Without Being Eaten Alive,* is a simple approach to gathering and organizing important information about every customer with whom the Mackay company does business.

For years, Tom Peters has advised business people that it isn't enough to be close to the customer; you've got to be glued to the customer. More and better information about each and every customer is that glue. The company with more and better information about its customers has a strategic advantage, assuming, of course, that the information is used.

So, where do you get this information? One of the best sources is your own people. Just as Dell gleaned information from customer interactions, anyone who has contact with customers — sales, telemarketing, public relations, accounting, and the service group — picks up bits and pieces of information. Everyone should be involved in gathering and updating customer information.

4. How are we utilizing our cumulative expertise to serve our customers better?

Dell decided to pursue a price-driven buyer. This shaped its service strategy. It was a novel idea to provide an exceptional service level in an industry where — up to that time — buyers were accustomed to trading quality of service for low price. Suddenly, Dell was offering both. The key was to determine how to provide service levels that were perceived as higher than those provided by alternative vendors and still do so cost-effectively.

Before you can design a strategy that will position you as the service provider of choice, you must find the answer to the following question

5. What do our customers expect?

Dell knew day-to-day not only what its customers expected, but what they wanted. There is a substantive difference: Expectations are based on past and current experience with other service providers and any perceptions about your organization created by sales, marketing, or public relations. Wants are based on needs and desires. Just because customers get what they expect doesn't mean they are getting what they really want. Once you've determined what your customers expect, probe further to answer this question:

6. What do our customers want?

Exceptional service addresses both expectations and wants. After any interaction with your organization, your customer will feel one of three ways:

1. Cheated: expectations remain unfulfilled.
2. Satisfied: the customer received only what was expected, nothing more.
3. Delighted: the customer received what was expected and then some.

There are several important implications here. The first is this: How customers feel depends not on how you treated them but on their experience relative to what they expected.

It is your job to find out in advance what your customers expect. Your service level relative to expectations is what determines which of the three emotional states will be achieved.

Is customer satisfaction a worthwhile goal? Frederick Reichheld, writing about customer loyalty in the March-April 1993 issue of *Harvard Business Review,* reported that 65% to 85% of customers who defect said they were satisfied with their former suppliers. The danger is clear: If the best you can do in your service strategy is to satisfy customers, you've got little customer loyalty and even less strategic advantage. You need to ask the question:

7. Do we consistently meet and exceed expectations?

Legendary service is not created by simply satisfying customers.

Service providers quickly give up hope of ever delighting every customer. It is an impossible goal. The good news is that you don't have to delight every customer, but you must delight some customers. Why not make it a goal and expectation of every employee who has customer contact to delight at least one customer each day?

You won't have to go far to find management gurus who taut the concepts of absolute quality or service: Provide the best possible product or service anywhere. While this is inspirational advice, it is decidedly bad advice. If Dell had attempted that, the cost incurred would have negated the sales margins. Providing the best possible service anywhere is a costly indulgence, and you don't need to do it. There is an alternative: Provide relative service. This is determined by asking:

8. What service levels will give us a relative edge over our competitors?

Your service doesn't have to be the best anywhere, but it does need to be perceivably better than your competitors. Relative service provides a cost-effective edge. The idea is to improve service without paying too much in the way of time and resources to do it. If and when your competitors begin to match the service level you've achieved, you bump efforts up to the next level, though not necessarily the highest level.

A jewel in the Dell crown has always been their ability to provide customer support very conveniently and quickly. In the early years, Dell's employees were able to solve over the phone 90% of the problems that their customers experienced. Today they have managed to bump up even that extraordinary rate.

Problem solving can be either reactive or proactive. Reactive is typical: A user experiences a problem and calls for help. Proactive is more powerful: The vendor searches for common and potential problems and attempts to address them in advance. How good is your organization at finding and solving problems? Have you focused your service organization on answering the following question:

9. How well do we solve the problems that our customers experience?

Dell's immediate feedback helped them identify defective parts quickly. Said one marketing manager, "I go about 130 feet to the people who design the thing. Within five to six hours, engineering has fixed the design, and within two or three days, the factory's got that change incorporated on the line." A key aspect of Dell's success is its ability to compete in time.

10. How and how quickly are we using customer information?

If there are limitations to the questions I've posed so far, it is that they are answered by those who serve rather than those who are served. The sentiment is expressed in the motto of another corporation, Techsonic: *Quality and service are what the customer says they are.* To create an exceptional service strategy means we must go beyond talking to ourselves. We need to find out what our customers are thinking.

How do we come to terms with our customers' expectations, experience, and evaluation of our service? The obvious solution is to ask them.

Comment cards and toll-free numbers are a first step, but nothing is more powerful than frequent direct contact with customers when you can ask them the following three questions:

11. What did you like most about doing business with us?
12. What did you like least about doing business with us?
13. What will you tell others about us?

The answer to question No. 11 will tell you what your customers appreciate. It will focus you and your team on those activities and benefits that should be continued and refined because they are valued.

Question No. 12 will direct you to those things you should stop doing or do differently. It points out weak spots in your service delivery and identifies mistakes that need to be prevented.

Finally, question No. 13 will tell you whether your word-of-mouth advertising is working for or against you in the marketplace. What your customers are telling colleagues and others in the marketplace can potentially overshadow your marketing efforts. It is amazing that so few companies make a legitimate attempt to find out what present and former customers are saying about them.

CONCLUSION

The same concepts that Dell utilized to build its business can be used to design or enhance your own service strategy. It begins with asking the right questions. Don't be content with cursory or superficial answers, as many businesses are. By being willing to dig deeper and consider more carefully, you'll find the information you need to craft a successful strategy for the delivery of superior service. That's a critically important piece of the puzzle for long-term business success.

EXERCISE
Applying the Answers

How to use these questions: I recommend that key service managers answer the first 10 questions independently before meeting as a group. The more and varied the sources of information tapped, the richer and more rewarding the outcome. Plan to meet as a group to discuss and challenge conclusions. Develop specific actions to take as a result.

ASK YOURSELVES:

1. Who do we want our customers to be?

_____

_____

_____

2. Who is our customer?

_____

_____

_____

3. What are the most important things we know about our customer?

_____

_____

_____

4. **Are we using our cumulative expertise to get glued to customers?**

_____

_____

_____

5. **What do our customers expect?**

_____

_____

_____

6. **What do our customers want?**

_____

_____

_____

7. **Do we consistently meet and exceed expectations?**

_____

_____

_____

8. **What service levels will give us a relative edge over our competitors?**

_____

_____

_____

9. **How well do we solve the problems that our customers experience?**

_____

_____

_____

10. How and how quickly are we using customer information?

_____

_____

_____

ASK YOUR CUSTOMERS:

Each service manager should interview a minimum of 10 randomly selected customers and ask the following questions before convening as a group and comparing notes.

11. What did you like least about doing business with us?

_____

_____

_____

12. What did you like most?

_____

_____

_____

13. What will you tell others?

_____

_____

_____

Third-Level Service

by Nate Booth

Back in the 1960s, the first rule of business was: Find a need and fill it. It was a simple rule for simple times. It worked well. Consumer expectations weren't very high so it was relatively easy to meet their expectations. This was First-Level Service.

Then came the increased global competition of the 1970s and 1980s. Now, just filling expectations was no longer enough. Japanese consumer products exceeded expectations. The Honda Accord set the standard for excellence in an entire industry. Giving people more than they expect is an example of Second-Level Service. To achieve Second-Level Service, the rule of business was: Find a need and exceed it. But by the early 1990s, Second-Level Service was the norm rather than the exception. The Honda Accord now had rivals in the Ford Taurus, the Toyota Camry, the Nissan Altima, and others.

To prosper in the 1990s, Second-Level Service is no longer sufficient. Your customers' expectations have now risen to the point that "value added" is expected. They expect more for less, and there are plenty of suppliers from all around the world who will give it to them. The rapid pace of change in the 1990s is leveling the playing field. Smaller, faster, and more flexible companies have the advantage in times of rapid change. Today, businesses must be prepared to deliver Third-Level Service.

To achieve Third-Level Service, a company must focus either on a problem or on a product/service. In the former, you actively discover a customer problem and then uniquely and quickly over-solve it. Let me give you a couple of examples to illustrate this level of service.

In 1986, personal computer sales were really taking off. Michael

Nate Booth, D.D.S., is head corporate trainer at Anthony Robbins Companies, in San Diego.

· 199 ·

Dell, age 21, knew he couldn't compete against the big boys head-on. He also knew he didn't have to. They were still providing Second-Level Service. He intended to provide Third-Level Service. He went to potential PC buyers and actively discovered a customer problem. They told Michael, "My company has unique needs that require customized solutions. All the other computer companies are trying to fit my needs into their systems. I want computers that are designed to meet my needs exactly!"

Once Dell discovered this problem, he uniquely and quickly over-solved it. He created a company in Austin, Tex. with a unique marketing and distribution strategy. He decided to telemarket directly to his customers. To this day, his telemarketers phone their business customers, discover exactly what they need, and suggest a system of customized PCs that will be assembled, tested, and shipped the following day. Considering that Dell Computer is now a $2.9 billion international business, it is clear that Third-Level Service can pay off in a big way.

In the late 1980s, Hewlett-Packard was stumbling. A large, lumbering corporation, Hewlett-Packard was missing new markets and creating too many products that customers didn't need or buy. Then the company changed focus. It started asking its customers what their problems were before it created solutions to them. Only then did it put its vast resources to work to over-solve those problems uniquely and quickly. Working with its customers, Hewlett-Packard discovered solutions it would never have found alone. Today, Hewlett-Packard is the leading maker of printers, number two in powerful workstation computers, and number eight in personal computers.

Third-Level Service can also take a product/service focus. With this focus, you direct your attention to creating products and services that people don't even know they need yet. In other words: Create a desire and then uniquely and quickly exceed it with value.

One of my favorite ways to begin a presentation is to ask: "How many of you have used a 3M Post-It Note in the past week?" Ninety percent of the people raise their hands. How would you like to have 90% market penetration? And 3M's 90% market penetration has come with a product that no one needed when it was introduced. An extensive marketing and sales campaign to office supply distributors in four test cities revealed that Post-It Notes were a loser. Nobody wanted to sell an unknown product with a comparatively high price (compared to staples and paper clips) and a low profit margin. Two men at 3M who loved Post-Its and couldn't understand why everyone didn't share their feelings went to Richmond, Va., one of the test market cities, to see what was wrong. In a last-ditch effort to save the product from the scrap heap, they took a couple of boxes of Post-Its and went up and down the business section of Richmond giving the product away. Once you use that little yellow pad, you're hooked. And soon Richmond was hooked too. Reorders came in at 90% — double the rate of the most successful office products.

The moral of this story is simple. One way to be successful in business is to create a desire for a product and then uniquely and quickly exceed it with value. That's what Federal Express did. The U.S. Postal Service, United Parcel Service, and Emery Express all asked their customers, "Will you pay what it's going to cost us for overnight delivery?" The answer was a resounding, "No! We don't need overnight delivery!" Fred Smith didn't believe it! He knew it would work and created Federal Express to prove it. I'm sure you've heard the story of the early years of Federal Express. The company barely survived. It was held together by a group of people with a common dream who finally created a desire for overnight delivery and then uniquely and quickly exceeded it with value. Federal Express is still doing it to this day. Even today, they keep one step ahead of the competition.

Whether you focus on a problem (actively discover a problem and then uniquely and quickly over-solve it) or a product/service (create a desire and then uniquely and quickly exceed it with value), it is absolutely critical to deliver Third-Level Service if you intend to start or grow a business in the 1990s. The next Dell Computer, Hewlett Packard, Post-It Notes or Federal Express awaits the person and corporation willing to aspire to Third-Level Service.

THE THREE LEVELS OF SERVICE

Level of Service	Time	First Rule of Business
First-Level Service	Pre-1970	Find a need and fill it.
Second-Level Service	1970-1990	Find a need and exceed it.
Third-Level Service	1990 and beyond	Actively discover a problem and then uniquely and quickly over-solve it, or create a desire, then uniquely and quickly exceed it with value.

EXERCISE I

Establishing Third-Level Service with a Customer Problem Focus:

1. List three problems that your customers have right now.

_____

_____

_____

If you can't come up with at least two off the top of your head, you're not close enough to your customers. Get out of your office and ask them these questions:

- What two or three changes, if they did occur, would take your business to the next higher level?
- If I had a magic wand, what two or three things would you like to see changed?
- What are your two most nagging problems?

2. From your unique vantage point, what are at least three problems that your customers have that even they don't know about?

_____

_____

_____

3. How are corporations in other industries solving their problems? Can you use these same problem-solving techniques with your customers?

_____

_____

_____

_____

_____

_____

_____

4. If your customers operated in a perfect world, how would that world be different than the world in which they are presently operating?

_____

_____

_____

_____

5. Based on what you have discovered, what unique and practical solutions can you create to over-solve these problems?

_____

_____

_____

_____

_____

_____

6. Take quick action! (If you don't, someone else will.)

EXERCISE II

Establishing Third-Level Service With a Product/Service Focus:

1. **What one product/service that you presently offer would create a tremendous desire if your customers began to use it?**

   _____

2. **What better way might your customers do business?**

   _____

   _____

3. **What product/service would revolutionize your industry?**

   _____

   _____

4. **What innovations in other industries would inspire you to produce similar products/services for your customers?**

   _____

   _____

   _____

5. **Based on what you have discovered, what unique products/ services could you create that would catch the interest of your customers?**

   _____

   _____

   _____

6. **Take quick action! (If you don't, someone else will.)** ■

Notes

5

The Smart Customer Survey

Dell Computer isn't the only company that is obsessive about customer surveys. Consider Deck House. For years, founder William J. Berkes groomed Michael Harris to take over as president of Deck House Inc., a home designer and builder in Acton, Mass. After working his way up the ladder for 18 years, Harris took the helm in 1989. His first presidential move was not exactly the gutsy directive one would expect from a newly minted president putting his stamp on a company, but it was a shrewd one. He conducted a customer survey. "You'll rue the day you did this!" Berkes warned. "You'll get so many outrageous customer demands you won't know what to do with them all." Harris stuck by his guns. The company hasn't been the same since.

Harris sat down with key managers and hashed out what kind of information they wanted to gather. The sales manager wanted to know how well salespeople followed up with customers. The marketing manager wanted more testimonials about how customers liked their houses once they were built. Designers wanted to find out which features customers liked and which they could do without.

The general tone running through the initial responses was that while the houses were wonderful, the designing-and-building process was a nightmare. "Common complaints were that there were too many choices, it took too long to plan the house, it wound up costing more than customers thought it would," Harris says. Many questionnaires came back loaded with tips on

To have a truly customer-driven company, you have to know what questions to ask and what to do with the answers. Here's how one CEO's customer survey transformed his company.

other, more specific problems Deck House needed to address: the product line was lacking, estimating costs was difficult, drawings were inaccurate, salespeople weren't around after the sale, builders were difficult to work with, windows were leaky, and making a warranty claim was a pain in the neck. "We didn't realize how far-reaching the implications of this questionnaire would be," Harris says. The customer feedback called Deck House's central strategy into question: "During the 1980s the mantra was 'The choice is yours!'" he recalls. "We felt that forcing standardized homes on customers was infringing on their freedom. But in reality, the variety of choices was overwhelming. Also, we were trying to sell '60s housing in the '80s. Those houses didn't possess the features our customers wanted, so we ended up doing a lot of custom work, which is costly and a hassle."

As a result, the Deck House staff designed a new line of standardized homes that met most customers' requirements without needing a lot of customization. The company also improved the quality of its service before, during, and after construction. Today only about 25% of Deck Houses are custom-built homes, compared with 75% a year ago, and the time it takes to process a piece of business has gone from 549 days to 370. "We are seeing an uptick in business even though the housing market is still flat," claims Harris, who reports that revenues have held steady at about $10 million annually. "We can now handle up to 250 homes per year with much lower overhead because we aren't reworking the designs."

5 ▽ GOOD FORMS

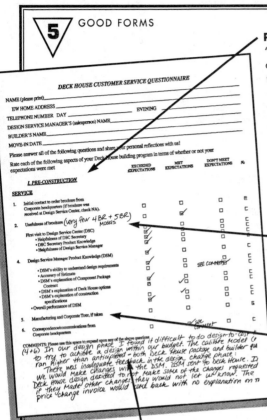

Preconstruction

"I found out a lot about my sales force from this section [satisfaction of preconstruction expectations]. It turns out they were around plenty during the preconstruction phase but were inattentive during construction, when customers can really feel lost. Now we withhold a percentage from salespeople's commissions until they make their final site visit. If they want that money, they have to send us a roll of film with pictures of the house on it. That gives our headquarters more feedback about the house and serves as proof that the salesperson actually visited."

Fine-Tuning the Product

"About a year ago we realized no one was ordering from the brochure, because we were trying to sell people '60s-style housing. Now we have a new line of homes that incorporate the most frequently requested custom features of the '90s. As a result, we've gotten back to our original focus — preplanned housing that anticipates and incorporates popular features and needs little or no customization."

Deal Closer

"We found out one of the things customers liked most was our manufacturing tour. So last year when we were conjuring up sales incentives, we designed one around it. If prospects build a Deck House after taking a tour, we'll give them roughly $1,500 off their house price to pay for plane fare and the time they took to visit. We put the tour on video for people who aren't able to come in person."

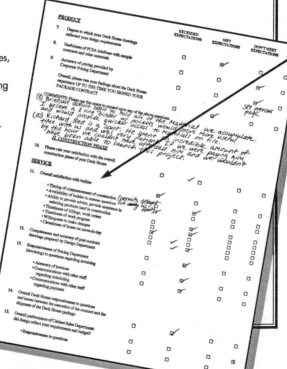

Eliminating Confusion

"Customers pick out their own plumbing and kitchen fixtures, and we build them in. This was a source of confusion for them. People would comment, 'I had no idea we were going to have to spend $5,000 for countertops; our salesperson said it would cost only $2,500.' Now, to make budgeting easier, we provide detailed sample cost estimates for bathrooms and kitchens. On a more basic level, others complained that the case of sample materials we sent them prior to beginning work on their house had been confusing. So we created a service handbook. It's inexpensive to produce — an 80-page photocopied book that answers most of the questions our customers kept asking and eliminates much of the confusion that made the process of building a Deck House difficult. We also found out we were not providing enough details on our invoices. The line items and totals were often a mystery to customers. Now we describe right on the invoice what the charges are for and what changes in the building process they might reflect."

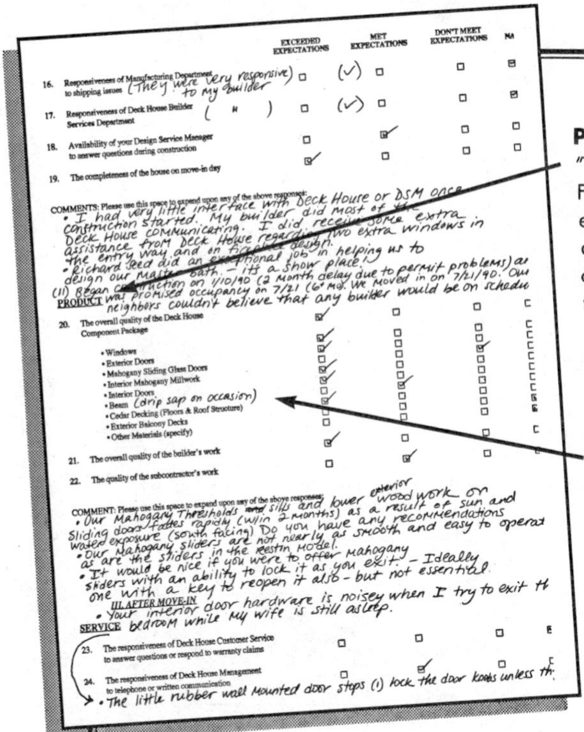

(top form, partial)

	EXCEEDED EXPECTATIONS	MET EXPECTATIONS	DON'T MEET EXPECTATIONS	NA
16. Responsiveness of Manufacturing Department to shipping issues *(They were very responsive to my builder)*	(✓)			☒
17. Responsiveness of Deck House Builder Services Department *(")*	(✓)			☐
18. Availability of your Design Service Manager to answer questions during construction	☑			☐
19. The completeness of the house on move-in day				

COMMENTS: Please use this space to expand upon any of the above responses: *I had very little interface with Deck House or DSM once construction started. My builder did most of the Deck House communicating. I did receive some extra assistance from Deck House regarding two extra windows in the entry way and an additional bath.*
• Richard Leed did an exceptional job in helping us to design our master bath — it's a show place!
(1) Began construction on 1/10/90 (2 month delay due to permit problems) and (11) Began was promised occupancy on 7/21 (6 wk we moved in on 7/21/90. Our neighbors couldn't believe that any builder would be on schedule

PRODUCT

20. The overall quality of the Deck House Component Package				
• Windows	☑			
• Exterior Doors	☑			
• Mahogany Sliding Glass Doors	☑			
• Interior Mahogany Millwork	☑			
• Interior Doors				☐
• Beam *(drip sap on occasion)*	☑			
• Cedar Decking (Floors & Roof Structure)	☑			
• Exterior Balcony Decks				☐
• Other Materials (specify)				
21. The overall quality of the builder's work	☑			
22. The quality of the subcontractor's work				

COMMENT: Please use this space to expand upon any of the above responses:
• Our Mahogany Thresholds and sills and lower exterior woodwork on sliding doors (within 2 months) as a result of sun and water exposure (south facing) Do you have any recommendations for mahogany sliders are not nearly as smooth and easy to operate as are the sliders in the Destin Model.
• It would be nice if you were to offer— Mahogany sliders with an ability to lock it as you exit — Ideally one with a key to reopen it also— but not essential

III AFTER MOVE-IN
• Your interior door hardware is noisey when I try to exit the bedroom while my wife is still asleep.

SERVICE

23. The responsiveness of Deck House Customer Service to answer questions or respond to warranty claims				E
24. The responsiveness of Deck House Management to telephone or written communication		☑		

• The little rubber wall mounted door stops (1) lock the door looks unless th...

Grading the Builder

"In this section [satisfaction with builder] the cleanliness of the house on moving day and the timeliness of billing and work orders have gotten the worst ratings. We now have a newsletter for builders, and we keep harping about how important it is to clean up the work site. We also include quotes from customers saying how nice it was to move into a clean house. To make billing easier, we now offer our builders standardized work orders. We have a list of 250 builders we recommend. About 60% of customers use a builder on our list. We've taken builders off our list because of feedback we've gotten from the questionnaire. The first time we get a really angry remark, we just make a note of it, but the second time it happens, we start to feel this person is really slipping. We don't wait for the third complaint."

Referrals

"Hardly anybody recommended prospects to us, so we'll drop this [section] in the next edition. However, we've found that when we ask for a referral from someone calling our Owner Assistance Center, we almost always get one. Our service manual has eliminated much of the confusion in the designing and building process that surfaced from this questionnaire, so our next edition will ask more questions about the handbook and about how customers like our new line of standard homes."

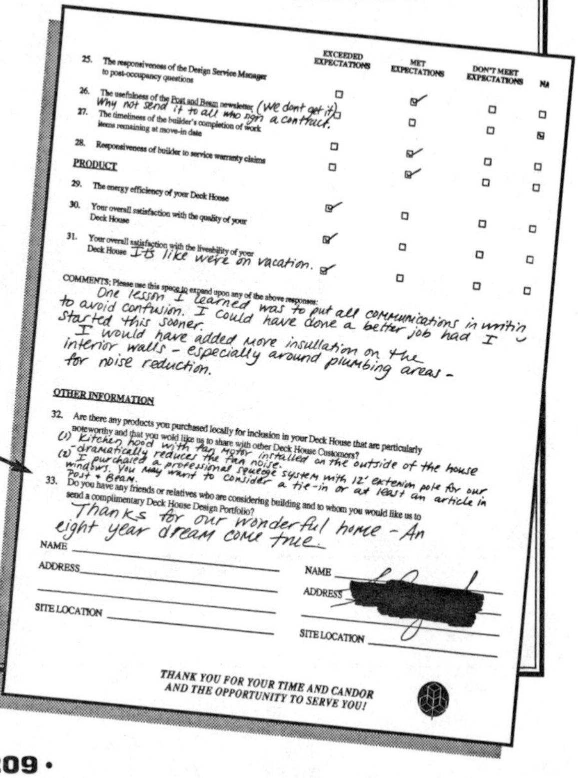

Product

"This is the heart and soul of Deck House [satisfaction with product]. Feedback from this section has alerted us to a number of weaknesses in our products we would have not known about otherwise, such as oceanfront homes having leaky windows on the sea side. This customer writes about how nice it would be to have a sliding door that you could lock but still leave open six inches or so. We now offer that type of door. Any comments made in this section I respond to in detail in a follow-up letter to the customer."

Warranty

"This questionnaire helped build our confidence in our product and prompted us to change our warranty process. The claims procedure had required too much information from the customers, and it was pretty frustrating for them. Now we make it easier, giving them a simpler claim form and asking them to take pictures of the problem so we know better how to fix it."

The Follow-Up Letter

"The letter I write to each person who sends in a questionnaire gives more detailed answers to their concerns about our product. This gives us one more point of contact with our customers and lets them know their comments and concerns are taken seriously. Also, anytime a customer mentions a specific employee by name, I make sure to get back to the employee about it. That's a great morale booster and gives recognition where it's due." ■

(lower form, partial)

	EXCEEDED EXPECTATIONS	MET EXPECTATIONS	DON'T MEET EXPECTATIONS	NA
25. The responsiveness of the Design Service Manager to post-occupancy questions				
26. The usefulness of the Post and Beam newsletter *(We don't get it. Why not send it to all who sign a contract.)*	☐	☑		
27. The timeliness of the builder's completion of work items remaining at move-in date	☐			☐
28. Responsiveness of builder to service warranty claims	☐	☑		
PRODUCT				
29. The energy efficiency of your Deck House	☐	☑		
30. Your overall satisfaction with the quality of your Deck House	☑	☐		
31. Your overall satisfaction with the livability of your Deck House *It's like we're on vacation.* ☑	☑	☐		☐

COMMENTS: Please use this space to expand upon any of the above responses:
One lesson I learned was to put all communications in writing to avoid confusion. I could have done a better job had I started this sooner. I would have added more insullation on the interior walls— especially around plumbing areas— for noise reduction.

OTHER INFORMATION

32. Are there any products you purchased locally for inclusion in your Deck House that are particularly noteworthy and that you wold like us to share with other Deck House Customers?
(1) Kitchen hood with fan motor installed on the outside of the house dramatically reduces the fan noise.
(2) I purchased a professional remote system with 12' extension pole for our windows. You may want to consider a tie-in or at least an article in Post + Beam.

33. Do you have any friends or relatives who are considering building and to whom you would like us to send a complimentary Deck House Design Portfolio?
Thanks for our wonderful home — An eight year dream come true.

NAME _____
ADDRESS _____
SITE LOCATION _____

NAME _____
ADDRESS _____
SITE LOCATION _____

THANK YOU FOR YOUR TIME AND CANDOR
AND THE OPPORTUNITY TO SERVE YOU!

Notes

Listening Your Way to Success

All too often, when just the opposite should happen, businesses patronize their customers. Too many business people make the fatal assumption that they know their business better than their customers do. Business people make the mistake of telling their customers what they need when they should be asking their customers what they want.

To patronize is to act superior. To serve connotes the opposite relationship. Tom Carns never made the mistake of acting superior to his customers, largely because he knew absolutely nothing about the printing industry before he went into the business. But this outsider's perspective proved to be a tremendous advantage. Carns had to listen to his customers. And what he heard surprised him.

Carns discovered that the printing industry was full of "craftsmen in ink-smudged smocks who are not business oriented." He reasoned that the upper end of the market, where professionalism and customer service are important, was wide open. So, in an industry that believed its product was a commodity, Carns began to sell service. By soliciting and being solicitous of professional clients such as physicians and lawyers, Carns won business from clients who expect to be treated as professionally as they treat their own clients. And business for Carns has exploded as a result.

It is Tom Carns's ability to ask questions and listen to his customers that is at the heart of the success of PDQ Printing, argues Joe Sperry (see p. 229). Sperry talks of in-depth account listening as the key to generating data that are strategic, reliable and valid, actionable, and finally, and most important, acted on.

Mike Wing (see p 238) contrasts Tom Carns' experience with that of the owners of a print shop in the Midwest. The difference between the shops, Wing points out, is that Carns asks customers how he's doing. And, once he has determined what customers want, he measures his firm's success in delivering that service. As Wing notes, "It is not the quality of service that you give, but the quality of service that the customer perceives that causes him to buy in the first place and then come back and buy again."

Consultant Harvy Simkovitz (see p. 245) argues that many companies understand the importance of creating a good impression — externally — to customers. But the reason Carns has enjoyed such pronounced success, says Simkovitz, is that he built the internal systems and supports that form the foundation for sustained, exceptional customer service.

Quick Study
Blitzes the Market

*When Tom Carns decided to go into the
quick-printing business in 1980, he had no experience
in the field. Yet today his PDQ Printing boasts sales
and margins that dwarf industry averages. Why?
Because Carns understands something his competitors
do not. Carns is not in the printing business. He's in
the customer-service business.*

In 1980, Tom Carns was a furniture retailer in Lynnwood, Wash.,
about 15 miles north of Seattle. As the recession began to bite, Carns realized that it was the wrong time to be selling furniture — which made it the
right time to find a new challenge. After all, he was in his early forties.
There might never be a better time to make a change.

When his wife, Carolyn, a native of San Diego, suggested they
move someplace where the sun might show its face for more than one
day at a time, Carns ventured to Hawaii. But Hawaii seemed less than
receptive to outsiders. He considered California, but California was just
too crowded. His wife then blurted out that she really wanted to move to
Las Vegas. Carns replied, "Nobody lives in Las Vegas." They moved on
April Fool's Day, 1980.

The move didn't exactly solve Carns's problem of what to do with
the rest of his life. After taking a couple of months off, he enrolled in a
six-week course to become a croupier. But then it dawned on him that

inhaling other people's cigarette smoke and venomous airs as their money ebbed in the direction of the casino's coffers wasn't exactly his idea of fun. On the day he was to report for his first shift of duty at a local casino, Carns simply didn't show up.

By then his mind was turning over another possibility. He knew a few people who ran quick-printing shops, those ubiquitous hole-in-the-wall places where photocopying equipment hums day and night, and the pungent smell of ink hangs in the air. The work was unexciting but steady. Carns, a man with a placid facade that conceals a churning interior, had developed high blood pressure up in Washington, and his doctor had warned him that if he wanted to keep on living, it might be a good idea to slow down. Carns thought that maybe starting a quick-printing business would be a good way to ease into the slow lane.

Carns Opens Pretty Damn Quick

In June 1981, with $25,000 in working capital, he opened PDQ Printing in a 1,100-square-foot space off a busy Las Vegas boulevard. After netting $82.56 that first month, he worried that maybe he should have taken a nearby 900-square-foot space instead. After all, he wasn't reinventing the wheel. There are some 40,000 quick-printing shops in the United States, and up to 25% of those are franchise operations. The average shop grosses $350,000, with net margins hovering around 8%.

Carns has done somewhat better. This year PDQ Printing will gross better than $6 million, or about 22 times the industry average. Although sales are not climbing 18% a year as they were in the late 1980s, PDQ continues to rack up consistently strong numbers. PDQ's net margin now approaches 20% — or 2.5 times the industry average.

It's no wonder that Carns was chosen Quick Printer of the Year in 1991 by the National Association of Quick Printers (the highest honor awarded in the industry and one you can win only once). Today, Carns is something of a guru to fellow quick printers looking to learn his secrets so they can turbocharge their businesses. Printers fly in for intensive two-day meetings, for which Carns charges $3,500. Printers come to Las Vegas, not just from around the country but from England, Scotland,

Australia, Canada, Bermuda, and elsewhere around the world, to see and hear how Carns serves customers.

How, exactly, did all this happen? How did Tom Carns, looking to put the brakes on his life, walk into a low-key, me-too kind of business he knew nothing about and build it into a smooth-running $6-million operation that now clears a cool $1 million a year?

Identifying the Market

Tom Carns owes part of his success to luck. When he arrived in Las Vegas it was just another mildly booming Sunbelt town. But in the decade of the 1980s, the growing popularity of gambling helped make Las Vegas the fastest-growing city in the country. Today, Las Vegas is a city of 880,000 people. Beyond good fortune converging with better demographics, PDQ owes its rise to the fact that Carns was an outsider who came to his new calling with a fresh perspective. He was a savvy businessman, walking into an industry dominated by craftsmen. That offered him insights many of his established competitors never had.

"The first business I owned was a used furniture business," says Carns. "I wore blue jeans and a kickaround shirt. I bought and sold used furniture. I sat on my duff." It was a fun business, especially the buying. Carns would tell friends he worked on a five "percent" markup: He would buy something for $5 and sell it for $25. He built up a very successful business, sold it, and bought a piece of a top-drawer furniture business.

"What I found fascinating was that these two businesses were located within a few blocks of each other," he says, "yet there was absolutely no crossover of customers. In the high-end business, I wore a suit and a tie and greeted customers differently than I had in the used furniture business. The ambience was entirely different."

When Carns began to look into business opportunities in Las Vegas, he went out and "shopped" every quick-printing shop in town — all 70 of them. He walked into each, looked around, and made copious mental notes "I watched how they treated their customers, what the business looked like, and how good the quality was," Carns recalls. And he liked what he saw "Most shops were dirty and disorganized.

> **HOT TIP**
>
> *Norman Melnick makes buyers his partners in business. As chairman of Pentech International, a $23-million manufacturer of inexpensive writing and drawing implements, in Edison, N.J., Melnick makes a point of sitting down with buyers to let them shape the final product. If they want pens in a 16-pack rather than an 8-pack, he's happy to accommodate them. If buyers feel the package takes up too much space on the shelf, he'll shrink it. As partners in the manufacturing and marketing process, Pentech's customers have a vested interest in the product's success.*

The people were sloppy dressers. They played loud rock music in the back of the shop. They were definitely lacking in customer service and commitment."

It was clear to Carns that every single quick printer in Las Vegas was selling used furniture. And that meant there was no competition in the high-end-furniture printing business. "With clean windows, employees in shirts, ties, and dresses, and a clean shop," he says. "I knew could prosper. The point is: I wasn't going into the commodity business. I was going into the customer business."

But fresh insight wouldn't be worth much without some attendant energy, which Carns indubitably has. At 57, he is a thoughtful, persistent, and quietly driven man. "Tom's a very dynamic, aggressive marketer. He watches trends, and he tries new things," says Buzz Warren, owner of Buzz Print, in Overland Park, Kan.

"Tom has this energy level that always keeps him going forward. He knows how to get to the people who will help him get things done," adds Patrick Leamy, a friend of Carns's who heads Econo Print, in Madison, Wis. More to the point, Carns is thorough. He leaves few stones unturned. When he set about getting into the quick-printing business, he immediately immersed himself in the industry to learn its nuances. To become a successful quick printer, Carns knew he had to be a quick study.

"This industry is dominated by craftsmen in ink-smudged smocks who are not business oriented," says Carns, adding, "if there's one thing I know how to do, it's read a financial statement. There was definitely room for a sharp, aggressive businessperson."

Zeroing in on the Professions

Reasoning that the upper end of the market, where professionalism and customer service were important, was wide open, Carns zeroed in on the professional-services market: medical offices, accounting firms, brokerages, and the like His thinking went as follows: Customers' needs vary widely. Many customers, seeing printing as a small part of their operations — yet reliant on good printing to keep things running — put great stock in a printer's expertise and professionalism. For that they will pay a premium. Small and midsize white-collar service companies best fit this profile.

But why not larger companies?

Larger companies, Carns figured, work in larger volumes — and think accordingly. "They don't want the printer to make much money," says Carns. They also might often have an employee whose principal duty is to buy printing services. Smaller companies could not afford such a specialist and thus would be reliant on the printer. Moreover, in white-collar service companies, printing, done right and on time, is more critical to the overall health of the operation than it is in other types of businesses.

Today white-collar professional operations such as doctors' and CPAs' offices, real estate and stock brokerages, and law offices constitute the core of PDQ's customer base. They account for about 75% of annual revenues, with the typical account doing about $1,000 worth of business per month.

The medical market is a case in point of how Carns's strategy to provide a custom-manufactured product, rather than a commodity, has paid off. Health-care providers routinely drown in paperwork, which they must complete expeditiously to stay in business and survive. As Carns studied that market, he noticed something interesting. Vendors sold complete "packages" to medical practitioners. Those included not only printed matter but software and related services to keep an office running. But then the vendors would disappear, and soon afterward, the printed forms would run out. Carns realized that certain oft-used forms relating to billing and insurance were critical. PDQ came in and offered to print specialized replacement forms on a timely basis. That filled a pressing need and gave PDQ an immediate toehold in the market. It also provided PDQ with a window on the medical market, so the printer could then appraise what other needs it could fill. Moreover, since workers in the health-care field tend to stay within the industry when they change jobs, PDQ started getting a lot of referral business. Today 20% of PDQ's sales are to medical practitioners. Carns estimates PDQ has as much as 50% of the Las Vegas medical market.

Gathering Grass-Roots Intelligence

More recently, PDQ has also made serious inroads into the legal market by filling a simple and very specific need — the timely photocopying of documents for litigation work. Like PDQ's entry into the medical market, that was the product of grass-roots research.

One day Carns spotted an empty 825-square-foot space in what appeared to be a strategic location — the ground floor of a prestigious building in downtown Las Vegas. Maybe PDQ could set up shop there? From talking with contacts in the legal field, Carns knew the building was home to four of the five top litigation law firms in the city. He knew litigation required a great deal of photocopying work to be done on short notice and to precise standards, or else the court wouldn't allow it to be filed. Thus, quality, timeliness, and confidentiality were paramount. Price was not.

Who Controls the Copy Flow?

Now Carns, who had been looking for an opening in the legal market, got interested. He wondered who, exactly, controlled the flow of copy in a law office. The answer, he discovered, was paralegals. He also discovered that paralegals in Las Vegas had their own professional organization. He contacted the head of the organization and invited her out to lunch. He told her he wanted to meet with her for perhaps two hours twice a month, for two to three months, to learn as much as he could about the market. He was willing to pay $500 for each consultation.

By the time those meetings were done, Carns knew plenty about the legal profession and its printing needs. He devised a brochure whose cover was stamped with the word "confidential" in bright red letters, since that issue, he learned, was of paramount importance to lawyers. He attached a copy of a document that all PDQ employees were required to sign when they began working for the company, agreeing, under threat of dismissal, that they would keep confidential all documents they handled. He then had his lawyer draft a one-page document holding PDQ itself liable for any breach of confidentiality. Last, he made it known that PDQ's facility would have a shredder, ready to devour any flawed or mangled copies.

> **HOT TIP**
>
> *Hugh Vestal, co-owner of Carbide Surface Co., a small machine-tool business, reorganized the company with one thought in mind. He wanted to let customers deal directly with the people who do the work. Now, when a customer needs a tool coated with carbide, he talks with one of five "impregnators" who actually do the coating. The impregnators schedule the job, arrange for delivery of the part, perform the work, and submit a job-cost form to Vestal. Customers like working directly with shopworkers. Shopworkers like the system because it challenges them and breaks monotony. Salespeople like the system because it frees them to focus on new business.*

Carns then saw to it that one of those packets landed on the desk of every paralegal and every partner in every law firm in downtown Las Vegas, days before PDQ opened its legal-services division. Meanwhile, Carns discovered that paralegals in Las Vegas had a monthly newsletter. He offered to redesign the newsletter and print it for free every month, in exchange for an exclusive ad in its pages. In early January 1991, the PDQ blitz hit in the form of the redesigned newsletter and the PDQ brochure, reinforced with the offerings of a local baker Carns had lined up. Every day for four weeks, boxes of doughnuts — compliments of PDQ — were delivered to the city's largest litigation firms, which Carns had dubbed PDQ's "10 most wanted." (Those firms account for about 70% of the litigation work done in Las Vegas.) By month's end PDQ had landed all 10 accounts.

In its first full month of operation, February 1991, PDQ's legal-services "division," operating three photocopying machines out of an 825-square-foot space, grossed more than $64,000. For all of 1991, it generated $600,000 in revenues, or more than twice the volume of the average quick-printing business in the United States.

Getting the Message Out

Back in the 1960s, after graduating from college, Tom Carns got a job selling advertising for the *Los Angeles Times*. That experience convinced him of the value of advertising and, even more important, the worth of advertising consistently.

Within a month of PDQ's inception, Carns was advertising in local media — something he has done with unfailing regularity to this day. He employs a broad media mix, using local broadcast and print as well as a healthy dose of direct mail and television advertising. PDQ's ads stress image, not price. Last year PDQ's ad budget was 4.5% of sales.

Advertising consistently and aggressively, Carns believes, tells the world you exist — a critical element in the crowded quick-printing business, where customers are accustomed to searching out copy shops as the need arises, and customer loyalty is far from a given. Carns knew PDQ couldn't just open its doors and expect people to show up — which is precisely the premise that most quick-copy shops operate on. Those shops do little advertising, and they certainly have no outside sales force.

Having an outside sales force in the quick-printing business is almost unheard-of. PDQ, however, has had one since its first month of operation, and today it numbers seven people. In 1990, Carns hired his brother, Rick, who used to own a print shop, to be PDQ's sales manager. Unlike most sales managers, Rick Carns spends little of his time behind his desk. Most of the time he is in the field with PDQ's sales force, calling on customers.

"Most quick printers are not successful at outside sales because they don't understand what sales takes," Tom Carns claims. "Even if they get around to hiring outside salespeople, they usually don't tell them much more than, 'Go out and sell some printing.' "

Nothing Happens Until the Eighth Call

Carns argues that successfully selling something as basic as printing requires as much product knowledge, initiative, and persistence as selling supercomputers. On his desk he has a small sign that reads, "Nothing happens until after the eighth call." Carns explains that bit of wisdom this way: Most salespeople stop calling after three calls. Most buyers will not buy until the sixth call. If you make at least eight calls, then you have outperformed the competition, and it's likely you've softened up the most reluctant of prospects. Equally important, and less understood, notes Carns, is this: "If you make eight calls on a prospect, then it will take someone else at least that many calls to get that prospect away from you." One of PDQ's major clients required 24 sales calls before signing up with the printer, but Carns knew the account was worth the effort. Today that client does $70,000 worth of business each year with PDQ.

The doggedness of the sales force at PDQ mirrors Carns's methodical persistence. When making a cold call (always in person), a PDQ salesperson simply introduces himself or herself to the receptionist (the gatekeeper) and asks for the name of the person in the company who buys printing (the prospect). Upon returning to PDQ that afternoon, the sales rep leaves the names off in the print shop. The next morning at six o'clock, PDQ's pressmen arrive for work and print up "from the desk of" sheets bearing the gatekeeper's and the prospect's names. The bindery workers arrive by seven, when they glue the sheets into notepads and shrink-wrap two sets of three, along with the salesperson's card. By 9 a.m., when the salespeople leave to make calls, they pick up the personalized note-pads and drop them off at the prospective client's company that morning.

The salesperson then follows up with a phone call two or three days later to ask if the prospect received the notepads. Then the rep asks if he or she can come in and talk, some days hence, not to sell anything but to determine the prospect's needs. A few days later the salesperson returns with a written proposal detailing how PDQ might be able to help. If the prospect demurs, then the PDQ salesperson simply asks, "May I be backup printer on your next job?" Notes Carns, "No one has ever said no to that."

By now PDQ has developed a mailing list of 10,000 names, including virtually every good prospect in the city, to which it tries to send PDQ's monthly internal newsletter. Periodically, PDQ has a month-long 2¢-per-photocopy sale for volume users so it can identify large copy users and then follow up with sales calls. As a result of these sales, PDQ has picked up dozens of sizable accounts.

Extending Service Beyond the Counter

Every PDQ employee who does not come into daily contact with customers must go out with a salesperson one day per quarter. "It's important that customer service extend beyond the counter," says Carns. So employees in the bindery, pre-press, press room, even accounts receivable, head out on the road four times a year. "Now, when billing calls a customer, that customer is not just a name, phone number, and a balance, but a real person." Once a year each salesperson visits half a dozen competitors' operations to discern what they might be up to.

Each week salespeople write thank-you notes to customers who have recently placed orders Carns himself used to do that, until the business grew too big.

Carns is convinced that what gets measured gets done. "When you stop measuring things," he says, "employees get the sense that those things are not important, and they stop doing them." Carns believes it's important to send handwritten thank-you notes out to customers, so he set up a system to measure that practice. In each store, there are boxes labeled 1 to 31. Each customer service employee is expected to write six thank-you notes every day. Employees insert their handwritten notes into envelopes which they then address, putting their initials where the stamp will go. At day's end, the store manager records how many notes have been written by each employee, puts a stamp on each envelope, and mails them out. Each month, the store managers hand Carns their record sheets.

Networking at Trade Shows Pays Off

Two months after starting his company, Tom Carns went to his first industry trade show. The National Association of Quick Printers (NAQP) has two meetings a year. One is its annual convention and trade show. The other is a midwinter series of seminars. Carns hasn't missed any of those semiannual meetings since he started his company.

Carns, a past president of the NAQP, finds such sessions ripe for intelligence-gathering because they're intensive and filled with people from noncompeting markets. "You talk with people at breakfast or the cocktail hour. It's a great way to learn a lot. On top of that, for obvious competitive reasons, if you talk to printers from Cincinnati, they're going to tell you a lot more about their business than printers from Las Vegas would."

At the 1982 convention Carns saw a manufacturer's thermographic printing press that produced raised letters on the printed page. He was pretty sure no one else in Las Vegas had such a press. He bought one. "We automatically did every letterhead and business card that way at no additional charge," says Carns. "That was the first thing that really differentiated us from the local competition." In 1983 PDQ's sales rose by 73%, largely because of the acquisition of that one piece of technology.

Over the years at industry conventions, Carns has gotten to know a handful of like-minded, fast-track quick printers. In 1990, Carns and seven other large, successful quick printers formed the TIP (Top Instant Printers) group, which convenes quarterly at different members' businesses to exchange ideas. A year later, the group began conducting intensive semi-annual top-to-bottom audits of each member's company on a rotating basis, to gauge how well the individual business was being run. Carns says the TIP group has been a great boon to his business, for obvious reasons. "Say we hired a Big Six accounting firm to look at our company, but it doesn't really know the industry. The help and knowledge I get from seven of my peers really can't be matched by someone coming in from outside the industry."

After the first audit, of Patrick Leamy's quick-printing business in Madison, Wis., Carns realized that finding and keeping good people was a concern in an industry with historically high turnover (45% to 50% is not uncommon), and it was an issue he hadn't really addressed. He hired a full-time director of training with a degree in human resources and beefed up PDQ's training program so it lasted a month and included a number of quizzes. "It really hit me over the head back in Wisconsin that no one's goal in life is to enter the quick-printing business, and there are fewer and fewer quality people to select from. So if we spent the money up front to hire the right people and train them well, then maybe we'd end up cutting turnover." It seems to have worked. Carns estimates that PDQ's annual turnover is only 12% or so.

Meanwhile, Leamy was so petrified by the prospect of his peers picking his business apart that he started looking at his operation two months before his fellow TIP members arrived for the audit. "I was able to cut $90,000 off our yearly overtime bill," he says.

Customer Service: Do It Their Way

Sitting in his office one day, Tom Carns leans forward on the couch, and with disbelief rising in his voice, says: "I went to a meeting a few years ago and one of the speakers said that 60% of all the printing that is done in America is either screwed up or late. What an indictment of an industry! There's a printer in Las Vegas with a sign that says, 'This is not Burger

King. Here you get it my way, or you don't get the sonofabitch at all.' Can you imagine?"

PDQ does everything it can to see that customers get it their way. Customer service is the foundation, the very fiber of Tom Carns's business. "We make sure that our commitments are kept," he says. "Customers don't have to call us. If we say a job will be ready by 4 p.m. Friday, it will be ready."

When customers come into one of Carns's shops, they are handed a claim check that lets them know the date and time the order will be ready. The customer service employee (all customer service employees wear name tags) writes his or her name on the order and tells the customer to "call me if there's any problem." Claim checks are color-coded to stores (customers often show up at the wrong store to pick up an order).

In a room at PDQ, a row of loose-leaf binders sits atop a set of filing cabinets. Those binders contain a copy of every form PDQ has printed for every one of its commercial accounts. Each form is numbered and indexed on a master list. The customer gets an identical book and a master list, so when running low on a certain form, he or she can simply call up PDQ and ask for a refill by job number. Conversely, PDQ keeps track of the quantities ordered and the dates they're requested; that way, if there is an abnormal interval between orders, PDQ can call customers and ask if perhaps they're running low on a certain form.

PDQ also assumes responsibility for proofreading customers' jobs before they go to press — virtually unheard-of in the industry. "Other quick printers make customers come back and proof jobs," says Carns. "Look, you don't go to a restaurant and have the waiter come out and say, 'The chef is ready to put your steak on. Do you want to come into the kitchen and see if it's being done right?' " Besides, he adds, "customers are terrible proofreaders to begin with."

Carns says that PDQ has always striven "to operate on the same level with our customers. That means not having them step down to deal with us." Assuming responsibility for such key tasks as proofreading, typesetting, and design affirms that sense of equality. Running a business where employees dress neatly and no radios blare from the back of the shop reinforces it.

> **HOT TIP**

Douglas A. Phillips, a bankruptcy expert with the accounting firm of Weber, Lipshie & Co., in New York City, advises paying attention to the warning signs in customer or vendor relations. Beyond such obvious red flags as the departure of key employees or inexplicable delays in shipments, Phillips warns of such dangers as:

• frequent changes in accountants or lawyers;
• unexpected sales of assets;
• a shift in financing, say, from a bank line of credit to factoring of receivables.

The best way to determine the health of a supplier or customer, notes Phillips, is to examine its latest financial statements, as certified by an accountant. And think twice about doing business with a firm that gives you inadequate financial information.

PDQ is nothing if not solicitous of its customers. With every job, it sends the customer a survey dubbed "Two Sides to Every Story." "In it," says Carns, "we tell our customers that we try to do things right and on time. The form has a blank side, with prepaid postage on it. We ask customers to give us their side of the story."

Every December PDQ also does its "defense defense" sales calls. "We go out in person to our 150 largest customers, thank them for their business, and ask how we can improve things," says Carns. "We ask them one other key question: 'What kind of printing are you buying elsewhere that you're not getting from us?'" A few years ago Carns found that "continuous forms" was cropping up frequently as the answer to that question. "So we bought a short-run continuous-form press in December 1989." Today PDQ sells continuous forms to 25% of its commercial accounts.

"Most print shops are in the printing business," says Carns. "Quite frankly, I don't give a hang about the printing business. It's just not a big deal. I could be in the tire business. The truth is, I'm in the customer focus, customer service business. Printing is simply the product I sell."

The difference between being in the printing business and being in the customer service business is dramatic. The average quick printer does about $350,000 in sales each year. "We do that by the 20th of each month," says Carns.

A New Paradigm

Tom Carns knows he couldn't have picked a better time and place to start a quick-printing business. Yet what is truly odd is that he seems to have spawned so few imitators. Carns believes not only that he caught local competitors flat-footed but that the quick-printing industry remains ripe for professionalization. "I think in the years ahead you'll see more people with M.B.A.s getting into this industry because the level of competition is so low," says Carns. "It remains an industry of mom-and-pop outfits, yet with the electronics and computers now available, it's potentially very dynamic."

As evidence, he points to the 120 quick printers with whom he has formally consulted — many of them highly successful. How many of those had ever written a business plan? One. Writing a business plan was one of the first things Carns did before starting PDQ.

Tom Carns could probably take PDQ on the road and set up shops in other cities, but he has no plans to expand beyond the Las Vegas city limits. He would rather strengthen his position by opening new stores (one per year starting in 1995) in Las Vegas.

While Carns makes it look easy, it is not. "You have to be a visionary to succeed in business," he says. "You have to develop the kind of vision you want for your company. Then you have to find people who buy into that vision. They have to understand what you're trying to do, accept it, and own a part of it. It takes a zealot to make a business successful."

And Carns is a customer-service zealot. ■

Measuring
Satisfaction

by Joseph P. Sperry

Tom Carns is a great leader driving a great company. PDQ is already doing most of the account-focused activities we suggest that our clients perform. What are PDQ's critical success factors? They relate to developing or improving customer listening and feedback systems.

Business-to-business accounts satisfaction measurement is a way to improve account loyalty, which in turn leads to increased profitability. Tom Carns has clearly made this connection — that all cash flow starts in the customer's pocket. He is primarily successful because he used disciplined, in-depth account listening to generate data that are:

- strategic
- reliable and valid
- actionable
- acted on.

Strategic Data

Tom Carns explored the quick print business. Searching for strategic information, he canvassed every competitor in his market area. Carns's thoroughness, as well as his disciplined business observation, allowed him not only to explore the business but to redefine it. He ended up seeing that printing was not the product — that printing was, rather, a solution to some other problem. Carns concluded that what customers really wanted was a kind of "custom manufacturing." This significant difference in approach allowed him to position his offering against the other suppliers in the marketplace.

Joseph P. Sperry is a principal with Shaffer Sherman Sperry & Swaddling Inc., in Westerville, Ohio.

ACTION POINT: Differentiation — and sustainable competitive advantage — happens when business people redefine their offering. Assume that what you sell is not your real product. Work to redefine your product by speaking to your key customers. Ask them what they expect, where you are exceeding their expectations and where you are not. The payoff: a new focus on your business that can help your positioning and your profitability.

Actionable Data

Actionable data are data which allow the supplier to prioritize action steps. Carns started with his newly defined service (custom manufacturing) and asked which customers should be targeted. Instead of following the market and trying to offer universal service, which would mean serving demanding and unprofitable customers, Carns focused on the small to midsize professional services market.

Why? Two critical reasons: Such firms tended to lack in-house dedicated staff, and they were willing to pay a premium if the service was done well. The inescapable conclusion is that marketing in the 1990s is "niche or be niched." Careful targeting or unlimited capital are requisites for small business survival. Carns focused on a segment that, if offered higher value, would generate correspondingly higher margins. And he was blessed with an industry service quality baseline that gave him a chance to really shine. His listening allowed him to act.

ACTION POINT: There is no such thing as a business without unprofitable customers. Work with your financial people to determine which of your segments is most profitable and least profitable. Don't forget those indirect support costs (set-up/servicing/logistics), as they are the ones that often make the difference and seldom show up on balance sheets.

Valid and Reliable Data

The next challenge for Carns was to gather valid and reliable data on how his target accounts defined the added value he needed to offer. Validity involves asking the right questions for the market, and reliability is a matter of consistently measuring those right things. The big question: How to determine those right things? How do you ask your customers the right questions in satisfaction measurement?

The answer: Let customers tell you what is important to them, and then design your listening system around that feedback. The best satisfaction research starts by examining critical interactions by the customer's definition and then isolating the customer's expectations within these interactions. Without such expectations, the provider may try to develop or improve the wrong service delivery systems, or the researcher may ask the wrong satisfaction questions.

Make a visual map of those critical interactions. Most organizations have complicated structural charts, showing organizational levels and who reports to whom. Companies need these charts much less than they need a map of their organization as their critical customers experience it. Such a map can be developed internally, but it has to be validated by the critical customers if it is going to generate valid and reliable conclusions. For an example of such a map, see the "Moments-of-Truth Wheel" (p. 232) for a printing company (not a quick print) that lists the critical interactions.

Carns's conclusions were particularly valid because he realized, as too many business-to-business marketing firms do not, that his account relationships were many-headed and that each of the critical account contacts had differing expectations. In the professional services market, for example, that meant developing a relationship with paralegals.

ACTION POINT: Fill in the blank Moments-of-Truth Wheel (see p. 233) with your critical customer segment. After you have determined the critical interactions:

1. Prioritize them from the accounts' standpoint.
   Identify the top ten.
2. Determine what account contacts expect within each interaction.
3. Compare those expectations with what you are actually delivering.
   Do the interactions have customer-focused standards? Are those who perform the interactions effectively trained and ready to perform to the accounts' requirements? Are there any internal barriers to that interaction's being successfully performed?

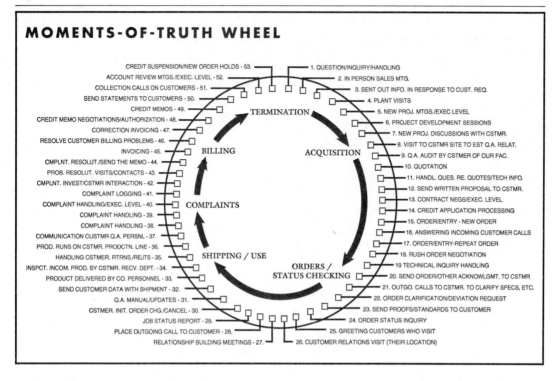

MOMENTS-OF-TRUTH WHEEL

CREDIT SUSPENSION/NEW ORDER HOLDS - 53.
ACCOUNT REVIEW MTGS./EXEC. LEVEL - 52.
COLLECTION CALLS ON CUSTOMERS - 51.
SEND STATEMENTS TO CUSTOMERS - 50.
CREDIT MEMOS - 49.
CREDIT MEMO NEGOTIATIONS/AUTHORIZATION - 48.
CORRECTION INVOICING - 47.
RESOLVE CUSTOMER BILLING PROBLEMS - 46.
INVOICING - 45.
CMPLNT. RESOLUT./SEND THE MEMO - 44.
PROB. RESOLUT. VISITS/CONTACTS - 43.
CMPLNT. INVEST/CSTMR INTERACTION - 42.
COMPLAINT LOGGING - 41.
COMPLAINT HANDLING/EXEC. LEVEL - 40.
COMPLAINT HANDLING - 39.
COMPLAINT HANDLING - 38.
COMMUNICATION CUSTMR Q.A. PERSNL - 37.
PROD. RUNS ON CSTMR. PRODCTN. LINE - 36.
HANDLING CSTMR. RTRNS./REJTS - 35.
INSPCT. INCOM. PROD. BY CSTMR. RECV. DEPT. - 34.
PRODUCT DELIVERED BY CO. PERSONNEL - 33.
SEND CUSTOMER DATA WITH SHIPMENT - 32.
Q.A. MANUAL/UPDATES - 31.
CSTMER. INIT. ORDER CHG./CANCEL - 30.
JOB STATUS REPORT - 29.
PLACE OUTGOING CALL TO CUSTOMER - 28.
RELATIONSHIP BUILDING MEETINGS - 27.

TERMINATION
BILLING
COMPLAINTS
SHIPPING / USE
ACQUISITION
ORDERS / STATUS CHECKING

1. QUESTION/INQUIRY/HANDLING
2. IN PERSON SALES MTG.
3. SENT OUT INFO. IN RESPONSE TO CUST. REQ.
4. PLANT VISITS
5. NEW PROJ. MTGS./EXEC LEVEL
6. PROJECT DEVELOPMENT SESSIONS
7. NEW PROJ. DISCUSSIONS WITH CSTMR.
8. VISIT TO CSTMR SITE TO EST Q.A. RELAT.
9. Q.A. AUDIT BY CSTMER OF OUR FAC.
10. QUOTATION
11. HANDL. QUES. RE. QUOTES/TECH INFO.
12. SEND WRITTEN PROPOSAL TO CSTMR.
13. CONTRACT NEGS/EXEC. LEVEL
14. CREDIT APPLICATION PROCESSING
15. ORDER/ENTRY - NEW ORDER
16. ANSWERING INCOMING CUSTOMER CALLS
17. ORDER/ENTRY-REPEAT ORDER
18. RUSH ORDER NEGOTIATION
19. TECHNICAL INQUIRY HANDLING
20. SEND ORDER/OTHER ACKNOWLGMT. TO CSTMR
21. OUTGO. CALLS TO CSTMR. TO CLARIFY SPECS, ETC.
22. ORDER CLARIFICATION/DEVIATION REQUEST
23. SEND PROOFS/STANDARDS TO CUSTOMER
24. ORDER STATUS INQUIRY
25. GREETING CUSTOMERS WHO VISIT
26. CUSTOMER RELATIONS VISIT (THEIR LOCATION)

Acted On

When customer listening and feedback systems have been put in place, they create an additional expectation that something will be done with the data gathered. If nothing is done, a supplier can weaken a relationship it was hoping to strengthen.

No such problem for Tom Carns, though. Once he determined that the critical expectations of small to medium professional firms included quality, timeliness, and confidentiality, he set up systems to provide them. He did not define these allocated resources as costs because he had determined that price was not critical to these customers. He correctly defined the allocation as a differentiating investment. In other words, he started to act on the data generated by his disciplined listening.

At this point, Carns came to the conclusion, which our research also supports, that product quality will get you onto the playing field, that service quality will score you a field goal or two, but that relationship quality will win you the game and ensure the continued operation of your franchise.

YOUR MOMENTS-OF-TRUTH WHEEL

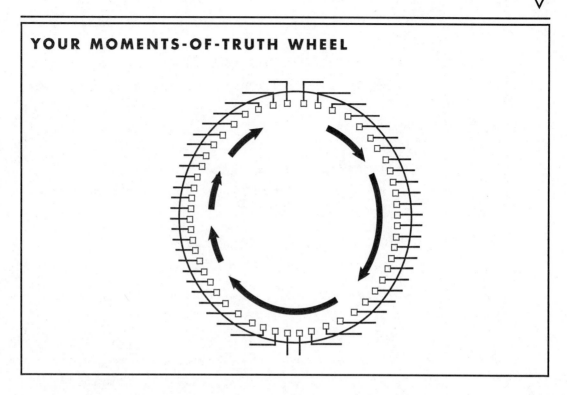

The same disciplined listening which allowed him to redefine his market now allowed him to redefine his customer relationships. For the legal market, paralegals are the critical account contacts, and so he focused his marketing efforts on them.

ACTION POINT: If you are serving business-to-business accounts, rather than retail customers, have you mapped out your account relationships? Our research has uncovered five roles you might want to explore:

- User
- Decision Maker
- Buyer
- Influencer
- Gatekeeper

Have whoever is managing your account relationships map out the relationship so all your critical account contacts know who plays each role. If you only have a relationship with one of these contacts, what happens if that person leaves/is promoted/gets angry with you? Identify the "paralegals" in your market relationships.

From the standpoint of customer listening and feedback systems, we believe the kinds of data Carns generated — strategic, actionable, valid, and acted on — were critical to his success. Here are three suggestions for developing and/or improving your own listening and feedback systems.

Three Suggestions for Improving Customer Listening

What is especially heartening about Carns's approach is that he has never stopped asking the questions:

1) What are my critical customers' expectations?
2) How can I continue to exceed those expectations?

He knows what we have seen again and again: Customers' expectations will continue to rise. This means the supplier needs to be aggressively searching for ways to add value now and in the future. If the supplier stops asking these questions, they will stop being answered, or some other supplier will do a better job answering them. When you rest on your laurels, you get your laurels shot off. There are three ways that Carns — or any fast-moving operation like his — can continue to grow.

1. Improve the After-Job Survey

The author describes PDQ's "Two Sides to Every Story" survey, which is included with every completed job. Asking customers to describe their needs and their sense of the process of working with PDQ is a good beginning. The difficulty with open-ended questions is that they tend to:

1) get low responses, as business people tend not to like to write (who looks back fondly on their essay examinations?);
2) highlight the very poor writing skills of the average American adult (it's hard to determine in many cases what the problem is);
3) generate qualitative data, useful for isolating expectations and needs but not good for prioritizing improvement action steps.

Carns should continue to ask his open-ended question, but along with it he might ask some focused and quantitative ones, which would allow him to generate account-prioritized improvement areas. If Carns has a good grasp on the expectations of his target segments, he could include 10 to 12 quantitative questions that get at the drivers of account satisfaction.

Let the questions be driven by the critical account contacts' critical expectations within the critical interactions. Then, consider this sort of survey response scale:

A Scale for Generating Actionable Data on Customer Surveys

DIRECTIONS

1. *In the box on the left, indicate the number on the scale that represents how important you feel each characteristic is.*

2. *In the boxes on the right, indicate the numbers that represent the level of performance that you expect from XYZ Department and the current level of performance delivered by XYZ Department.*

3. *Use the Don't Know/Not Applicable response where appropriate.*

0	1	2	3	4	5	6	7
DON'T KNOW/NOT APPLICABLE	VERY LOW	LOW		AVERAGE	HIGH		VERY HIGH

EXAMPLE:

Importance	To what extent does Firm X:	Level of Performance Delivered	Level of Performance Expected
6	1. Hit its promised delivery dates?	2	6

It is of high importance to this person that Firm X hits its promised delivery date (Importance = 6). Firm X's performance delivered in meeting this person's service needs is low (Delivered = 2). This person expects a high level of performance from Firm X in meeting his/her service needs (Expected = 6). The responses are computed by measuring the gap between performance and expectation (in this case 4) and then multiplying it by the importance (6) for an overall gap (24).

Send out your survey to a number of key contacts, perform this computation, and then start averaging your responses. What would your highest average gap be? It's the largest gap between expectation and performance x the greatest importance. Another way of looking at it, though, would be that your highest average response on a given question would be what you are doing worst, and that is most important to your targeted segment. The scale would thus give you account-prioritized action areas.

2. Improve and Leverage Expectation Research: Video Focus Groups

Carns has again leaped ahead of his competitors by realizing that, along with account relationships, his employee relationships are PDQ's critical assets. He wants to keep those assets appreciating and so is concentrating on human resources. There are some ways he can continue to get systematic customer expectation data and improve both training and performance. One particularly effective approach is video focus groups.

Most people know the focus-group technique, where customers are brought together and asked their opinion by a professional facilitator. In initial business-to-business satisfaction focus groups, we usually ask key account contacts a number of pointed questions about their expectations and how well the supplier is meeting them. You will get wonderful data, as Carns did.

The difference is that this focus group is videotaped, which means that there will be an edited record of customer responses whose uses are limited only by the firm's creativity. Such tapes can be used to:

1) tighten and align the questions on satisfaction surveys;
2) bring the "voice of the customer" directly into internal training programs;
3) help determine which internal delivery systems are out of alignment with customer expectations;
4) develop quicker employee buy-in for any process or system improvement effort.

Video focus groups are among the most powerful ways to create a sense of urgency about service quality. Employees tend to listen to customers more than they listen to their own supervisors. At the same time, video focus groups are a powerful way to capture targeted customer expectations systematically. There's no better way to leverage a research investment.

3. Use Satisfaction Surveys

After systematically gathering targeted expectation data, Carns should consider using this information to design a quantitative survey. Here are some guidelines for that survey:

1) Obtain inside agreement as to the purpose of the survey. Too many have eight purposes, none of which is served very well by a short survey. Firms need to ask all critical stakeholders: How do you think we should use the satisfaction data? Then consensus should be reached before the survey is designed.

2) Keep the survey fairly short. The response rate drops significantly when a survey starts to take more than 10 to 15 minutes to complete. At 10 or 15 minutes, though, you can achieve an average response of 65% to 75%.

3) Send the survey to more than one contact within the account. If this is not done, you run the risk of getting high levels of satisfaction and then having the relationship ended by a dissatisfied and unsurveyed account contact.

4) All responses need to be confidential. The rule of research is that unless confidentiality is guaranteed, you are probably not going to get the whole truth

5) Use the scale we suggested above to generate actionable data: account-prioritized improvement areas. A comparison of performance data with expectations provides comparison of the most robust improvement data. ■

6

How Do You Know
How You're Really Doing
Unless You Ask?

by Mike Wing

When you read about a company like PDQ Printing, it all looks so obvious and easy. In fact, what Tom Carns has accomplished is both obvious and easy. Carns asks his customers what they want and how they want it delivered, and he does exactly what they tell him to do. Carns has the golden touch. Or, perhaps we should say he has the golden ear.

It should be easy to listen to your customers and deliver the product they want the way they want it delivered. What's hard is keeping your ear to the ground. It's a constant process. You're not finished this week or this month. You must constantly monitor your customers. You must look for new ways to surprise them. Their wants and needs change, and you must be ready to change with them.

Often the difference between runaway success and dispiriting failure is not the effort that is put into a business, but the direction of that effort. Let's look at another entrepreneur, also in the printing business. In this case we're talking about Steve and Susan, owners of a print shop in a suburb of a large Midwestern city. Steve had had a successful career as a mid-level executive. Desiring a change and looking for something he and Susan could do together now that the kids were gone, Steve decided to buy a small printing/copying company.

Over a three-year period, Steve and Susan had poured a substantial amount of their accumulated capital into the business as well as a considerable amount of their time. Working 14- to 16-hour days, six days a

*Michael Wing is
president and
CEO of InfoPlan
International Inc.,
a Houston market
research firm.*

week, was not unusual. However, after an initial upward trend in revenues in the first year of operation, the store hit a plateau. Over the next two years, revenues and earnings remained relatively flat. Steve and Susan weren't working any less intensely, yet, much to their frustration, they began to see an erosion in their profit and loss statement.

As part of a national franchising concern, Steve and Susan's operation was regularly compared to other units in the system. Despite their considerable efforts, during the last two years their shop ranked in the lower quartile of franchisees in the system. Regardless of the unit of measurement (i.e. revenue per square foot, number of pages copied, etc.), they seemed to reside permanently in the lower quartile.

Unprofessional Front-Line People

Frustrated and seeking some insight, Steve contracted with a research firm to conduct an analysis of his outfit with respect to customer perceptions of product service and quality offered by his printing company. The research found that customers were "unimpressed" with his front line people, phone calls were often not handled in a professional manner, and many customers felt as if they and their needs were more of a bother than an opportunity for business.

To their credit, Steve and Susan used the statistical information and qualitative comments from customers to make several modifications within their company. The result of those changes? Business has never been better. "I was so busy working hard to build my business that I didn't know I had a problem until it was reflected in my monthly financials over a period of time," Steve says. "I am definitely going to ask my customers more frequently in the future."

In any business, the people who deal directly with customers can make or break a business. Make a good impression and the customer buys, comes back, and multiplies. Make a poor impression and he or she goes away (sometimes telling as many as eight to ten other people about a bad experience). The more service-oriented a business is, the more important it becomes to have front-line people who know how to present themselves — and the company — in a favorable light.

You may have an efficient, dedicated workforce. You may care about your customers. But until you make customers aware that you are taking special care of them, until you make customers realize you are giving them good value for their money, your efforts may be wasted. It is not the quality of service that you give but the quality of service that customers perceive that causes them to buy in the first place and then subsequently to come back and buy again. When it comes to winning and keeping customers, it is the perception of the quality of service that determines to a large extent how successful your company will be.

The only reliable way for a company to be sure of a customer's perceptions is to ask. The only sure way to know how your customer sees your business is to look at your business from your customer's perspective. (Don't forget, however, that for such information to be meaningful and reliable, it must be sourced properly, and administered and analyzed with appropriate methodologies.)

Understanding how to improve service quality demands a two-step approach: measuring customer satisfaction and gauging the firm's actual performance in delivering that service. Timely research and measurement can reveal new market opportunities and disclose hidden service problems before unhappy customers migrate to competitors. In an increasingly competitive economy, customer expectations of service quality are constantly increasing, while customer tolerance for poor service is falling.

Assessing Firm Performance

Assessing firm performance against customer expectation can be both insightful and humbling. It is very important that company-held assumptions of customer wants and perceptions be measured against actual customer wants and perceptions.

The data Steve and Susan gained from polling their customers ranged from the simplistic (employees should wear name tags, employees should give their name when answering the phone, the company should publish price lists along with printing suggestions) to the profound (price versus quality tradeoffs; awareness of and interest in the range of products and services offered).

Such information enabled Steve and Susan to move into a more "congruent" relationship with their customers. This required them to curtail some product and service offerings that had marginal interest so that capital (both human and financial) could be shifted to areas of greater interest. These changes resulted in a greater return on investment.

This customer congruency produced greater customer loyalty (as customer turnover was reduced substantially), along with a steady growth in the customer base as increased customer satisfaction created significant word-of-mouth traffic.

Realizing how hard they worked to get a customer, Steve and Susan began to understand the cost of losing a customer. That realization strengthened their commitment to measuring customer satisfaction on a regular basis to gauge their firm's performance, not only against financial benchmarks but also against customer satisfaction benchmarks. A quantitative exercise that paints a vivid picture of the financial implications of losing a single customer is provided on page 244

Conclusion

"The future belongs to people who see possibilities before they become obvious," Theodore Levitt, of the Harvard University Graduate School of Business Administration, once said. Steve and Susan found that their customers were a great source of ideas as well as a tool of accountability. Your customers, too, are a source of valuable information concerning your company's strengths, weaknesses and possibilities.

How do you know how your business is doing unless you ask...and ask...and ask... ■

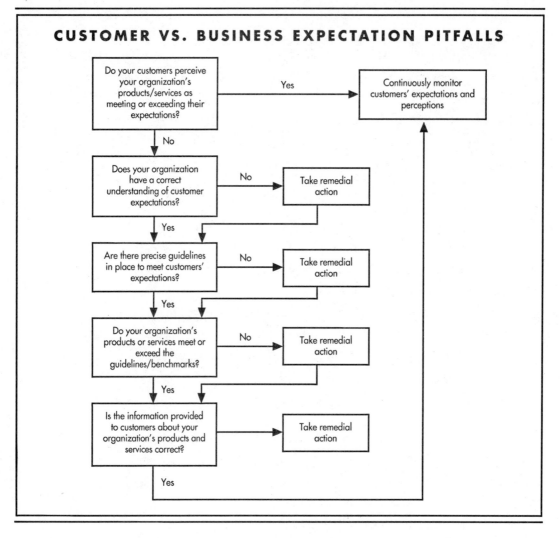

CUSTOMER VS. BUSINESS EXPECTATION PITFALLS

Do your customers perceive your organization's products/services as meeting or exceeding their expectations? — Yes → Continuously monitor customers' expectations and perceptions

No ↓

Does your organization have a correct understanding of customer expectations? — No → Take remedial action

Yes ↓

Are there precise guidelines in place to meet customers' expectations? — No → Take remedial action

Yes ↓

Do your organization's products or services meet or exceed the guidelines/benchmarks? — No → Take remedial action

Yes ↓

Is the information provided to customers about your organization's products and services correct? — Take remedial action

Yes

EXERCISE

Customer Satisfaction Scorecard

Use survey information in conjunction with this scorecard. Values are as follows:

(A) These values refer to how a business scored in the survey in each category. The average performance score in the aggregate is used.

(B) These values refer to what customers expect in each category. The average expectation score in the aggregate is used.

(C) This value is a ratio of (A) over (B)

(A) Performance Score	Categories (for reference only)	(B) Customer Expectation Score	(C) Customer Satisfaction Ratio (A/B)
_____	Shipping	_____	_____
_____	Product quality	_____	_____
_____	Price	_____	_____
_____	Phone service	_____	_____
_____	Sales force knowledge	_____	_____
_____	Frequency of contact by sales force	_____	_____
_____	Professionalism of staff	_____	_____
_____	Expertise	_____	_____
_____	Problems handled effectively	_____	_____
_____	Responsiveness	_____	_____
_____	Understanding customer needs	_____	_____
_____	Accessibility of personnel	_____	_____
_____	Reliability of products	_____	_____

$$\text{Customer satisfaction ratio} = \frac{\text{Performance}}{\text{Customer expectation}}$$

The desired objective is a customer satisfaction ratio greater than one, in each category and as an overall score.

EXERCISE

The Cost of Losing Customers

Information required:

(A) = Number of customers lost. (Choose the
appropriate time period for your firm —
monthly, quarterly, biannually, or annually.) _____

(B) = Average revenue per customer.
(You can divide an annual figure
to get the amount equivalent to
the time period selected.) $ _____

(C) = Profit margin.
(This figure should be derived
as a function of the revenue figure.) _____

(D) = Administrative costs — amount to open
accounts, amount to close accounts +$ _____

(E) = Estimated marketing cost per customer
(cost associated with securing the customer). $ _____

Calculation — Financial Cost

```
        _____  (A)
x   $   _____  (B)
=   $   _____  Lost annual revenue
x       ___X___  % (C)
=   $   _____  Profit lost
    $   _____  (D)
x       ___Y___  (A)
=   $   _____
```

X + Y = Financial impact of lost customers

Calculation — Marketing Cost

```
$   _____  (E)
x   ___X₁___  $
= S _____  Marketing expense lost
```

**Assumption of having to replace lost
customers requires the firm to repeat:**

```
$   _____  (E)
x   _____  (A) Number of customers
        X₂          lost = number of customers
                    to regain.)
= $ _____  Market expense lost
```

$X_1 + X_2$ = Marketing cost of lost customers

Assessing and Developing Your Customer Service Capabilities

by Harvy R. Simkovitz

Before a company can embark on any organization improvement program, its leaders must believe that such improvement will enhance the company's customer service, competitive advantage and, as a result, the bottom line. PDQ Printing is a case in point. Tom Carns, president of PDQ, instinctively knew that the best way to make money was to invest time and resources, not only in his (external) sales and marketing efforts but also in his (internal) equipment/technology, work environment, employees, and operating systems. Without this fundamental belief in customer service, no leader will spend the necessary time, energy, and money to assess and develop the organization's capabilities to achieve that excellent service.

Tom Carns knew that in making an investment in customer service, he would achieve not only immediate customer satisfaction but also long-term customer loyalty, both of which generate repeat business and referrals and are usually more cost-effective than trying to find new customers. Tom Carns also knew that, *externally,* he could not be all things to all people. Therefore he chose to be a custom house to small and mid-sized professional service firms. He had to decide where and how to make investments *internally* (e.g., technology, human resources, training, systems) that would yield returns for the customers and increase the effectiveness of the organization.

Harvy R. Simkovitz, CMC is president of Innovative Management Systems, in Arlington, Mass.

The External Game: Where Improving Customer Service Begins

In developing your company's customer service capabilities, you need to decide which of your customers to focus on initially. Rather than trying to improve service to all customers simultaneously, the wiser strategy is to begin with certain customer types. There are five customer types from which to choose:

1) *Suspect* customers are all plausible customers within the universe of customers;

2) *Prospective* customers are high potential customers;

3) *New* customers are recently converted prospects;

4) *Existing* customers are repeat users of your products and services (grouped as low, medium, or high users, and fully or not fully saturated users);

5) *Discouraged* or lost customers are those who have gone elsewhere.

At PDQ Printing, from among a much larger realm of suspect firms that need printing, Tom Carns chose to target medical offices, accounting firms, brokerages, legal, and other white-collar service firms within Las Vegas city limits. He further narrowed the range by deciding what size firms to pursue as active prospects. He chose, for example, the top ten law offices in his city when he opened a new downtown site. Then, to attract these prospects, PDQ used a varied mix of "push" (e.g., direct sales and direct mail) and "pull" (e.g., print and radio advertising) marketing techniques targeted to the right decision makers in each niche (e.g., paralegals in law offices).

To maintain and grow new and existing customers, PDQ surveys every customer at the end of each job. The company asks its top 150 customers both how PDQ can improve and what kind of printing they are buying elsewhere. Salespeople also personally thank customers for their orders. These practices reduce the likelihood of customers leaving, and they increase PDQ's share of a customer's printing business.

Tom Carns undoubtedly did not implement all his marketing, sales, and service approaches simultaneously. You can use the following worksheet to help set priorities for your business. Once you have completed the worksheet, go back and indicate areas of high, medium, and low priority for your company. (Ask key people in your company for their opinions as well.) The areas of high priority are the places where you should begin to focus your external improvement efforts.

WORKSHEET
Identifying Your Priorities

I — GENERATING NEW CUSTOMERS

A. Who comprises your *realm of suspect customers*, as defined by specific market niches, customer size, geographical territory, etc.? (Leave no stone unturned for this part of the exercise.)

_____

_____

_____

B. From the realm of suspects above, who are your *highest potential prospects?*

_____

_____

_____

C. What current, possible marketing strategies can you use to *generate individual prospect leads?*

_____

_____

_____

D. What current or new-sales activities can you use to attract your targeted prospects and convert individual leads into new customers?

_____

_____

_____

II — GROWING (OR PRUNING) EXISTING CUSTOMERS

A How do you distinguish your *new and existing customers* in terms of:

1. Low, medium, and high users of your products and services?

_____

_____

2. Fully and not fully saturated users?

_____

_____

B. Within each area above, what current and possible service activities can you use to *increase your new and existing customers' involvement* in your company's products and services?

_____

_____

_____

C. What current and possible service activities can you use to *rekindle discouraged or lost customers?*

_____

_____

_____

D. What activities do you, or could you, perform to help you decide *which customers and products or services to prune* **each year?**

_____

_____

_____

The Internal Game: Six Supports

Before you can decide what to work on internally, you must decide where you need to improve your customer service performance externally. There is little sense in improving internal parts of your business unless those improvements have an appropriate impact on those customers you wish to target. Once an external choice has been made, it should be clear where you must direct your internal efforts.

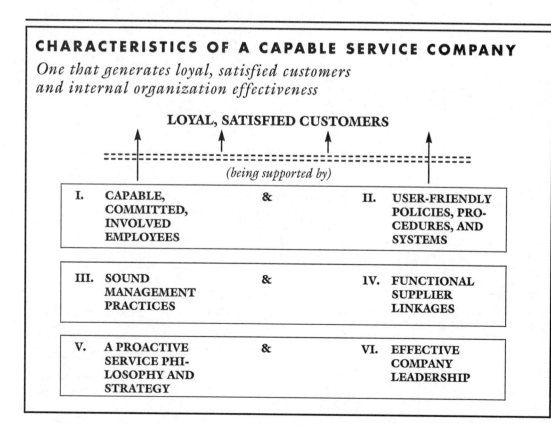

CHARACTERISTICS OF A CAPABLE SERVICE COMPANY

One that generates loyal, satisfied customers and internal organization effectiveness

LOYAL, SATISFIED CUSTOMERS

(being supported by)

I. CAPABLE, COMMITTED, INVOLVED EMPLOYEES	&	II. USER-FRIENDLY POLICIES, PROCEDURES, AND SYSTEMS
III. SOUND MANAGEMENT PRACTICES	&	IV. FUNCTIONAL SUPPLIER LINKAGES
V. A PROACTIVE SERVICE PHILOSOPHY AND STRATEGY	&	VI. EFFECTIVE COMPANY LEADERSHIP

To create real customer service capability, a company should look to invest its limited resources in any of six different areas internally. These six supports to customer service are presented visually on the preceding page. These are the areas where opportunities for improvement exist. That improvement, in turn, will enhance external customer sales and service.

Customers confront the first two supports every time they contact your company:

1. **Capable, committed, involved employees:** The degree to which employees are helpful and effective, working with intelligence and enthusiasm.

2. **User-friendly policies, procedures, and systems:** These should facilitate development, sales, delivery, and support functions.

The next four supports create, sustain, and reinforce those elements of customer contact, working to ensure a viable organization. These are:

3. **Sound management practices:** The degree to which financial control systems and personnel practices support and sustain employee empowerment and improvement.

4. **Supplier linkages and relationships:** The degree to which these relationships are functional and reliable.

5. **Proactive service philosophy and strategy:** The degree to which everyone in the company understands what business the company is in and what is expected of them.

6. **Competent, credible leadership:** The degree to which the leaders of the firm provide the vision, energy, and inspiration that builds trust.

These six supports are the fire fighters holding up the safety net that will catch and carry a company's customers. If any of the supports are weak, customers may fall through the net. All six supports are needed to attract and retain customers. However, all six supports do not have to be strengthened simultaneously. A company can focus on those supports that require the most improvement.

At PDQ, here is how Tom Carns is building his internal supports:

1. Capable, committed, involved employees

In an industry where employee turnover averages between 45% and 50%, Carns has worked to hold his turnover to 12%. He has done this by hiring a competent director of training and "spending the money up front to hire the right people and train them well." He expects employees to dress neatly, and he runs a clean and relatively quiet shop, all of which reinforce quality and professionalism. Internal PDQ employees also go on regular sales calls with sales staff to improve their understanding of customer needs.

2. User-friendly policies, procedures, and systems

Carns instituted systems that help customers "get their own way." He keeps a loose-leaf binder of all past orders for each account. He creatively uses this system to fill repeat orders more quickly, as well as to call up customers when they have not reordered stock for some time. PDQ also proofreads orders before going to press, an unheard-of practice in the printing industry, yet one that adds value, presumably allowing PDQ to command a higher price for its services.

3. Sound management practices

The PDQ case study does not reveal how Carns controls the financial aspects of his business, or how he manages and rewards the performance of individuals and groups within the organization. How a company treats its employees and manages their performance determines their productivity, work quality, commitment, and loyalty to the organization.

4. Supplier linkages and relationships

In order to provide good customer service, a company must develop strong supplier relationships. Successful companies make suppliers their partners in business. Although supplier relationships were not discussed in any detail in this case study, Carns undoubtedly has created and maintained healthy supplier relationships.

5. Proactive service philosophy and strategy

Carns is clearly a master of proactive service philosophy and strategy. By targeting professional service firms and providing varied, convenient, secure, and custom-tailored printing services, Carns maintains and builds his customer base in ways that no other Las Vegas printer has. He also works to ensure that his printing is always "right and on time," a very important concern for his target market.

To keep customers loyal, Carns stays aggressively in contact with them through a variety of creative sales and service techniques. He provides guarantees (confidentiality to legal firms is guaranteed) and works to build lifelong relationships (the sales force calls on PDQ's top 150 customers every year, and every customer is contacted through surveys). Also, he treats his best customers well (with offers such as volume discounts). He wins customers over by exceeding their expectations about what a printing company can do for them.

To stay in the strategy forefront, PDQ gathers competitive intelligence through its sales force by having them visit and learn from competitors. Carns also has a way of making good business decisions seem altruistic. He redesigned, for free, the newsletter for the Las Vegas paralegal association, which provided him with an opening to the local legal market. He also helps to maintain a network of top quick printers throughout the country to share ideas and help each other.

6. Competent, credible leadership

As business associates have attested, Carns provides intelligence, creativity, and a quiet dynamism to his business. He is thorough and aggressively persistent, qualities critical to success. As one colleague said, "Tom has this energy level that always keeps him going forward. He knows how to get to people who help him get things done." With an eye to the future, Carns never stops learning. This attitude has helped him maintain his edge in the market. ■

TEN (PLUS ONE) STEPS TO IMPROVING YOUR COMPANY'S CUSTOMER SERVICE CAPABILITY

Now that we have examined *what* to improve within your business, here are 10 ideas (plus one) on *how* to move those efforts forward.

1. **Decide which types of customers (and product/market areas) to focus on** initially. Do not take on more areas than your organization can realistically handle at once.

2. **Assess and analyze your organization's current internal capabilities** with regard to the six supports. Start meeting with executives/managers, then appropriately involve customers, suppliers, and employees in assessing *what's working* and *what needs improvement* within your organization.

3. **Get the right high-leverage people in the room** to come to a reasonable consensus on analyses and plans. This helps build employee commitment to your improvement efforts. Keep minutes of all meetings to log and keep track of efforts and commitments (stuff written on paper gets more attention than stuff said into the air).

4. **Fully understand what currently makes your company's customer service strong.** Reinforcing and building on these positive capabilities generates positive motivation.

5. **Prioritize areas for improvement,** i.e., where the greatest needs are for improved customer service. If appropriate, simply take an executive or manager vote on necessary short-term and long-term initiatives.

6. **Solicit improvement ideas from all appropriate staff.** They can be a wealth of ideas.

7. **Implement easiest improvements first.** Focus on areas where smallest time, money, and energy investment will achieve the greatest customer and company returns. Don't bite off more than your company can chew at once. Build your muscles for the more strenuous efforts.

8. **Eventually involve all staff in improvement efforts,** and teach them skills in data gathering/analysis, problem solving, and solution implementation. Educate and help your employees to help your organization.

9. **Measure the results** of the changes being instituted in terms of internal productivity/efficiency and external quality/service to customers. Tracking results helps you learn about your business and lets you know if your efforts are making a difference.

10. **Shift focus as priorities change.** Keeping your focus on what things to do next keeps the long customer service improvement voyage more manageable and endurable.

11. **If you need help, get it.** Look to business colleagues, advisers, books, or competent consultants to help you along the way. ■

Notes

The Model
Damage–Control Letter

At PDQ Printing, Tom Carns will do almost anything to make it up to a customer for a botched job. *Almost* everything.

But, to restore that lost confidence, how much should you concede? How much do you spell out? And what do you do about compensation?

Like all delivery companies and most other businesses, Sterling Courier Systems, a provider of same-day-delivery services based in Herndon, Va., occasionally fails to meet its deadlines. Sterling uses commercial airlines to transport the parcels it takes on, so the delays are usually the result of packages' being misplaced in airlines' tracking systems. The fact that it happens is beyond Sterling's control, but from a customer's vantage point a missing box is Sterling's problem — end of discussion.

For several months back in late 1990 and early 1991, Sterling experienced a spell of bad luck. Several packages disappeared in transit, and Sterling had to report late deliveries to three accounts. Even though the packages eventually turned up, the delays meant real cash losses to the customers.

Sterling president Glenn Smoak says he hesitated to pay out compensation. "We normally make it right by not charging the customer for that particular shipment, and if they need another shipment done to rectify the problem, we do that, which we did with all of these folks. But in these cases it wasn't enough; they had suffered downtime." What made Smoak's decision more difficult

In the wake of a botched job, the right combination of explanation, apology, and compensation can make a world of difference to your customers and to your business' chances of success.

was that because the packages weren't permanently lost, neither Sterling's insurance company nor the airline that handled the transport was obligated to pay damages. If Smoak elected to reimburse his customers, the total hit would be about $30,000, an amount that would push his then five-year-old $5-million company into a loss for that quarter. On the other hand, "one of the customers," says Smoak, "had 23 plants around the country. This fellow was so ballistic that all it would have taken was one E-mail message to the other plants, and 10% of our business would have evaporated."

Often damage control for such problems can be handled with phone calls, apologies, and make-goods. But because the gods had conspired to make similar and sizable problems happen concurrently, and because it took several months for Smoak to confirm that the company's insurer, Lloyds of London, definitely wouldn't cover the damages, he decided to draft one letter to all three customers to explain the company's situation.

In the end Sterling did give out $30,000 in gratis service and did take a hit to the bottom line that quarter. But the customers stayed, and Sterling continued to grow, to $7.5 million in 1993. Smoak still deals with problems on an ad hoc basis. "We tell people during our sales pitch that there will be problems, that we're not infallible, but that we guarantee to fix them for them." On the pages that follow, he explains why he included what he did in this particular sample letter.

6 GOOD FORMS

Explain the situation.

"Without trying to pass off responsibility, we always let customers know where the problem was: with the airline, with one of our agents, or with a computer person in our office.

"I tried to make a presentation that indicated what our dilemma was. The verbiage was for drama, to say that we have a lot of problems here: that, as you know, our insurance company, one of the best in the world, will not cover this, that nobody will cover consequential damage but that we'll make up the difference.

"I was very proud to make this offer, because I knew that it was an investment in the future. So I agonized over this letter. I really did want to get across that we didn't have to do this, but we were going to, anyway."

Explain what you're doing about the basic problem.

"There still is no insurance company that will cover downtime because of a delay. We have an agent still looking around, but all the insurance companies say that someone would take advantage of a guarantee like that big time, and they don't want to be involved with that someone. The point here is that we wanted our customers to know they wouldn't get better coverage from another carrier, in case they were thinking about switching."

Say this.

"We say this because we do. We're in such a highly competitive field that the loss of any customer means something."

On the other hand, don't beg.

"I think it leaves a better taste in the customer's mouth when you're not saying, 'We'll do anything; can I put your kid through college? Just don't drop us.'"

STERLING *Courier Systems*

847 STATION STREET   HERNDON, VA   (800) 633-6666   (703) 471-4488

May 1, 1991

REF: ▮▮▮ Magazine Shipment 1/17/90

Dear Mr. ▮▮▮

I have had long, fairly intense discussions with our insurer, Lloyds of London, regarding your claim, as well as insurance for air cargo in general. Air cargo insurance covers tangible physical damage or actual loss of the item shipped, be it from theft, weather, or whatever. Sterling Courier Systems is the most specialized shipper in the business, for we ship ONLY same-day, rush items. However, ALL POLICIES CURRENTLY WRITTEN BY ANY INSURER WILL NOT COVER LOSSES SUSTAINED BY DELAY. This sort of loss is described as consequential - loss due as consequence of the delay, which tends to be open to subjective judgment.

Had your shipment been damaged, stolen, destroyed, or lost, you would have been compensated long ago. But because we eventually found your shipment in the American Airlines system, there was no "loss," as is currently defined by insurers.

I have been in contact with Lloyds, as well as Allstate and the Fireman's Fund, asking them to write Sterling Courier Systems a specific policy to cover losses sustained in the delay of a rush shipment. If it is feasible, it will be announced soon.

We value your business. We do not want to see you look elsewhere for your rush shipping. Therefore, I am offering $7,875 in rush shipping to you, and hope this will sufficiently compensate you for the loss you sustained due to the delay of your shipment. If this is satisfactory, please deduct as you see fit, and note it on future invoices. I would appreciate a confirming call.

Best regards,

STERLING COURIER SYSTEMS, INC.

Glenn M. Smoak

Glenn M. Smoak
President

GMS:pc

Lay out exactly what you're doing for them.

"We decided to pay the customers in full for their losses. Earlier, we had asked them to send us documentation as though they were making an insurance claim, with a receipt saying what the loss cost them. I think it's good to do it that way, so that they take what's being done seriously and realize we're not just pandering to them. I think they respect you a little more if you show you understand the temptations in your offer. But our customers are straight with us because we're straight with them.

"We offered credit in order to spread the cost out, but if they had asked for cash, I would have written out checks. None of them did."

Respond when you have complete information.

"This wasn't our first communication. I'd been handling this problem personally, getting the barometric pressure from each customer and finding out how much of a problem each delay was. We're in touch with these folks almost daily anyway, but we kept them up to date while we had all the back and forth with Lloyds, which was busy with Exxon at the time and in no mood to deal with this. We had worked to develop trust with our customers, so that when we said, 'We're working on it,' they didn't think we were giving them the runaround. We had, of course, told them that somehow we were going to make it right for them and wouldn't leave them twisting in the wind."

Benchmark yourself against a Bad Form.

"This, in contrast, is the letter we got from American Airlines. I had sent the airline copies of my letter, saying, 'This is how we stand behind our customers; how about you?' And we got no call, nothing. I would have appreciated a gesture, but the airline did only what it had to, refunding 50% of the air-bill charge, which was $75 or $100 for the three claims. It was a learning experience. Seeing how much American infuriated me — and we're a $20,000-a-month customer — I knew how angry my customers would have been if we hadn't come through. If I didn't have to use American anymore, I wouldn't, but sometimes you just don't have a choice."

Ask for an acknowledgment.

"I suggested that they call me because I wanted them to know that if they had something to say, they could say it to me. I also wanted to reemphasize that I was directly involved. Instead they called the salespeople they already had relationships with, which was fine. And they were extremely pleased; it was very heartwarming."

American Airlines

May 12, 1992

Re: Airbill 62575111
Airbill 62629722
Airbill 68780843

Sterling Courier Systems
459 Carlisle Drive
Herndon, VA 22070

Attention: Glenn M. Smoak, President

Dear Sir:

This is in response to your letter regarding claims on the above shipments.

Per your letter, Sterling had earlier filed claims for delay and had been reimbursed fifty percent of the freight charges for these shipments in accordance with our tariffs. Unfortunately, we cannot reimburse you for the credit amount issued to your customers. These items are by legal definition "special damages" not contemplated by or known to the carrier when it receives a shipment. Under Common Law and our Conditions of Contract, we are not liable for special damages.

Please let me assure you that our handling of the above shipments was not typical of American Airlines' Cargo service. We hope that we shall have an opportunity to prove that to you soon.

Sincerely,
AMERICAN AIRLINES, INC.

Administrator
Cargo Claims Administration
Mail Drop

JS:mfs

Notes

The Experts

Nate Booth
The Anthony Robbins Companies
9191 Towne Centre Drive, Ste. 500
San Diego, CA 92122
(800) 445-8183 or (619) 535-9900

Nate Booth is the head corporate trainer for The Anthony Robbins Companies. Dr. Booth received his D.D.S. degree from the University of Nebraska in 1971 and was in private dental practice for eight years. He has consulted for some 150 corporations and is the author of numerous articles and the book *Turning Resolutions into Realities.*

JoAnna Brandi
Integrated Marketing Systems, Inc.
P.O. Box 59
Sea Cliff, NY 11579
(516) 674-3356

JoAnna Brandi is president of Integrated Marketing Systems Inc., a customer care company committed to helping companies build better relationships with customers through the strategic use of marketing, research, and training. She has given talks for many industry groups and corporations. She is a regular columnist on customer care for the *Business Council Newsletter,* as well as the author of two other newsletters, *Dare to Care* and the *Customer Care Bulletin.*

Margo Chevers
Northeast Leadership Enterprise
P.O. Box 1584
Plainville, MA 02762
(800) 858-0797 or (508) 695-8687

Margo Chevers specializes in seminars, workshops, and keynote speeches to corporations and associations. Since 1986 she has been delivering professional development programs on the skills of quality customer service and goal achievement. The author of numerous articles, Chevers has also produced and hosted her own television show, "Against All Odds." She edits the *Success Report,* a customer service newsletter based on personal in-

terviews with companies that thrived despite the recession. Her book, *What Do You Want to Be When You Grow Up? A Creative Approach to Choosing Your Life's Goals,* was recently published by Grand Publishing Co., and Kendall/Hunt published her new book, *Stop the BS (Bad Service),* in May 1994.

Susan Clarke
Motivation Unlimited
2110 Sunset Cliffs Boulevard
San Diego, CA 92107
(800) 747-7417 or (619) 224-0906

Since beginning her consulting and training company in 1982, Clarke has developed and coordinated national personnel policies and full-scale training programs for companies throughout the country. She is the author of *The Secrets of Service,* which focuses on the development of customer service skills.

Bruce Hodes
CMI
711 South Boulevard, Ste. 9
Oak Park, IL 60302
(708) 383-7970

As president of CMI, Bruce Hodes helps companies and work groups thrive in the 1990s. He works with firms in the areas of leadership, strategic planning, team building, customer service, productivity, and culture shifts. Hodes is the author of numerous articles as well as *The Coach's Handbook.*

Howard E. Hyden
Hyden & Hyden
7415 Hyde Park Drive
Minneapolis, MN 55439
(612) 942-0980

Howard E. Hyden is president of Hyden & Hyden, a Minneapolis-based firm specializing in providing marketing services to businesses that want to be market-driven. His services include seminars, training programs, and a full range of implementation programs designed to increase customer focus throughout the culture of an organization.

Lori Laub
Excellence by Design
227 Old La Honda Road
Woodside, CA 94062
(415) 851-3660

Lori Laub is founder of Excellence by Design, a firm dedicated to helping companies maximize their service efficiencies. Since 1983 Laub has created a new and dynamic vision in the service and support field, creating and implementing programs designed to enrich customer service, improve vendor relations, and maximize company profits.

Linda Miller
Development Dimensions International (DDI)
1225 Washington Pike
Bridgeville, PA 15017
(412) 257-0600

Linda Miller joined DDI in 1987. As manager of the Strategies for High-Involvement Leadership product line, she consults on topics such as leadership skills, performance management, labor-management relations, and training analysis. Before joining DDI, she served as director of management development for a management holding company in the financial services industry.

Don Peppers
marketing 1:1
Ten Overbrook Lane
Weston, CT 06883
(203) 221–7534, voice mail: (203) 348-6252

A former executive with the New York offices of Lintas: USA and Chiat/Day, Don Peppers now heads up his own consulting firm, marketing 1:1. Peppers works with clients in business development and marketing technology. He and Martha Rogers have written a book about the technology of marketing and the future of business competition, *The One to One Future: Building Relationships One Customer at a Time* (Doubleday/Currency, 1993). *The One to One Future* is contracted for publication in ten languages and is the subject of a PBS special. *Inc.* magazine editor-in-chief George Gendron has called the Peppers-Rogers book "one of the two or three most important business books ever written."

Martha Rogers, Ph.D.
marketing 1:1
65 Back Bay Road
Bowling Green, Ohio 43402
(419) 823-8856, voice mail: (203) 348-6252

Martha Rogers, Ph.D., a founding partner in marketing 1:1, is associate professor of telecommunications at Bowling Green State University, in Ohio. A former copywriter and advertising executive, she is co-author, with Don

Peppers, of *The One to One Future: Building Relationships One Customer at a Time* (Doubleday/Currency, 1993).

Mark Sanborn
Sanborn & Associates
c/o Kingsbury Enterprises
12625 High Bluff Drive, Suite 203
San Diego, CA 92130
(619) 481-3322

Mark Sanborn gives about 100 speeches or seminars a year on topics such as leadership, teambuilding and service. In addition to producing nine videos and four audio training programs, he is the author of *Teambuilt: Making Teamwork Work*. Sanborn was recently selected by ECI/Westcott as one of the top business motivation experts in the country for the "Masters on Motivation" Business Television Series.

Harvy Simkovits, CMC
Innovative Management Systems
17 Russell Terrace, #2
Arlington, MA 02174
(617) 648-2021

Speaker, writer, and consultant, Harvy Simkovits has assisted more than 50 independent, small to midsize firms shift from surviving to thriving in today's tough economic times. A certified management consultant with the Institute of Management Consultants, Simkovits has authored dozens of articles on issues of productivity, efficiency, quality, and service.

Joseph P. Sperry
Shaffer Sherman Sperry & Swaddling, Inc.
575 Copeland Mill Road, Ste. 2-C
Westerville, OH 43081
(614) 794-3311

Joseph P. Sperry, Ph.D., is a service and relationship-quality consultant with 16 years' experience. Since 1986 he has been a principal at Shaffer Sherman Sperry & Swaddling Inc., which improves its clients' profitability by increasing their accounts' satisfaction and loyalty. They have helped some of the largest and most successful firms in the world: American Electric Power, AT&T, Bank One, Dun and Bradstreet Software, Eastman-Kodak, GE Capital, Hewlett Packard, Nationwide Insurance, Swiss Bank and many others

Deborah B. Taylor
Taylor Consulting Group Inc.
P.O. Box 597
Glen Ellyn, IL 60138
(800) 284-9566 or (708) 790-0847

An international business consultant, Deborah Taylor brings cutting-edge expertise and experience to the clients she serves. As managing partner of the Taylor Consulting Group Inc., the creators of the Taylor More (than) Satisfied Customers Matrix, Taylor's client list includes an array of *Fortune* 500 companies as well as smaller entrepreneurial companies. She is the author of *More (than) Satisfied Customers*

Michael J. Wing
InfoPlan International Inc.
14505 Torrey Chase Boulevard, Ste. 420
Houston, TX 77014
(800) 321-8425

Michael Wing is the president and CEO of the international market research firm InfoPlan International Inc. In his career, Wing has enjoyed success as head of four different companies in four different industries. He has appeared on numerous national business telecasts, and is the author of several articles as well as the book, *Talking with Your Customers*. He has just completed a one-year appointment as a White House Fellow.

Wesley W. Zimmerman
WZA Inc.
11060 N. 77th Street
Scottsdale, AZ 85260-5644
(602) 948-3015 or (800) 328-7629

Wesley W. Zimmerman is founder of WZA Inc., a sales and marketing consulting firm, where he directs his clients to focus on perception of difference when promoting their product or service. It is this perception, he feels, that motivates customers to choose their suppliers. A former theologian, Zimmerman has also spent part of his career as a salesperson in the computer industry.

Notes